Policing the Urban Underworld

Policing the Urban Underworld

The Impact of Crime
on the Development
of the American Police,
1800–1887

David R. Johnson

 Temple University Press, Philadelphia

Library of Congress Cataloging in Publication Data
Johnson, David Ralph, 1942-
    Policing the urban underworld.

    Bibliography: p. 233
    Includes index.
    1. Police—United States—History—19th century.
2. Chicago—Police—History—19th century.
3. Philadelphia—Police—History—19th century.
4. Crime and criminals—United States—History—19th
century. 5. Crime prevention—United States—History—
19th century. I. Title.
HV8138.J58   363.2'09748'11   78-31220
ISBN 0-87722-148-0

Temple University Press, Philadelphia 19122
© 1979 by Temple University. All rights reserved
Published 1979
Printed in the United States of America

To
Ralph G. Johnson
Teacher, Friend, and Father
In Memoriam

Preface

This book examines how criminals shaped police behavior in the nineteenth century. It is not, therefore, another study of the origins of preventive policing; it is instead an attempt to understand how the theory of crime prevention worked in practice. In general, we will see that the theory was not a particularly effective guide to crime control because its advocates assumed an overly simplistic view of the relationship between policemen and criminals. More specifically, I will argue that various types of criminals had, and have, the ability to negate the theory's promises because of the underworld's complexity and growth in an urban setting. The primary focus of this book therefore is on the interaction between policemen and criminals, rather than on reformers and policemen. We must consider the experience of the police in dealing with criminals if we are to obtain a full understanding of the reasons why our police behave as they do.

In the process of assembling the materials for this study I have accumulated a number of debts. The staffs at the libraries of the University of Chicago, the Historical Society of Pennsylvania, and the Philadelphia City Archives were generous with their time and assistance. Several friends and colleagues gave uncounted hours of their valuable time to reading the manuscript in whole or in part. Warren Billings, at the University of New Orleans, provided pungent, constructive criticism at a crucial point in my writing, and

listened patiently and sympathetically to my early efforts
to organize my ideas. Mark Haller, at the University of
Chicago and later at Temple University, offered valuable
insights into the structure and implications of this study
and has been a source of constant encouragement as the work
progressed. John Schneider, at the University of Nebraska,
provided a close and critical analysis of the manuscript which
saved me from many errors. I am also grateful to Roger Lane,
at Haverford College, for his gracious and stimulating com-
ments on various early versions of my ideas. Ken Arnold,
editor-in-chief of Temple University Press, by his patience,
sound advice, and encouragement, greatly diminished the
final hurdles in the path of publication. I have not incorporated all their suggestions into the final version of the text,
but I appreciate their efforts to save me from its worst pit-
falls. Finally, I want to acknowledge my greatest debt to my
wife, Peggy, who has been a constant source of strength and
encouragement throughout this endeavor. This book would
not have been possible without her help.

Contents

Policing the Urban Underworld

Introduction

Studies of policing's formative years in America have concentrated on the impact which politics (in its generic as well as its specific sense) has had on the police. As a result, we now know a great deal about how ideology, partisanship, and social values shaped the structure, administration, and policies of the police.[1] Perhaps inevitably, the impression which emerges from these works is that politics and the political process are the keys to comprehending police behavior. Although there is considerable truth to this view, it ignores the underworld's contribution to molding the police, or assumes it to be simply a chronicle of corruption. While that assumption identifies a salient feature of the ties between policemen and criminals, it does not do full justice to a complex relationship in which corruption is only part of the story. We cannot fully appreciate the reasons for police attitudes and conduct unless we attempt to understand the structure of criminal behavior and how it, too, influences the police.

The underworld's specific contributions to the development of modern policing varied according to the kind of criminal who came in contact with the police. Since it would be impossible to detail the effects of all types of crime on the police, this study will concentrate on three general categories of unlawful behavior which many urban residents wanted suppressed: professional theft, street crime, and illegal enterprise (gambling and prostitution). These are certainly not the only crimes which existed in the nineteenth century (public drunkenness was also very important in shaping police be-

havior), but each played a major role in defining the limitations of police reform.[2]

Criminals from these three categories comprised a highly
visible part of an urban underworld whose existence was
unquestioned but whose composition and extent were unknown. Aside from the fact that a diverse assortment of
unruly juveniles, thieves, and other undesirable persons
harassed them, urban residents knew little about these
people; nor did they make any serious effort to investigate
this subculture. Had they done so, they would have discovered an amorphous society consisting of individuals and
loose-knit groups who were classified as criminals by personal
choice, by circumstances, or by social prejudices. These
people were neither passive participants in the attempt to
deal with them nor a cohesive class capable of collective
resistance. But certain of their characteristics and advantages would make them extremely resistant to reforms designed to enhance the effectiveness of the police. Their
behavior in fact affected the patrolman on the beat as well
as the organization and administration of the police departments which emerged in most large American cities during
the mid-nineteenth century.

The geography of cities was one important advantage
criminals had, especially because of the changes which rapid
urbanization wrought in the uses of land, in the distribution
of social classes, and in the kinds of people who were attracted to the burgeoning cities.[3] Urbanization increased
dramatically between 1800 and 1890. Of the three largest
cities in the United States by 1890, Chicago had existed
only as a small military post at the outset of the century
while both New York and Philadelphia had numbered fewer
than 100,000 inhabitants. All three contained more than a
million people in 1890, and in the nation as a whole urban
residents had increased from about 5 to 35 percent of the
total population. This growth reflected the increasingly
crucial role which cities played in an expanding nation.
As centers of industry, trade, and culture, cities helped
shape both the economy and society of the United States.

In the process of ministering to the needs of the country
and of their local populations, cities also changed their in-

ternal organization. Land uses became more specialized, as wholesale, retail, and financial districts appeared and "downtowns" emerged for the first time. Districts offering specialized services, such as rooms for single men and women and entertainment areas, also developed. The introduction of mass transit revolutionized the distribution of social classes. Wealthy and middle-class citizens began moving to the urban periphery, leaving the older areas to the poor. Ethnic diversity increased, as thousands of immigrants flocked to America and sought their fortunes in the cities. Whole areas of New York, Boston, Chicago, Philadelphia, and other metropolises became ethnic enclaves whose inhabitants' cultural values were at odds with those of their host society.

These changes enhanced criminals' opportunities for crime and compounded the predicament of controlling it. At a time when few public institutions existed to care for unassimilated members of a rapidly urbanizing society, many people formed a large group in the underworld which was responsible for much of the street crime of the century. Street arabs, gang members, vagrants, and the unemployed begged, stole, and fought among themselves. Respectable citizens resented their importunities, their thefts, and their rowdiness. Yet how were they to be controlled? Gangs, for example, appeared in widely scattered areas of the city and frequently had roots in ethnic neighborhoods. Although they usually confined their activities to their immediate areas, that was not always true, and in either case they could count on some measure of local support against outside authority because they helped defend their neighborhoods from the aggression of competing ethnic groups. Relatively secure in their geographical enclaves, they could defy efforts to suppress them.

Professional thieves and vice entrepreneurs also profited from the changing geography of cities. Urbanization increased the number of people and businesses worth plundering, while the sheer size of the downtowns and wealthy residential sections made it relatively easy for thieves to find victims. Since carelessness among potential victims was not predictable or confined to specific places, criminals appeared to strike randomly throughout the metropolitan area. Urban geography thus helped to mask the activities of these thieves. Gamblers and prostitutes, on the other hand, found the emergence of highly visible specialized entertainment districts particularly useful to their enterprises. Major brothels and gambling houses located in these areas because they could draw upon nearby businesses, hotels, restaurants, and rooming houses for their customers. Specialized land use had concentrated the people interested in gambling and prostitution, thereby ensuring a high level of profits for vice entrepreneurs.

The geography of crime was not the only obstacle to coping with criminals. Their organization and skills also created difficulties. The professional thief's inventiveness, for example, matched his opportunities, and he became an expert at methods designed to enrich himself at the expense of others. Moreover, these techniques constantly improved as thieves evolved solutions to new defenses. Beginning with fairly crude equipment, professional thieves developed extraordinarily sophisticated devices for separating a property owner from his possessions. The public's ability to protect itself from the depredations of these criminals was therefore in constant doubt.

As gambling and prostitution expanded to satisfy customers' needs, their organization became more complex and sophisticated. Alterations in the structure of gambling which laid the foundations for modern "organized crime" were especially important. By the mid-eighties gamblers had adopted most of the devices which they would need to maintain their influence not only over the more ordinary forms of gambling like card games but also over other important kinds of urban entertainment such as sporting events. Vice's success in consolidating its position in society perplexed those Americans who regarded gambling and prostitution as two of the root causes of crime because they did not understand that changes in the organization of vice brought illegal entrepreneurs into the mainstream of urban life.

This was especially due to the fact that, as gamblers transformed their activities into efficient businesses, they became important sources of money and manpower for local politicians. Some gamblers, in fact, became politicians. These men usually managed organizations in the downtown wards, but occasionally they held important state and even national offices. Gambler-politicians were in a key position to exploit representative government to their own advantage. Ward and police precinct boundaries usually coincided. At a time when the ward politician controlled appointments to city jobs in his district, these men had little trouble finding candidates for the police who would sympathize with their business interests. Any officer who attempted to enforce laws against gambling or prostitution without the consent of his sponsor could be fired or transferred. Indignant moralists who regarded lax law enforcement as simple corruption therefore missed a critical point. The gambler's influence derived as much from his participation in the political system as from a policeman's personal venality.

The growing diversity and complexity of the underworld required a flexible response which existing agencies of social control lacked. If urban growth spelled opportunity to criminals, it meant disaster for the watch and constabulary, which were the only law enforcement agencies in existence at the beginning of the century. Both dated from the colonial era. Borrowed from earlier English and European traditions, neither had changed much prior to 1800. Watchmen, patrolling from dusk to dawn, guarded towns by suppressing dancing, drinking, loud singing, and similar violations of public decorum. One of their most important duties was to warn of fires. But they were extremely inefficient even in these limited tasks. Watchmen slept on duty, reported for work drunk, and frequently refused to make their rounds. Constables carried the main burden of law enforcement. Guarding the cities during the day, their strenuous duties included supervising the hue and cry after criminals, apprehending drunks, vagrants, and other disorderly persons, and commanding the watch. In addition, constables enforced all the local ordinances encompassed in the phrase "the police of the town." That is, they looked after the condition of streets, sidewalks, privies, slaughterhouses, and the mis-

cellaneous activities which affected the health, safety, and
well-being of the urban population. Citizens deemed duty as
constables so onerous that the towns had difficulty finding
men willing to serve. Increases in the geographic size and
population of cities like Boston, New York, and Philadelphia
undermined the reputations of both institutions. Behavior
among watchmen and constables which had been tolerable in
the colonial city quickly became unacceptable after 1800.
Both had to be replaced now that increasing numbers of citizens thought crime was becoming a major challenge to urban
society.

Interest in tackling this task did not coalesce to any
significant degree until the 1830s. Then an accelerating urban
growth rate, along with rising numbers of urban riots, intensified concern over public order. Wandering juveniles,
rowdies, and gangs seemed more common as city populations burgeoned. In the absence of a neutral agency capable
of arbitrating disagreements, individual and neighborhood
disputes were settled by violent confrontations. The rise of
popular political parties complicated the problems of maintaining the public peace. Competing groups frequently resolved their differences by force. Many city dwellers increasingly thought they needed some means of controlling
the chaos on the streets and creating a tolerable peace in
their communities.

Prodded by their fears, Americans tinkered with a wide
variety of existing ideas for dealing with crime. Many people
who had long regarded liquor as the root of all crime now
became even more vocal advocates of temperance. Others
thought education was the key to social order and directed
their efforts toward creating viable public school systems.
Yet another group tried to reform individual offenders using
such organizations as houses of refuge, Rosine societies, and
newboys' homes to instill proper behavior in certain members
of the "dangerous classes."

All these proposals looked toward a general reformation
of large numbers of people who displayed socially obnoxious
or vaguely criminal behavior. But these reforms would take
time to become effective. In the interim, the basic problem

of controlling crime remained. Recognizing this, some citizens began agitating for a more immediate solution which necessitated a complete overhaul of the philosophy, organization, and techniques of policing. They proposed that cities adopt the idea of crime prevention embodied in Sir Robert Peel's reform of the London police in 1829. This theory emphasized centralized direction of a large body of men whose collective efforts to suppress crime depended upon their ability to establish a pervasive, visible presence in all areas of a city at all hours of the day or night. In principle at least, crime prevention promised to control criminals for the first time in history. Slowly gathering support over several decades, the advocates of crime prevention finally succeeded in supplanting the antiquated watch with a presumably more effective approach to policing.

The reformed police departments which emerged during the 1850s and 1860s were not, however, pristine exemplars of crime prevention theory. Advocates of a new police had to adjust this theory to the realities of nineteenth-century American society. Ideology and politics, in particular, seriously compromised the theory. Proponents of public order had to come to terms with their own and their neighbors' commitment to individual freedom and a belief in decentralized political authority. The interplay between freedom, order, and republicanism produced a police initially less committed to the suppression of criminals than to a due regard for the sensitivities and interests of its sponsors.

A laudable concern for basic social and political values had unintended consequences because the kind of police which urban Americans created presented criminals with several opportunities to influence law enforcement. What should be done, for example, about professional thieves? Property owners had sought a way to protect themselves even before the movement to reform policing began. Around 1800, those who had the financial means devised a private solution to the threat by inducing constables to pursue criminals.

Once begun, this process of changing constables into detectives had long-range consequences for policing. Victims, constables, and thieves became enmeshed in a complex relationship whose often noisome methods created a fundamental dilemma for police reform. Corruption became a byword of this relationship quite early. Public distaste for detectives' methods, which often involved bribery and collusion in crimes, did not, however, solve the basic problem of how the police should deal with professional thieves and their victims. The problem was resolved by grafting the detectives onto the newly reformed police departments, but this solution compromised the organization, conduct, and integrity of those departments by, in effect, legitimizing certain types of corruption.

The new police discovered that dealing with street criminals would not be easy either. Theory and perhaps a cursory riffle through newspaper and pamphlet accounts of the London police were their only guides. Pervasiveness, visibility, and discipline existed merely as goals, not realities, in the initial years of each department's development. Administrative personnel had to learn how to implement generalized ideals. In the meantime, the public's reactions to the continuing crime problem also influenced the ways in which administrators solved the day-to-day problems of establishing a credible police presence on the streets. The answers they derived from experience helped to shape their police into a uniquely American institution.

While police officials learned to solve their problems, individual patrolmen struggled with their own difficulties. Since no governmental agency had effectively mediated the spontaneous disputes of urban residents prior to the emergence of a preventive police, few citizens knew what to expect or respect in their new protectors. The patrolmen had to create practical solutions to theoretical promises. In the best of times, preserving public order can be a delicate task, but the new policemen began work in an extraordinarily tumultuous and violent era. The unsettled nature of their environment profoundly shaped the first patrolmen's efforts to establish authority on the streets. By the 1860s they had evolved a fairly coherent body of arrest tactics, but in several important respects, especially in their use of physical force, the results were not entirely what their superiors and supporters had expected because the patrolmen learned more from the criminals they policed than from the public and administrators who supposedly controlled them.

Finally, the new police had to confront the enormous popularity and sociopolitical influence of vice entrepreneurs. In a diverse urban society, the police were under considerable, though fluctuating, pressure to eliminate these activities which so many people enjoyed. Balancing the demands for suppression against the reality of vice's power to affect policies and careers, the police struggled to evolve a solution which would not compromise their institutional mandate in some disastrous way. The struggle was complex in large part because of the structural ties with legitimate society which gamblers and prostitutes had created by mid-century and which they were not loath to use in shaping law enforcement in their own best interests.

By neglecting to study the evolution of such relationships between the police and criminals in the nineteenth century, we have had an incomplete understanding of how and why the police in urban America behaved as they did. Current attitudes and tactics which the police share amongst themselves have their historical roots in the lessons which patrolmen learned while walking their beats over one hundred years ago. We also have an insufficient knowledge of and appreciation for the ingenuity and resources of our criminal classes. While no one book can hope to explain adequately all the nuances of the relationships between policemen and criminals, the following pages sketch the broad outlines of their emergence and the consequences for modern law enforcement.

One   Police Reform, 1830–1860

It was no accident that crime prevention became an important idea in antebellum America. Cities on the eastern seaboard had not been immune from crime and disorder prior to 1830, but reactions to both problems were qualitatively different before and after that date. Part of the reason for this difference lay in the perceptions of city residents whose experiences spanned the transformation of urban society between 1800 and 1860. During the first three decades of the century, criminal behavior increasingly seemed to disturb the prevailing tranquillity of urban society; in the next three decades, many people became convinced that crime was about to undermine their society. Whether this was in fact true is questionable, but irrelevant, since these people acted upon their belief rather than upon a careful analysis of the actual situation. The reasons for the intensification of the reaction to crime lay in the real changes which occurred in the cities. As cities grew, their sheer geographic size made them seem less manageable to residents accustomed to the more compact walking city they had known. Then, too, the number and visibility of strangers, in both the literal and symbolic senses of the word, disturbed many people. Newcomers from diverse ethnic and religious backgrounds were especially suspicious to a society which was still predominately Anglo-Saxon and Protestant. These strangers posed potential dangers to accepted values and norms of behavior, and their numbers seemed to increase too dramatically beginning in the 1830s.

Americans concerned about these problems turned to the theory that crime could be prevented. This idea seemed to offer an opportunity to infuse law enforcement with a philosophy more appropriate to a complex urban society than the inefficient, outmoded watch and constabulary. Prevention implied prior decisions as to whom society regarded as prone to crime. This aspect of the crime prevention theory was especially attractive to its advocates because they assumed that their social values and political influence would determine who the criminally inclined were. The police could use those decisions as a basis for concentrating their efforts on those people, who would in turn be discouraged from committing a crime because of the likelihood of being promptly arrested. In theory, then, crime prevention would preserve the essential character of American society by placing those who seemed to threaten its existence under the supervision of a re-invigorated police.[1]

There were, however, several obstacles to police reform in the United States, and the structure of politics was one of them. A decentralized form of government resulted in piecemeal action as small groups of reformers worked within the confines of their local political situation to achieve change. As only one interest group among many, they had to marshall public opinion behind them in order to convince politicians to reshape the police. Shifting political alliances in a volatile urban environment further complicated matters. Politicians searching for new votes found it necessary to pledge hostility to law enforcement reform as one means of attracting partisans to their cause. Finally, battles for control of city government were fiercely fought, and violence was typical during elections. No party wanted to create a police which would be used against them to defeat their candidates.

Reformers also had to balance their requirements for public order against the sensitivities of those constituents who perceived a more efficient police as a threat to freedom. Fear of centralized authority and an emphasis on individual rights were basic tenets of republican ideology. Some people thought that a strong police would "in ordinary times . . . put in peril the liberties of the citizens."[2] Local authorities, especially native-born Americans from the upper classes, tended to reinforce fears regarding the abuse of personal freedom because they had a history of trying to suppress seemingly trivial transgressions of public order. They frequently objected to groceries staying open on Sunday, for example, because this practice violated the Lord's Day. But workingmen who received their pay late Saturday needed Sunday to buy their families' food and other necessities. Groceries which served liquor complicated the problem by contributing to drunkenness. Closing such places, the authorities claimed, helped reduce crime.[3] An expanding electorate, aware of these types of enforcement, would be extremely loath to enhance authority at the expense of their understanding of individual liberty.

The large number of policemen required for crime prevention raised other ideological objections which were reinforced by economic considerations. The militia and the outmoded watch were the only sizable bodies of men which republicanism would tolerate. Though unpopular except for parades, the militia in theory offered "sometimes the only weapon that can quell the mob, the riot, the rout, the unlawful assembly; sometimes the only shield that can be interposed between the lawless and the administrators of the laws."[4] According to this belief, the best defense against domestic disorder was "civil volunteer companies" composed of men "whose worth and labor give them an interest in society, and society in them."[5] The watch antedated the evolution of a distinctly American political theory and was therefore simply part of the colonial heritage which had become an accepted institution in early nineteenth-century cities. Since it worked only at night, the average citizen had little knowledge of, or personal experience with, its activities. Because the watch was both obscure and ineffective, it did not attract any attention as a potential threat to liberty. In fact, both characteristics probably made it seem to be an eminently democratic means of law enforcement.

The militia and the watch shared another characteristic: they were inexpensive to maintain. Economy in government became a primary consideration after the depression of 1819, and the concern over city expenditures continued unabated throughout the antebellum era. Militiamen did not have to be compensated for their work; it was part of their responsibilities to help suppress public disorder. The watch remained a fixture until the 1850s because it seemed so cheap. The men worked at other jobs during the day, and while this reduced their ability to stay awake at night, it obviated the necessity to pay a living wage. The cost of preventive policing, especially when compared to existing law enforcement agencies, would be an important impediment to reform.

These ideological and practical objections prohibited any rapid changes in policing. In the years from 1830 to the 1850s each American city evolved its own police department, whose form was the product of compromise and experience. Local circumstances, especially the incidence of "crime waves" and rioting, dictated the pace of reform in each city. Those people who wanted safety and tranquility in their streets had to proceed a step at a time toward that goal, and at each stage the difficulties which remained unresolved created the impetus for further changes in the structure of law enforcement.

The first efforts to reform policing grew out of generalized fears among many contemporary observers before 1830 that crime was increasing in American society. In their estimation, a wide range of criminals terrorized the inhabitants of cities. Public officials and private citizens complained that "the morals and manners of youth are neglected and . . . corrupt, society is poisoned at the fountain, and all its channels and branches will soon become infected with the deadly taint."[6] Teenagers harassed and assaulted respectable persons, set fires in the streets, fought among themselves, and engaged in petty thefts. Petitioners and editors drew a dismal portrait of a crime-ridden environment: "It is a fact against which we ought no longer to shut our eyes, that we have in the very midst of us, a population of the most abandoned kind."[7] Garroters lurked in the shadows of ill-lit lanes, springing upon the unsuspecting to murder and rob. Highway robbery was common; burglary frequent. No reliable statistics survive in sufficient quantities to verify these charges, and the picture of a crime-ridden society was probably exaggerated.[8] But the rhetoric indicates a widespread belief that crime had become a major problem, and in the absence of any contrary evidence, that attitude became an important justification for changing the existing law enforcement machinery.

Philadelphians were the first to give concrete expression to these generalized fears. In early 1830 Philadelphia seemed threatened by a crime wave: "The numerous acts of violence and outrage upon the persons and property of our peaceable citizens, and the boldness with which many of these acts are committed, . . . are sure indications that we are infested at this time by an unusual number of villains, of the boldest and most daring character."[9] Grand juries had become impatient with seemingly impotent city authorities. Philadelphia's law enforcement apparatus stirred no confidence. An independent commission controlled the outmoded watch, which performed "a routine of duty limited certainly by custom, and perhaps by the terms of their engagement, to a narrow compass."[10] Unable to command the watch or discipline its members, the mayor had only two high constables to stem the growing number of offenses. With local variations, this situation existed in Boston and New York, where these same officers carried the main burden in fighting crime.[11]

Prompted by complaints, Recorder Joseph M'Ilvaine began the movement toward police reform. Reminding critics that the courts were helpless unless they had an effective means of bringing offenders before them, M'Ilvaine proposed that the city establish a "regular police" which would have three distinct duties: collection of information regarding crime, investigation of all details necessary to prepare a legal case, and arrest of culprits. He emphasized centralized command of such a force, explaining that the key to supressing disorder lay in a *"system* constantly in motion— a something which by the laws of its *own organization* must act uniformly upon the same subject at all times."[12]

M'Ilvaine's proposals might have gone untested except for a fortuitous circumstance which gave Philadelphia the opportunity to experiment with his plan. Stephen Girard, one of the city's richest men, died in 1833. In his will Girard set aside an income to "provide more effectually than . . .

now . . . for the security of the persons and property of the inhabitants of the said city by a competent police."[13] The select council asked M'Ilvaine, Mayor John Swift, and former Mayor Joseph Watson to investigate the best means for implementing this bequest.

The report which this committee issued on November 2, 1833, showed that M'Ilvaine, Swift, and Watson were well informed about the changes which Sir Robert Peel had introduced to the London police in 1829. But their recommendations also indicated a sensitivity to peculiarly American circumstances which would prohibit a similarly sweeping reform in Philadelphia. The committee members suggested that the city councils should pass an ordinance "for the establishment of an efficient preventive police," but they recognized that many of their fellow citizens would interpret prevention to mean suppression. Seeking to reassure the public, the committee asserted that the advantages of the London reform "have not arisen from any additional or arbitrary powers conferred upon the officers, but are entirely referrable to its regular, organized and systematic operation." In fact, they argued, the British system bestowed "less power upon the individual policeman," left "less to his discretion," and afforded him "less opportunity to oppress the citizen" than "those which have always prevailed in Philadelphia, in reference to the nightly watch."[14]

Having dealt with a major objection to a preventive police, the committee members then tried to combine experience with new ideas. Apparently using M'Ilvaine's 1830 proposal, they concentrated on redefining the role of the constables in law enforcement. Arguing that "it has become necessary that in every large town there should be several intelligent and experienced men devoting their time and skill to the pursuit and arrest of the higher order of offenders," the committee recommended that the councils assign to the constables "as their principal duty, the business of tracing and arresting culprits, and executing the process of the Mayor's office." Because constables had become *de facto* detectives prior to the 1830s, this suggestion only recognized what had become accepted practice. But it incorporated a

detective approach into policing at a time when the committee was trying to introduce the preventive concept to
their fellow citizens.[15] Furthermore, while M'Ilvaine, Swift,
and Watson severely castigated the watch as "inadequate
even to the limited service at present expected, and consequently incapable by any extension of its duties of supplying
deficiencies in other branches of the Police," they did not
recommend its abolition. Because the watch constituted an
important source of patronage, the committee members
were probably accepting the political realities of the day.
But again this diluted the impact of their main goal concerning a preventive police. In order to achieve that objective,
the three men recommended that Philadelphia establish a
day and night police which would be sufficiently numerous
to implement the theory of prevention. Since this idea
simply created yet another law enforcement agency in
addition to those which already existed, the committee
urged that the mayor be given complete control over the
organization, recruitment, and command and dismissal of
the constabulary, the watch, and the new police.[16]

The councils showed considerable reluctance to embrace
the committee's report completely. Although the report
asked for an "efficient preventive Police," the politicians
passed an ordinance on December 26, 1833, designed to
establish "an effective police." The difference in wording
was not merely a matter of semantics. Rather, it showed
that few people at this time considered the London model
with favor. Though recognizing the need for change, the
councils did not want to create an agency which would
affront republican ideology. To prevent that, the enabling
ordinance severely limited the size of the new force to 24
policemen, 120 watchmen, one captain, 4 lieutenants, and
12 inspectors. This was hardly the "sufficient number"
requested by the committee. London in 1833 had 3,389
men, or one patrolman for every 434 inhabitants. Philadelphia would have one for every 3,352 persons.[17] This
ratio of patrolmen to residents would ensure that the police
would not appear to be a standing army in disguise. Girard's
bequest also helped keep the number of officers small. His

estate had authority to pay for only one-half the cost of the new police. The councils, having to pay the other half, adopted a frugal approach to reform lest they be accused of spending tax monies too liberally.

The new police was not, however, a complete defeat for the reform-minded trio, M'Ilvaine, Swift, and Watson. In 1830, M'Ilvaine had argued that "the only basis" for effective law enforcement was "constant, accurate and detailed information as to all persons, places and things, which are, or probably may become, the subject of criminal prosecution." The committee had incorporated this concept of prevention into its final report, and the ordinance creating a revised police showed the influence of this view. That law specified that the new patrolmen should walk the streets, question strangers, beggars, and disorderly persons, and arrest those who could not adequately explain themselves. The constables had performed those tasks prior to 1833. By assigning these duties to the policemen instead, the ordinance helped differentiate between detective and preventive concepts.[18] This enabled the constables to devote their full time to the pursuit of professional thieves. It also gave city officials the ability to regulate, however inadequately, those people who had become accustomed to using the public arena to settle their disputes, or who were obnoxious to respectable citizens because of their status as vagrants, juveniles, or paupers.

There was surprisingly little resistance to the new police in Philadelphia for a variety of reasons. The "crime wave" of 1829-1830 had stirred demands for a solution from many quarters. Grand juries were not the only interested citizens. Some workingmen had called for a competent police to protect their meetings, and would not therefore consider the new organization dangerous.[19] Then too, the policemen were not numerous, and they did not suddenly appear on the streets dressed, as in Britain, in a uniform, which would have shocked many Americans.[20] Finally, the lack of hostility testified to the wisdom of tempering new ideas with experience. M'Ilvaine, Swift, and Watson had achieved as much as they could within the constraints imposed by politics, economy, and ideology.

The general lack of opposition among Philadelphians to a new approach to policing may also indicate that public opinion had begun to shift in favor of greater controls over some population groups in the cities. That change was not yet very pervasive, but subsequent developments would convince many more people that further reforms were necessary. Beginning in the 1830s, nativism and anti-Negro attitudes emerged as major sources of social disruptions. Each prejudice affected wide areas of society in a variety of ways. Rioting was, of course, the most spectacular form of conflict. In Philadelphia, for example, black-white relations took a decided turn for the worse beginning with the first major race riot in the city in 1829. Additional flare-ups occurred in 1834 and 1839. While not yet as potent as it would shortly become, nativism also helped provoke such riots as the attack on Boston's Ursuline Convent in 1834. The hatreds stirred by this form of prejudice would later culminate in virulent outbreaks of violence in the 1840s.

But rioting was only the more spectacular expression of the conflicts generated by nativism and racism. As broad social phenomena, both helped create an atmosphere of fear and hatred which pervaded many aspects of urban life. Nativism became an important consideration, for example, in the temperance crusade, in the growing violence among fire companies, and in the increasingly common gang fights which terrorized neighborhoods. Racism became intertwined in the abolitionist campaign, and it contributed to the incidence of physical assaults in urban areas where the races lived side by side—in Philadelphia's South Street, for example.[21]

Hatred thus contributed in various ways to the general problem of social order, but concern over more ordinary crime did not entirely disappear. At some point in each decade an editor surveyed the situation and concluded that the "increase of crime is becoming one of the most startling notices in our daily newspapers."[22] A variety of offenses continued to alarm the authorities and various urban dwellers. Chicago's mayor complained of "gross violations of the Sabbath day; such as the firing of guns within the limits

of the city, and the keeping open of groceries."[23] Petty
thieves abounded, stealing clothing, junk, and metal. Burglars
and robbers continued to operate with apparent impunity.
Murders were so common that "Veritas," a local citizen,
claimed that Philadelphia had become known as "The Murder
City."[24]

At first, city governments responded to these problems
in severely limited ways. The Philadelphia councils actually
reduced the number of day police in 1835 because they
deemed the force too expensive. New York's councils rejected a plan proposed by Police Justice O. N. Lownds in
1836 to reorganize that city's unwieldy mass of watchmen,
marshalls, and constables. They argued that a London-style
police might be necessary sometime in the future but not
then. Boston made a halting step toward reform in 1838,
when the state legislature authorized appointment of "Police
officers with any or all of the powers of Constables, except
the power of executing a civil process." This established a
police with no connection to the watch, consisting of a city
marshall and six men (later increased to thirteen). Far to the
west, Chicago did not take advantage of its 1837 Charter
provision for seven constables, using only two or three until
1839, when the first city watch—two men—appeared on the
streets.[25] Of these cities, only Chicago escaped the increasingly large riots which punctuated the decade, but
even Chicago, a small town at the time, experienced disorder.

Ambivalent public opinion probably dictated the politicians' cautious response to crime and disorder during the
1830s. In spite of Philadelphia's limited success in introducing a preventive police, most Americans had not yet
given up on other means of social control. They expected
the authorities to utilize existing agencies to maintain order.
In 1840, for instance, a New York newspaper praised a
former mayor because he "had all the police officers, marshalls and constables, so well organized, that he could assem-
ble them together at any part of the city, at a few minutes'
notice. . . . In short [he] organized one of the most remarkable systems of police that was ever known in a republican
government."[26]

If existing agencies failed to cope with a problem, republican ideology supplied an alternative—vigilantism. During the antebellum years mobs attacked gamblers, abolitionists, Irishmen, and Negroes. These rioters were often led by "men of wealth and professed learning" who regarded these assaults as socially beneficial.[27] But vigilantism suffered from many defects. Directed mobs appeared only sporadically, and usually dealt only with unpopular groups or individuals in summary fashion without getting at the central problems of crime and disorder. Moreover, this approach had a dangerous tendency to justify personalized retribution. One editor urged his readers "upon all occasion" to shoot "riotous ruffians . . . like so many mad dogs, as pests to the community, whose deaths are a common blessing."[28] Capricious personal justice threatened the fabric of society. Some observers quickly recognized the limitations of the vigilante as a means of social control. Almost as soon as extremism began to appear, many people began to warn that "ere long, popular violence will be regarded by all as part and parcel of our institutions."[29] This concern generated a fear that crime, combined with popular justice, would "nullify all civil government, and render all rights unsafe."[30] In these circumstances, some contemporaries perceived the limitations of ideology. They concluded that the threat to *all* government and *all* rights required that *some* groups and individuals lose *some* freedom.

At the same time that Americans were beginning to recognize some limits to republicanism in law enforcement, the detective approach to policing came under heavy attack. A New York investigation in 1840 revealed the possibilities for corruption among constables for the first time.[31] This was the first probe of the police in America, and it set the pattern of exposé, public indignation, trials, and meager results. The constables had remained undisturbed for forty years as they developed and perfected their ability to solve crimes. Philadelphia's reform of its police had in fact helped make the detective approach more dominant in that city by freeing constables from their more onerous duties and by giving them explicit permission to pursue certain types of

criminals. The revelations of the 1840 investigation, however, helped to destroy the credibility of detection, and hence had enormous importance in the development of preventive policing.

This investigation derived from political conflicts. A Whig-dominated New York legislature, desiring to secure a better hold over patronage in New York City, sent a committee to examine the city's judicial system. The committee reported that the aldermen's control over the legal process, and the lack of any officers to bring offenders before the courts, had handicapped the judges. They recommended a reorganization of the courts and the appointment of fifty policemen to correct these problems.[32]

The New York *Herald* opposed this report, saying the Whigs wanted to drive the Locofocos from power. But the *Herald* did not defend the police; instead it demanded reform, remarking, "it seems that nearly all connected with the Police Office get rich very soon." This editorial catalogued the evils of the existing police system. The list of charges ran from "retaining fees to stool pigeons," to "bribes from unfortunate women, unfortunate thieves, and unfortunate vagabonds of various descriptions, for liberty to exercise their lawful vocation." Hoping to counter the legislature, the city council appointed its own committee to look into abuses. Thus began a six-month inquiry. The key issue was the fate of an established, detective-style police, and the *Herald* placed itself on the side of progress: "What we want is a *preventive* day and night police; not one corrupt system changed for another corrupt system, with every change of party."[33]

The council investigation started with revelations that some men made $50,000 in five years by being police officers. But the sessions were secret, so the press had to rely on informants and rumors. The police were accused of prior knowledge of robberies, sharing plunder, protecting favored criminals, even an early "third degree" procedure of taking suspects "into the back room, or star chamber of the police, there to take down their depositions themselves, although the Revised Statutes expressly forbid any one doing so." In

March the committee formally charged one man, Justice Henry W. Merritt, with six criminal charges involving participation in robbery and freeing known criminals in return for cash. Merritt lost his position, but he seems to have been the only man to suffer for his sins. An attempt to keep the inquiry going failed in June, and the political dust settled.[34]

Philadelphia also investigated police corruption. A grand jury found evidence that "police officers go bail for felons arrested by themselves; in some cases compounding felonies with thieves, and dividing the stolen property between themselves, thieves, and the plundered."[35] Spurred by the developments in New York, a second grand jury inquired into this system and concluded that it had reached the point of gross abuse.[36] Neither jury returned any indictments, but their revelations further undermined the dominant police arrangements.

After these exposés the *Herald* showed the general feeling of the press by demanding that any reforms should endeavor "to make the system hereafter a preventive system of police."[37] But though favoring the theory, its advocates were still reluctant to adopt the organization required for its implementation. The *Public Ledger* asked for "some plan, . . . some organization which will be entirely under the control and direction of the civic authorities." The *Ledger's* editor recommended a thorough consideration of the problem so that "the very best plan of protection" could be adopted.[38] Shortly afterwards, the *Ledger* joined general press opinion in a call for a new police whose main objects would be "permanency, discipline, vigilance, and the skill and ability to prevent crime. These objects, experience teaches us, can only be attained by a regular and systematic police establishment."[39]

Indignation over corruption and growing concern about the problems of crime made possible more changes in the structure of policing. John Swift, one of the men responsible for the reform in Philadelphia's police in 1833, returned to the mayor's office in 1840. In January he used his executive authority to detail sixteen men from the watch to day duty "with the view to prevent riots, fights, omnibus and hack

racing, petty thieving, particularly on the wharves; to repress immediately all exhibitions of drunkenness and generally to preserve order, decency, and quiet throughout the
city." Then the following June, Swift ordered the remain-
ing watchmen to day patrols with the same responsibilities.
The success of this innovation, "operating chiefly as a preventive to petty crimes and violations of the city ordinances," encouraged another change.[40] In 1841 the city
councils created a special force of ten day and twelve night
police, whose main objective was the suppression of serious
crimes.[41] The constables and the watch remained undisturbed by the new arrangements. During the years from 1841
to 1844 various New Yorkers advanced several proposals
which more or less advocated a London-style police.[42]
Political considerations weighed heavily against reform, and
again the executive branch exerted its authority. Mayor
Robert H. Morris informed the councils in 1842 that he
would use his marshalls (the only force he controlled directly) as a preventive police until a new police organization was
adopted.[43]

   The reaction to crime had reached a point where "the
proper maintenance of order by an efficient police is a
subject which has engaged much attention in all our large
cities."[44] But local politicians seemed unable to respond
to the challenge except to tinker with the existing structure
of law enforcement by executive fiat. New York's councils
considered and rejected a proposal for a force of 600 men in
1843.[45] In January 1844, a Mr. Tustin, a state legislator,
introduced "An Act to Establish a Preventive Police for the
City and County of Philadelphia" in the Pennsylvania lower
house. Although Tustin's plan retained the watch, and his
only innovation was to suggest more police judges for the
metropolitan area, he did attempt to "condense the police
business into an efficient system." Mayoral initiatives had
created unwieldy organizations to protect the cities by the
early 1840s. Philadelphia's department had criminal, municipal, day, night, special, and watchmen divisions. New York's
combination of constables, watchmen, and marshalls was no
less complicated and ineffective.[46] The complexity of these

organizations made efficiency an important consideration in
police reform. Something had to be done to eliminate conflicts among the various agencies and to streamline the
administration of policing so that it could be more effectively
utilized in the campaign against crime.

Tustin's bill never became law, and at this point Philadelphia ceased to lead the way in police reform. In 1845,
New York, after a long struggle, finally accepted a state
law passed in May 1844, establishing a metropolitan police
organization. Both the need for greater efficiency and republican ideology influenced this act. It abolished all previous
law enforcement agencies, replacing them with a day and
night police commanded by a chief administrative officer
subordinate to the mayor. The law also ensured that the
average citizen, through his duly elected representative,
would control the new police. Aldermen, assistant aldermen,
and the assessors in each ward controlled nominations to
the department, and all nominees had to be residents of
the ward which they would patrol. Thus, while the law
streamlined the structure of policing, it also decentralized
the administration of law enforcement in keeping with
democratic theory.[47]

Efficient law enforcement in a metropolitan area proved
easier to achieve in New York than in Philadelphia. New
York City and County were almost contiguous, but Philadelphia was surrounded by several independent boroughs and
liberties, each with its own government. This arrangement
allowed rowdies and rioters to raid neighboring jurisdictions
and escape into their own district with near impunity. No
watchman or police officer of Philadelphia had the power to
arrest any person, regardless of his actions, who was within
the boundaries of Moyamensing, Southwark, or Northern
Liberties. The districts were further divided from the city
by politics. Philadelphia voted Whig; the districts went
Democratic. The move for a metropolitan solution to crime
began in Philadelphia at approximately the same time as in
New York, but while New York took five years (1840-1845)
to accept that answer, Philadelphia took fourteen (1840-
1854).

Philadelphia's very large and very brutal Nativist Riots in May 1844, intensified debate over police organization. The riots culminated several years of intense antagonism between the city's Irish and nativist communities. Bitter feelings between the two had not merely been based upon religious differences; rather, the friction derived from fundamental conflicts embedded in contrasting cultural, social, and political differences which had generated hostility even before 1844.[48] Because the riots grew from such complex roots, they symbolized many of the tensions which characterized urban society generally in the years after 1830. And they provoked a sharp departure within Philadelphia from previous reliance upon informal safeguards and inadequate police agencies to maintain public order. Advocates of the old system did not disappear. One concerned citizen, for example, proposed a vigilante-type volunteer corps which would serve during riots. But public opinion was slowly shifting to the view expressed by "A Citizen of Philadelphia," who wrote that such private associations "would only be called out to *suppress*" riots. This writer advised the city to adopt a London-style police whose first duty "would be to *prevent* a tumult."[49] Temporary, voluntaristic solutions to crime now began to give way to demands for a total restructuring of public law enforcement.

In July 1844, a county court judge directed the grand jury to consider some plan "which would be practicable for an organized force, to support the laws and suppress disorders." The jury submitted a report suggesting that 450 men should be apportioned among the several districts with Philadelphia's mayor acting as chief executive officer of this force. The plan included a day and night police for the city, with the latter group replacing watchmen instead of supplementing them. The jurors, reflecting the concern over economy, argued that the "increased value of property consequent upon establishment of permanent peace and security will fully compensate for the increase in taxation." They also felt that such a force would obviate the need for military intervention, "a result much to be desired, not only because of the general expense, but because the interposition of the military . . . always tends to a greater or lesser degree to draw a line of distinction between the citizen and the soldier, and to build up in the community an order of men distinct from the great body of the people."[50] These arguments differed notably from many prior statements against preventive policing. Two major institutions, the watch and the militia, were shunted aside for the first time, and the objection to the cost of any major change was turned around. It had become more expensive not to institute reform. Finally, the jurors disposed of the ideological objections to the police by asserting that use of the military in civil upheavals produced an undemocratic distinction between the citizen and the soldier.

As a result of these debates and suggestions a public meeting resolved on November 11 to push for consolidation of the metropolitan area. Led by distinguished citizens, this meeting appointed a committee consisting of representatives from each district to draw up a bill for passage by the state legislature.[51] But not everyone was convinced that consolidation was the answer. The reformers' desire for a sweeping governmental reshuffle as well as a new police aroused immediate opposition. To counter this proposal, the opponents submitted their own bill, much narrower in scope, asking that only the police be reorganized.[52] The debate over more adequate crime control now became deeply enmeshed in the party battles of the era. Reform-minded citizens had to convince both the Democrats and the Whig politicians that a more efficient police transcended partisanship and that consolidation was the only sensible solution to the crime problem.

The opponents of consolidation won the first round. On April 12, 1845, the state legislature passed an act "for the better regulation of police" in Philadelphia and the adjacent districts. This law dealt exclusively with the powers and duties of municipal and county officers in suppressing riots.[53] New York's police reform had restructured the entire department in order to provide for "the more effectual prevention of crime."[54] By comparison the Philadelphia reformers had failed dismally. Even the authorized increase in the number of officers does not seem to have helped. In late October 1845, Mayor Peter McCall complained that the police lacked sufficient strength. During the day, only four high constables and eleven policemen patrolled the entire city, and at night a mere twenty-seven officers were on duty. McCall neglected even to mention the watch; by this time he and others regarded a new police as the only legitimate guardians of the public safety.[55]

Progress in other cities remained slow. New York's reform was not popular even in that city. In 1846 opponents tried, but failed, to make policemen elective, just as the watchmen had been.[56] Mayor William V. Brady recommended in his 1847 inaugural address that the councils reinstate the old watch system because the changes made in 1844 had "failed to meet the just expectations of the community" and because the added expense was unnecessary.[57] Both attacks showed that the new department had not yet convinced many people of its ability. In other cities the New York reform was either misunderstood or ignored. A St. Louis newspaper commended a private detective agency to its readers on the grounds that this type of organization was similar to New York's new police.[58] Boston reorganized its force in 1846, but retained the dual system of day and night police which only supplemented the watch.[59] Chicago adopted an elective system. In 1845, Philip Dean won the post of city marshall and street commissioner, and the voters selected seven men to act as constables. Two years later the city council appointed a special night watch, but disbanded it within three days.[60]

In the late 1840s the Philadelphia area's problems with crime control seemed to increase. Gang depredations became especially severe, as their activities reached a peak in the years from 1845 to 1849.[61] The district of Moyamensing "was particularly afflicted" by these groups.[62] This large lower-class Irish and Negro area on the south side of the city was well suited to the operations of rowdies. Sparsely settled, it offered large open spaces for the gang battles which erupted so frequently. The police force was in no position to break up these fights. The first policeman did not even appear until 1844.[63] This lone officer's attempts to suppress disorder could not make a great difference, and the district's reputation for violence consequently grew steadily during the late forties. "Scarcely a night now passes without the perpetration of some outrage by a gang of Moyamensing desperadoes called 'Killers,'" one observer commented. "Brutal assaults, robbery, stabbing and murder help to make up the catalogue of their crimes."[64]

Politicians in the metropolitan area responded to mounting public concern over these disorders by trying to improve the efficiency of the police. Between January and April 1848, Philadelphia, Spring Garden, and Northern Liberties officials adopted various means to deal with the crime problem. Spring Garden's commissioners merely appointed a committee to confer with Philadelphia's mayor on ways to unite their respective police forces in order to halt firemen's riots. The authorities in Northern Liberties adopted a more immediate solution, ordering their police to arrest all disorderly persons. This reputedly had the effect of routing "loafers and young rowdies . . . from their old haunts." Philadelphia's councils decided upon the most sweeping reform yet attempted. They passed an ordinance dividing the city into four police divisions, each commanded by a captain. The watch quietly disappeared. Instead, two hundred policemen were to patrol at night, and thirty-four during the day.[65]

These changes did not solve the problem of disorder. Firemen, for example, continued their battles. The Moyamensing Hose achieved wide notoriety in the late 1840s by its exploits in street battles. Its favorite enemy, the Weccacoe Engine Company, rivaled the Moyamensing in its reputation for combativeness. As with gangs, the district suffered numerous firemen's battles, but with growing impatience. In June 1849, a major riot among firemen erupted in Moyamensing and lasted all day. Using bricks, stones, and firearms, the combatants fought from Eighth to Eleventh streets, and from Christian to Fitzwater, before finally dispersing.[66]

This riot triggered a new round of public indignation. On June 19, 1849, Moyamensing citizens met and passed resolutions to establish a vigilante-type ward organization to suppress future battles. The meeting paid no attention to the existing district police as a means of achieving order. That same day, the County Court investigated the riot to establish whether or not the district had complied with the provisions of the 1845 Police Act. In spite of the conclusion that the district had, the judge " advised the Commissioners to re-organize the police . . . and related several instances which had come under his own notice . . . to show the necessity for a thorough re-organization."[67]

In August, disorder reached a point where "fights and rows are of daily occurrence between the various organized gangs of ruffians by whom the districts are infested." Matters were in such disarray that in one riot "the mob was put down by employing the villainous clubs . . . of a rival district as police."[68] The Philadelphia councils debated, but postponed, a resolution asking the Police Committee to inquire into these outbreaks and report whether the police systems of the city and districts were insufficient.[69] A grand jury decried the "alarming increase of riots, disorder and unlawful assemblages of persons, many of them of the most depraved character," and suggested that consolidation would produce an "increased vigorous execution of the laws, a cheap government, and officers fearless in the discharge of their duties." The September grand jury agreed.[70] Frustrations over official inaction had resurrected the consolidation issue.

Racial tensions supplied another example of the need for a more effective police. Prior to the fall elections, rumors of an impending attack circulated in the black community. On election night, October 9, 1849, whites boisterously paraded into the Negro area, and the residents, regarding this as a prelude to white violence, assaulted the procession. Retaliation came swiftly, centering on the California House at Sixth and St. Mary, where the Negro proprietor lived with his white wife. The House was barricaded and stoutly defended. While the battle raged, a police detachment appeared. The mob turned on the officers and routed them. Returning to their work, the rioters finally destroyed the House and several surrounding buildings. The state militia intervened, but withdrew too early, and the riot flared up again the next day. The militia returned, but had to cordon off the whole area for two more days before the authorities could declare the emergency over. Four persons died and twenty-five wounded were counted.[71] The ease with which the mob had scattered the police dramatically underscored their ineffectiveness.

The mounting tensions over disorder needed only some final, precipitating incident to channel generalized fears into concrete demands for change. The turning point came in November, when forty rowdies savagely beat an old Northern Liberties man. A public meeting called on the surrounding districts to help suppress the bands of marauders who raided with impunity. The Northern Liberties Police Committee sent a memorial to the state legislature "praying for an act creating a uniform police establishment for the city of Philadelphia and adjacent districts" and offered to confer with any police committees which the other districts might appoint. Philadelphia, Southwark, and Spring Garden quickly authorized such committees.[72]

Capitalizing on the growing dissatisfaction with the existing police, proponents of consolidation held a public meeting to advertise and organize their cause. This gathering differed from the earlier movement for consolidation in attracting a wider base of support. Many prominent men had opposed the earlier effort to achieve a metropolitan government because they thought it would result in a city "governed by the mob of the districts and its own mob combined."[73] Now these same people perceived a threat which overcame their previous objections: disorder had begun to affect property values. John Swift, twelve times mayor of Philadelphia and a man with long experience in police problems, recognized this crucial concern in his address as chairman of the meeting: "Let us have a consolidation of the districts and a union of the police, and real estate in Moyamensing will pay a fair interest." There were fortunes to be made in a rapidly growing city in which the demand for housing exceeded the supply. New subdivisions, especially in the underdeveloped districts, promised adequate homes for new Philadelphians and handsome profits for developers. But disorder made land there less desirable because decent people shied away from areas which might threaten their personal safety. Thus this meeting to promote consolidation contained a number of "citizens of standing and influence, all of whom have a deep and abiding interest in the prosperity and character of Philadelphia."[74] These people combined with the more ordinary Philadelphians who simply wanted an end to disorder.

In spite of growing public support for consolidation, and a personal appeal to the legislature by "gentlemen of influence and character in both political parties," the result was another compromise.[75] The legislature rejected consolidation; instead, on May 3, 1850, it created a "Marshall's Police" which would have men from every district on it and which would have the power to make arrests and suppress disorders throughout the metropolitan area. The law created a Police Board, also composed of representatives from each district, to maintain this new force. The Marshall's Police did not replace existing organizations; it acted somewhat like a permanent posse ranging over the county.[76] Though authorized to appoint men up to the ratio of one to 150 taxable inhabitants, the new board fixed the number at 172 (1:400).[77]

The new law encountered immediate opposition from advocates of consolidation. "Franklin," a constant correspondent favoring union of the districts and the city, warned that the Marshall's Police would become embroiled in the rivalries between the districts. He predicted that if "policemen from another district are sent into Moyamensing, they will be looked upon by the people of that district as foreigners and interlopers, having no business there, and they in turn will treat the people of Moyamensing as a band of rowdies and rioters."[78] Other writers restated the argument that metropolitan government was the best way to run the police and reduce taxes. Those most dissatisfied with the new arrangements for public law enforcement, and fearful of continuing disorders, fell back to arguments in favor of citizen patrols and overt vigilante tactics. The political fight also continued. Though the Democrats refused to bind candidates to a consolidation stand, they agreed to submit the issue to a metropolitan-wide referendum. A public meeting in the fall passed resolutions reaffirming the goal of union. Having suffered a second defeat, the advocates of consolidation now began to insist that any legislative candidates they supported would have to pledge themselves to vote for metropolitan government.[79]

Opposition to the Marshall's Police assumed other forms as well. The residents of Moyamensing held a public meeting to denounce continued disorders and voted to form a citizens' patrol on each block to prevent further outrages.[80] This was hardly an encouraging endorsement for the new force which had just begun work in November. The Philadelphia council's Police Committee administered another blow in 1851, when it advised against reducing the city's force because the Marshall's Police did not provide "an adequate and reliable substitute for our present means of protection."[81] More difficulties occurred on the street. Conflicts arose over who had the right to arrest when two men from different police forces were present. One watchman rescued a prisoner taken by one of the marshall's men. In a more petty instance of antagonism, other officers petitioned to have the new policemen confined to the station house space set aside for them.[82]

By 1854 the reforms of the last fourteen years had created unwieldy police organizations totaling 705 men serving nine metropolitan districts.[83] The conflicts of jurisdictions and the inability to achieve concerted action against rowdies, firemen, gangs, and rioters finally convinced enough legislators that a total restructuring of the government was needed. On February 2, 1854, the districts ceased to exist and became parts of the city proper. The act established a new form of government headed by a mayor and governed by a select and common council. The new law abolished the Board of Police and eliminated the marshall's office after the term of its incumbent expired (1857).[84] In July the city councils established a police force of 820 men, exclusive of officers. The select council originally had the power to nominate candidates (the mayor later acquired this authority), while the mayor appointed and commanded the men. The councils decided that each of the twenty-four wards would constitute a separate police district and gave the mayor the power, with the consent of the police committee, to alter district boundaries. Under this arrangement, the mayor created sixteen districts.[85] Philadelphia had finally obtained a police similar in structure and philosophy to that of New York.

Chicago did not experience the more spectacular forms of violence such as organized gang warfare and firemen's riots. But the city had its share of trouble. In 1849 the new mayor devoted part of his inaugural address to the problem of rowdies and urged the council to establish a more effective police.[86] By 1850, Chicago had acquired a reputation for violence. Robberies became a nightly occurrence, and the town suffered from a "flood of vicious characters that are continually pouring in upon our city."[87] The intensity of these problems does not seem to have approached the magnitude of disorders in eastern cities, but the participants in Chicago's police reform movement shared with their eastern brethren a similar concern over the tensions inherent in rapid urbanization.

The existing police arrangements did little to inspire confidence. A day police did not appear until March 1853, and then it had only nine men. These officers had little time for combating criminals. Their main duties consisted of quelling "the confusion and quarrelling at the bridges, . . . the imposition on strangers by hackmen, . . . and the general disorder so common at the Depots."[88] The council did pass a new ordinance on May 12, 1853, but this law only served to coordinate the activities of the marshall, constables, policemen, and watch. As in other cities, Chicago was having trouble keeping its multiple police divisions from competing with one another. While the ordinance introduced a greater degree of efficiency to policing, it did nothing to institute the preventive model of law enforcement to the city. The council, however, seemed unconcerned about the crime situation. An earlier law, which merely gave the mayor power to appoint policemen and watchmen "from time to time," remained in force.[89] Without a mandate for change, the elected marshall and constables remained the backbone of the police.

Nativism played an important part in creating a new police in Chicago. Philadelphia's nativist movement had culminated in the great riots of 1844, but its political power had remained rather diluted. Robert Conrad won election on a Whig-Native ticket in 1855, after the police reforms in that city had been completed. This was not true in Chicago. During the 1850s almost half of Chicago's population was foreign born. The city welcomed these immigrants, but the Catholic Irish quickly distinguished themselves as a disorderly group. A newspaper column in 1849, listing the previous day's police report, claimed eleven of the twenty-one persons arrested were Irish.[90] Another account asserted that Irishmen were "imbued with a most remarkable and striking fondness and passion for riots and rows." The only reason for this behavior seemed to be "the influence which the Catholic priesthood exercises over the majority of the Irish in our country."[91] The nativist movement, fed by this kind of reporting, grew quickly in the early 1850s.[92]

Temperance provided another source of prejudice and political strength for advocates of police reform. The Maine Law Alliance, a group of Chicagoans who wanted the state to pass a stringent prohibition law patterned on Maine's, lent its support to the movement for change. As in other cities, Sundays had become a day for fighting and heavy drinking among local rowdies. Citizens like "Pro Bono Publico" complained against these activities in places like the "Irish groggery" on LaSalle Street. "Public Good," another writer, agreed that saloons blatantly presented "the most disgusting and debasing scenes" to decent people walking along the avenues. Foreshadowing a nativist victory in 1855, he declared that "it surely behooves the moral part of the community who value sobriety, purity of language, and the general well-being of society . . . to decide whether such public vice" should continue unchecked.[93]

The Know-Nothings and the Maine Law Alliance joined forces to elect Levi Boone mayor on the Law and Order ticket in 1855. Boone promptly asked the city council for a reorganization of the police. He argued that rivalry between the day and night police made both forces inefficient and necessitated a thorough reform. Boone cautioned the council's Police Committee to choose men of "strong physical powers, sober, regular habits, and known moral integrity" to serve on the new force.[94] These qualities might be admirable in themselves, but they were also characteristics which the nativists felt the immigrants, particularly the Irish, did not possess.

Boone precipitated the only major riot in Chicago's antebellum history shortly after making his recommendations on the police. He raised the saloon license fee from $50 to $300 annually and used the existing police to round up almost two hundred tavern keepers who did not buy the new license. This ordinance, aimed at the low dives and saloons which seemed such a prolific source of disorder, also struck at the legitimate tavern owners who could not afford such a high rate. Most German proprietors, who fell into this category, became greatly agitated by Boone's new regulation. On April 21 a test case under the revised ordinance brought a procession of several hundred small saloon owners into court in an effort to intimidate the judge. After a demonstration, they withdrew and blocked an intersection. Acting under Boone's orders, the police cleared the mob off the streets. But the crowd returned later in the day, armed for battle. A force of regular and special police met them and in the ensuing riot one German was killed and one officer had his arm blown off by a shotgun blast.[95]

The deliberate confrontation between the Germans and Irish, on the one hand, and the native Americans in control of the city government, on the other, produced the desired police reforms. The nativist-dominated council passed an ordinance creating a force of eighty men plus officers. The mayor had the authority to appoint all the men with the consent of the police committee, and to make all rules and regulations regarding the department. In addition all candidates had to be United States citizens who could speak, read, and write English. The first eighty men were all native-born Americans.[96] Chicago now joined a growing list of cities which had adopted unified police departments.

By 1855 the structure of policing in northern cities had emerged. In most cases the process had been slow, responding only to pressure from a continuing chronicle of crime. Riots provided the most spectacular reasons for reform, but they represented only the worst features of unruly urban life. The advocates of change believed that their society required better regulations than the old watch and constabulary provided. These people believed in a disciplined society in which the rights of property were protected. In 1855 a Philadelphia councilman summarized these beliefs by asserting: "We can truly say that the reign of law and order is established and maintained among us. Our religious rights, our social rights, are secured and protected. The Sabbath day is remembered, and our people are allowed to keep it holy. Violence and outrage, once so familiar to our streets, are almost unknown."[97] While the councilman's optimistic assessment of a tranquil city was a little premature, his enthusiasm did reflect the pride which many urban residents felt in their achievements. After so many years of struggle, they had at last introduced a major change in the structure of policing, and they now had more hope than before that their cities would indeed become more orderly.

Although each city had to cope with its peculiar combination of local problems in creating a preventive police, the basic organization of each department was remarkably similar because of certain shared characteristics. In the first place, the principals of democratic politics operated in basically the same fashion everywhere. The new police departments reflected that fact in their internal structure. Each was tailored to respond to decentralized popular control by giving ward politicians control over appointments. Chicago proved to be an exception to this general rule. The mayor had only to consult the city council's Police Committee on the matter of appointments. This more centralized approach revealed nativist distrust of a more democratic police organization which would have given immigrant voters some voice in the selection of patrolmen. But the turbulent nature of local politics guaranteed that the Irish and the Germans would have their chance to influence police appointments in the future.

The problems inherent in implementing a preventive police also forced each department to assume similar characteristics. This approach to law enforcement required large numbers of men on constant patrol. In order to ensure that the goals of the preventive model were carried out, the departments had to adopt roughly military chains of command. Other practical considerations, such as the need for regulations and uniforms, imposed a further degree of standardization upon the police.[98] Thus, while local considerations would result in minor variations in the organization of departments, their basic structure did not vary significantly from one city to the next.

While perhaps frustrating to its proponents, the long struggle to establish preventive policing in American cities probably contributed to a general acceptance of the new departments. The debate over crime control helped to inform the general public as to the alternatives while the chronicle of gang wars, firemen's battles, and the increase in ordinary crime convinced voters that something had to be done. Then, too, impatient reformers learned how to adjust their ideas to political realities in order to achieve change. Although opposition did not cease once the new police departments appeared, there was no concerted effort to return to prior forms of law enforcement.

Although this general agreement on the theory of policing represented a major victory, reformers had failed to address themselves to serious problems. First, public understanding of crime prevention had not proceeded very far beyond its original conception. Throughout the long years of debate, the theory of crime prevention had been more a campaign slogan than a concrete program. The phrase itself seemed self-explanatory, creating expectations that crime would be suppressed without specifying precisely how that would be done. In addition, crime prevention meant different things to different people. Some looked forward to the eradication of intemperance, gambling, and prostitution; others hoped for control over the "dangerous classes," especially the immigrant poor; and still others merely wanted protection for their property. The failure to define crime prevention more adequately may have been unavoidable. The phrase had the distinct advantage that it could unite otherwise incompatible groups under a single reform banner, but it also meant that the American public had no generally accepted understanding of what their preventive police would now prevent.

Finally, the struggle to reform the police paid no attention to actual criminal behavior. Recorder Joseph M'Ilvaine had offered a cogent analysis of the ways in which a preventive police ought to deal with criminals, but reformers who came after him increasingly spoke of crime as an abstract threat to social order. This was perhaps inevitable, since the debate over crime prevention became enmeshed in conflicting themes of republican ideology, economy, politics, and prejudice. Granted this inevitability, it still did not obviate the fact that a criminal, whether a burglar, a gang member, or a drunk, was not only a representative of some ethnic group, religious sect, or social class, who needed supervision. He was also a person who posed immediate and practical problems to an officer who had little time to consider broader social issues while he attempted to arrest him. Reformers assumed the relationship between offenders and policemen would be one-dimensional—that is, the criminal would always submit to the officer's higher authority. In fact, the relationship proved to be multi-dimensional because the criminal had resources which the supporters of crime prevention had not even considered. It remained to be seen whether the theory could deal with the reality of criminal behavior in an urban environment.

| Two | **Professional Thieves and Policing** |

Theoretically, crime prevention made constables obsolete. Their duties, in general, had been assigned to the new patrolmen, who would now report public nuisances, streets in disrepair, health hazards, and other common urban problems as part of the process of preserving public order. The constables' power to arrest criminals had also been transferred to the patrolmen. In sum, there was no room in the structure of the preventive police for this ancient officer.

And yet the constables persisted, albeit in altered form, and made room for themselves in the new police departments because the advocates of crime prevention had miscalculated. They had failed to take into account the constables' role in law enforcement prior to, and during, the debate over the new police. By the 1840s, many of these officers had developed an extensive practical knowledge of crime; they had in fact become detectives who practiced an approach to policing diametrically opposed to prevention because they intervened in a crime only after, not before, it was committed. Since crime detection was fundamentally at odds with crime prevention as a theoretical basis for reforming the police, the proponents of reform had refused to incorporate it into their campaign to re-organize law enforcement.

Unfortunately for the purity of prevention theory, detection was in fact vital for two reasons: society's preoccupation with the sanctity of property, and the professional thief's skill at acquiring other people's belongings. The possession of property did not merely mean a man could care for himself and his family; it also meant he was a responsible member of American society. Republicanism rested upon the man whose ownership of property guaranteed his independent judgment in governmental affairs. The safety of property was therefore a critical concern not only to the individual, but to the republic as well. Any threat to property struck at the foundations of society.

But professional thieves were adept at acquiring property illegally. They had a wide variety of ways for doing so, and their methods tended to become more complex as time progressed. Perhaps because they were so completely dependent upon their own resourcefulness to earn a living, these thieves displayed a high degree of skill and a willingness to learn new techniques. Technological advances designed to thwart them often had the opposite effect as professional criminals turned such changes to their own advantage. In addition, their work created a subculture which had its own language, sales network, and protective devices. The average citizen could not hope to penetrate such a self-contained society.

Property owners faced with the difficulty of protecting themselves from illusive, skillful professional thieves had few resources available to them prior to the advent of preventive policing. Individual intelligence and caution were insufficient to this challenge, as numerous encounters demonstrated. Casting about for a solution to their problem, some victims turned to those constables who were willing to chase thieves for a fee rather than enforce miscellaneous city ordinances. In doing so, however, these citizens unwittingly raised important questions about the nature of the services which law enforcement should render to their communities.

The emergence of constable-detectives confronted these questions directly. In order to capture thieves, constables had to consort with them. What should be the proper relationship between criminals and lawmen? The answer was not obvious because the constables' clients were less concerned with the tactics of their hired help than with their results. That ambiguity raised other problems. Did the public want crime suppressed or property recovered? Were these different services incompatible? If so, what could be done to resolve the conflicts between them? The advocates of crime prevention had not forseen these problems because they had assumed that the theory, once implemented, would control all types of criminals by vastly expanding the presence of the police at all hours of the day and night—thus supposedly increasing the safety and sanctity of a city's homes. Experience proved them wrong and forced them to make important changes in the structure of the new police in order to accommodate theory to reality.

Professional criminals set traps of varying complexity for the unwary. The drop game was an early favorite. One man would drop a bank note next to the intended victim, and pretend to find it. While the citizen wondered why he had not noticed this treasure at his feet, the partner arrived and declared that "this honest man is entitled by rule to one half." Following an apparent protest, the first thief would agree, and ask the stranger if he could make change for the bill. If he did, the pair walked off with their profit, leaving the victim holding a counterfeit bill. Its numerous variations and simplicity made this confidence game quite common by 1812.[1]

Counterfeiting was probably the most lucrative, widespread, and complex crime in the early nineteenth century. It required considerable quantities of ink and paper, an engraver to make the plates, and some kind of printing press, but the absence of a national monetary system and the incredible profusion of local banks of issue provided counterfeiters with a wide variety of bills to copy and practically guaranteed them success. One gang stockpiled notes for eight city and county banks in New York, four in Pennsylvania, and two in New Jersey and passed the bogus money in New Hampshire and Massachusetts.[2] Authorities discovered counterfeits only when they came to the bank of issue, or when they were so poorly made as to attract attention. The relative safety of this crime resulted in large operations, as well as individual efforts. Some industrious gangs established well-equipped shops in a city or in the countryside.[3]

Picking pockets was a common activity among professional criminals, who worked so quickly and with such finesse that the victim did not notice his loss. The basic procedures developed before 1830. Pickpockets (known as "files" or "dips" to their peers) operated alone or in small groups. When working together, one person acted as a stall to distract the victim's attention while another man did the actual robbing and then passed the loot to still a third accomplice. This crime was relatively common because its simplicity and its many opportunities in cities promised quick profits. Inadequate credit and checking systems forced visitors, businessmen, and residents to carry large sums of cash. Each new development in transportation offered an additional means of making money. Pickpockets frequented steamboats, omnibuses, ferryboats, and, later, trains. Anywhere a crowd gathered, such as at a fire, there was a potential bonanza, but these thieves also congregated at transport depots, along parade routes, and in theaters.[4]

Burglars organized and equipped themselves well. Some labored alone, but groups of three to five were common. Bulky plunder, like silverware and clothing, seemed to dictate this number. One man could not hope to carry off a great pile of booty, whereas accomplices guaranteed swiftness and a large take. The implements for this crime varied. A crowbar to force doors and windows was a basic tool, and by 1818 burglars were using false keys.[5] Armed with this equipment and organization, burglars took advantage of the growing mobility and anonymity of cities. Nathaniel Russell, John F. De La Roy, and John Hale, all habitual offenders, raided homes in New York City and hid their loot in Philadelphia.[6] By 1836 such men as these had established a seasonal work schedule. As one newspaper put it: "The honorable society of burglars are [sic] now in their usual winter professional tour, and as every attention should be paid to such distinguished guests, we hope that they may be entertained at the public expense."[7]

Before thieves could convert stolen items into cash, they had to store, alter, and dispose safely of their loot. The storage problem required someone to care for the property.

Receivers of stolen goods ("fences") probably appeared before 1800; certainly they were active after that date. The fence was essential; pawnbrokers, old clothes merchants, and junkmen commonly fulfilled this role. Though not all such dealers were accessories to crime, contemporaries noted their connections with all types of brigands. Whether accidental or deliberate accomplices, these tradesmen provided valuable services to pickpockets, burglars, and assorted offenders who brought them everything from fine jewelry to scrap iron. Without their services, criminals would have been hard pressed for cash.[8]

The emergence of a habitual criminal class required similar specialization on the part of law enforcement agencies. Only the constabulary had the potential to respond to this need. Since they worked during the day, constables theoretically had the time available to develop a case against a thief. And they had greater latitude than watchmen in common law to make arrests with or without warrants.[9] The problem was how to capitalize on this potential in order to combat the professional criminal.

Money proved to be the solution to the problem. Ordinary citizens realized that they would have to pay for protection. As some New York petitioners to their Common Council in 1811 recognized, "capital criminals may, through the want of competent remuneration to . . . inferior officers of justice, baffle pursuit and escape the penalties of the law."[10] Pay scales of fifty cents to a dollar a day were not sufficient compensation for the arduous task of coping with professional thieves. Urban residents therefore aroused the constables' interest by offering additional amounts of money.

Reward notices, rare in the 1790s, became commonplace after 1800.[11] Hardly a day passed without someone announcing the theft of valuables. Each of these bulletins contained descriptions of the stolen goods and of the thief, if that information was available. The reward was the most important item in each of these announcements. Sometimes the advertiser offered separate sums for the return of his property and the capture of the criminal: "[$200] will be paid for securing the thief in the jail of this city [and a] reasonable and generous reward [for the return of the stolen goods]," read one such ad.[12] The amounts of rewards ranged widely: six dollars for the capture of a burglar; five hundred for a robbery suspect. Two hundred dollars was not an uncommon offer, though sums ranging from fifty to one hundred dollars appeared more frequently.[13] A lucrative source of income, rewards gave constables a reason to apprehend the professional criminal.

The constables needed more than financial stimulus to become a successful thief-taker. He also required certain basic skills: a good memory for faces so that he could recognize individuals with criminal records; a knowledge of those areas of the city where thieves gathered; an acquaintance with the methods by which criminals operated; a sharp eye for suspicious actions; and, in a rapidly urbanizing nation, intercity cooperation to keep pace with a highly mobile criminal class. This list is not exhaustive, but the items included here were prerequisites for law enforcement in the early nineteenth century. The police organizations which developed after 1840 did not invent these means of crime control; they inherited them.

The constables developed most of these techniques and talents for coping with professional thieves by 1830. As early as 1800 their investigative work began to appear in the daily press:

> A person was apprehended on Tuesday last, on suspicion of counterfeiting money [counterfeiting equipment was found in his possession]. He was on the point of proceeding to business, having the metal melted in the crucible, when the officers of justice interrupted the process. . . . He is an old offender.[14]

This is an example of the methods involved in early detective work. The "officers of justice" had some knowledge of this suspect's activities, for they were able to catch him redhanded. And the man had a reputation for criminal activity. Other news accounts indicate the progress of constables subtly turning into detectives. In 1803 they located a repository for stolen merchandise, and by 1810 they were watching the activities of dealers in such goods.[15]

In these and other cases, a constable's success depended upon his ability to obtain accurate information regarding criminal activities. To obtain that kind of data, he became increasingly reliant on informers in the underworld. The use of informers was not new to law enforcement. City authorities had long used private citizens as a source of information regarding violations of ordinances. The usage continued into the nineteenth century, but officials relied upon this system less and less. Two factors gradually eased ordinary citizens out of the informing business. Malice toward one's neighbors or a desire to obtain half the fine for ordinance violations (as provided by law) prompted many unjustifiable complaints. As a result, various legislatures began to restrict the use of informants in civil cases.[16] Secondly, the average urbanite did not usually have the kind of information necessary for the pursuit of professional criminals. As Philadelphia's Recorder Joseph M'Ilvaine noted, "it is not safe to rely exclusively upon voluntary communications from private citizens, because regularity cannot be secured, and because inexperienced individuals are constantly liable to deception and mistake." The best solution to the problem of regular and accurate information was, according to M'Ilvaine, "a class of officers . . . moving rapidly and quietly from place to place as the exigencies of the service may require."[17] As the constables devoted an increasing amount of time to earning rewards, they became more expert than the ordinary citizen in acquiring knowledge of criminal activities.

The constables' ability to extract data from underworld figures was related to their strong bargaining position. They had the power to disrupt the business of crime by arresting an offender. On the other hand, the constables' primary interest in a case was the reward. To achieve his goal, the constable could offer a potential informer a deal: no arrest in exchange for information. The exact details as to when these arrangements became standard procedure is understandably vague and probably depended upon the skill of individual constables. New York's Jacob Hays, one of the most successful and famous of these men, had sufficient contacts within the underworld by 1818 that he was able to range beyond the city limits. In that year he

journeyed to Canada in search of counterfeiters, and his
information was so accurate that he proceeded to "the
principal manufactory" of the criminals. During the 1820s,
George Reed developed a reputation as Boston's greatest
thief-taker because of the reliability of his informers.[18]
Hays and Reed were only the best known among many
constables who pioneered in the development of detective
methods.

     Although a response to a specific need, the trans-
formation of the constable into a detective raised a complex
problem which contemporaries failed to perceive until the
late 1830s. Circumstances had altered the nature of a constable's duties, and by the end of the 1820s some urban
authorities recognized that it had "become necessary that
in every large town there should be several intelligent and
experienced men devoting their time and skill to the pursuit and arrest of . . . robbers, housebreakers, pickpockets,
and other felons."[19] The operative words for these city
officials were "pursuit *and* arrest," but there was a conflict
between this view and that of the victim of a property
crime. Ideally, the arrest of the thief should have resulted in
the recovery of his belongings, but many victims apparently
did not think so. Some of their advertised rewards included
an "and/or" clause which provided one amount for the
return of their property and another, sometimes smaller,
sum for the apprehension of the criminal. The choice in
effect turned the constable, a public employee, into a private entrepreneur.[20] Because his main interest lay in collecting extra compensation for official duties, and because
there was likely to be more money in capturing the pur-
loined property than arresting the thief, the constable was
encouraged to compound a felony by arranging a deal with
the criminal: return of the stolen goods in exchange for no
arrest. Thus the principal concern of the general public, the
arrest of felons, assumed secondary importance. This conflict between the public and the private interest (which
now included both the aggrieved property owner and the
constable) became the basic theme in the development of
the detective after 1830.

The general public did not become aware of this conflict until 1840, when two investigations in New York and Philadelphia revealed the abuses which a detective system could produce. These almost simultaneous inquiries found that a few officers were getting rich working something called the stool pigeon system.[21] As described by one newspaper editor, this arrangement was a partnership between a lawman and the criminal:

> It amounts in fact to this—keeping of a set of rogues in pay, for the benefit of police officers. The operation is well understood. A robbery is committed, or a pocket is picked, a reward is offered, the officers seek out the thief, and the goods or money are restored to the owner, the thief remains *unknown*, the reward is paid, and the officer and the thief divide the spoils.[22]

The New York inquiry, which was the more detailed of the two probes, indicated there were variations to this scheme. Policemen occasionally had prior knowledge of some crimes; in other instances they either received stolen property or knew of its location, and refused to surrender these goods until the owner paid a suitable reward.[23]

These arrangements cannot be dated precisely. One contemporary account claimed that they had been in existence since at least 1830.[24] In addition, the New York inquiry occurred behind closed doors, and a Philadelphia grand jury only issued a generalized condemnation of the system. Thus we have no testimony as to why stool pigeoning developed, but we can speculate. This partnership introduced an element of stability into a situation in which both the criminal and the constable had a similar objective: making a living. Both parties gained their goal by agreeing to cooperate. The officer, by working with a small number of thieves, reduced his work load and still guaranteed himself a steady income from rewards. A criminal avoided the occupational hazard of arrest and received compensation for his labors. Aside from the corruption which became possible under the stool pigeon system, these partnerships represented a logical step in the trend toward private entrepreneurship in detection work.

As a consequence of the 1840 investigations, some attempt was made to force the constable-detectives to recognize their public responsibilities. As part of this trend, the courts moved from an equivocal stand on rewards to an outright prohibition of them. Prior to 1840 there had been some question whether a constable's efforts to track down stolen property constituted a normal or extraneous part of his official duties. If the latter, he was entitled to rewards as a private citizen. At first some courts had been inclined to favor the idea that such work did qualify the constables for extra compensation.[25] Beginning in 1835, however, the judiciary gradually reversed this attitude.[26] Reflecting this changing opinion, the Massachusetts Supreme Court ruled in 1845 that public employees could not collect rewards. Three years later, Pennsylvania's highest tribunal summarized the recent trend by stating that officers "must do their utmost to discover, pursue, and arrest offenders . . . without other fee or reward than that given by the law itself."[27] These rulings placed legal obstacles in the way of maintaining the old, corrupt relationships between lawmen and thieves and reminded the detectives that they had an obligation to arrest criminals, not bargain with them.

Local laws and ordinances, though enforced haphazardly, reflected the trend toward greater control of rewards. New York's legislature stipulated that officers could receive extra compensation only by the prior written consent of the mayor. Boston's experiences with constables had been entirely different from that of other cities. There the aldermen had offered rewards for the detection of criminals since 1829, and private arrangements between detectives, victims, and thieves had flourished without any outcry into the 1840s. But in 1846 Boston joined the movement toward greater regulation by requiring a special council vote for payment of these fees. Philadelphia, which initially prohibited all gratuities, conformed to these developments by adopting New York's example in 1855.[28]

The revelations regarding stool pigeons also contributed to a shift in popular attitudes toward policing. Prior to the 1840 scandal the concept of crime prevention had made little progress in America. The constables, working on the detection principle, had managed to give property owners some sense of security. But the New York and Philadelphia inquiries helped to discredit detection as a major approach to policing. Public opinion (as expressed in the daily newspapers) turned against it because, as Philadelphia Mayor Peter McCall noted, collusion between officers and thieves would "inevitably bring the police into disrepute and materially injure its efficiency."[29] The official trend in the 1840s was firmly against what had once been accepted practice.

Although public opinion and official acts expressed a hostility toward constable-detectives, that animosity did not obviate the need for their services. Professional crime seems to have entered an era of maturity and prosperity by mid-century. There are no reliable statistics to prove that burglary, robbery, and swindling became more frequent; and it may be that people became less tolerant, and hence more willing to complain, of crime as preventive policing, with its implicit promise to suppress thievery, spread throughout the nation. But even with these considerations in mind, the available evidence indicates an increase in the sophistication of professional criminals which had not been present before 1840.

Confidence men continued to find many opportunities for profit in the burgeoning cities. Charities, for example, usually solicited funds during the winter months when the poor had the greatest need for aid. These organizations sometimes discovered that someone had preceded them through a neighborhood asking for contributions. Naturally, these "representatives" never turned over their collections. Immigrants bound for the West might encounter a polite "official" on the train who would inform them that they had the wrong tickets. He would offer to exchange their tickets for the correct one, and he generously asked only a little extra cash to make up the difference in price. The furor over the draft during the Civil War inspired another thief to pose as a government agent who could exempt a man from service for a mere twenty-five dollars.[30] Many people thus remained vulnerable to swindlers. Sympathy for the poor, ignorance of geography in a new country, and anger over a law might provide the thief with his opportunities. But these were ephemeral attitudes, or had seasonal limitations, and they did not furnish steady employment. To be successful, the underworld entrepreneur had to find more substantial work.

Confidence men did a brisk business by catering to their victims' desire to make a quick profit. The "drop game" continued to be a favorite means of cheating gullible city visitors.[31] Watch stuffing became common during the 1850s. In this game, a thief plated a cheap timepiece to look like gold. Armed with his device, he persuaded some pedestrian that he would part with the watch for a fraction of its "true" value. Others advertised their wares by mail. Some ingenious circular swindlers offered counterfeit money for sale at discount prices. They boldly pointed out the advantages of defrauding one's friends and local merchants by paying for goods and services with bogus cash. If the dupe accepted the proposal, he usually received a package of sawdust for his troubles.[32]

Other swindlers victimized merchants in a variety of ways. Some would order merchandise sent, along with the bill, to the house of a prominent citizen. The thief then gave an address where he could meet the goods, or he persuaded the delivery boy to surrender the merchandise to him en route. Check and money order forgers were among the most resourceful criminals by the middle of the century. One man obtained a storekeeper's signature by pretending to be an employee from a nearby shop whose owner wanted some information from his neighbor. Soon after the businessman sent a written reply, he discovered a four hundred dollar check had been cashed in his name. Fradulent drafts drawn on banks of other cities became so common by the mid-1850s that brokers in Philadelphia and New York devised a secret code to verify the authenticity of particular notes.[33]

The counterfeiting business began to change after 1840 because of technical improvements in manufacturing money. Many counterfeiters ceased operations when they found themselves unable to match the increasing skill of honest engravers who made products of superior design and complexity.[34] Although this competition drove many lesser talents out of business, counterfeiting remained a major problem.[35]

The Civil War, by creating an urgent demand for a sound national currency, brought the federal government into the battle against this crime. Neither side seemed able to gain a permanent advantage in this contest of skills. The Treasury Department employed the finest engravers available, and their talents provided the principal protection against bogus bills until the mid-1860s. Few criminals had the ability or patience to duplicate their work. But that defense weakened with the emergence of equally proficient underworld technicians. One of these men, Charles Ulrich, came to public notice with his arrest in 1867. According to one commentator, Ulrich represented a "new school of counterfeiters, who seem to be as highly skilled as the regular and honest engravers."[36] Ulrich's work shook the government's confidence. Beginning in 1869 the Treasury Department buttressed its product by issuing all notes on a fibre paper manufactured by a special patent process. Undaunted, the counterfeiting fraternity produced another coup. John Peter McCartney discovered a chemical wash which removed the ink from authentic one dollar bills, thereby giving him genuine paper for his own creations. In spite of the Secret Service's best efforts, counterfeiters with the necessary skills and technical knowledge continued to plague the nation.[37]

Thus the race continued as confidence men found new ways to defraud their victims, and they in turn sought more effective means of protection. Checking accounts seemed a good way to handle business transactions until the thieves stole a few canceled drafts, reproduced them, and then cashed them to the discomfiture of merchants and banks alike. Telegraphic communications between cities improved the chances of discovering fake money orders; but the swindlers countered by arranging to have accomplices deliver forged confirmations. If novel techniques temporarily frustrated the underworld, the con man could always purloin a few dollars working the simpler forms of deceit while someone solved the problems posed by the new developments.

Picking pockets continued to develop as a profitable career. During mid-century, these thieves began to develop specialties in their calling. By the 1840s "files" who worked alone had developed a small knife with which they silently sliced pockets to obtain the contents. This operation was known as "nicking." In addition to this refinement in methods, there is some evidence to indicate that pickpockets had begun to specialize. The underworld referred to those "dips" who worked in churches as kirkbuzzers (or autumn divers). For instance, William Jones, alias "Boots and Shoes," concentrated on crowds at funerals and other sacred occasions. Mollbuzzers victimized women, reader merchants operated in and around banks, and groaners administered to people at charity sermons. Finally, the carbuzzers practiced their craft in railroad coaches and omnibuses. Except for these specialties, the basic structure of pickpocket gangs remained unchanged throughout the century, and the business returned handsome profits. Eddie Jackson, one of Chicago's most adroit files in the late nineteenth century, cleared about $1,500 a week in his prime.[38]

Shoplifting had developed into a flourishing trade by mid-century. Its practitioners had invented several interesting devices which enabled them to steal articles even while being observed by a clerk. Male thieves wore special coats whose pockets appeared normal on the exterior, but which opened into a large cavity in the lining. Women used pouches concealed under their skirts. In an age of voluminous dresses, the technique allowed the "hoister" to carry off considerable quantities of goods. Organized groups of shoplifters, containing members of both sexes, moved from city to city plying their craft.[39]

Streetwalkers and inmates of the less respectable parlor houses frequently stole from their customers.[40] Some ingenious criminals decided to elaborate on this practice by making robbery the essential part of an offer of prostitution. The panel game may have been an American invention.[41] In

1859 to 1884. John D. Grady's career (1865 to 1880) spanned nearly as long a period. He dealt only with the top professionals, protecting his clients by informing on their competitors and acting as their banker for important jobs.[62] These receivers, and a few others of like stature, made a very decent living in this business. They obtained quality materials in bulk, and at discount prices. Snow, for example, paid Clendaniel $1,100 for property worth $5,000 to $6,000. Clendaniel testified that at other times Snow had given him $300 for $2,000 worth of laces, and the same sum for furs valued at $2,000.[63]

The fence was not the only person who performed valuable services for the underworld. By the 1840s a class of bail bondsmen had appeared who spent their time obtaining the rapid release of captured criminals. Arrest had become a routine hazard for some felons, and "straw bail" (a bond which the thief had no intention to honor) developed as a response to that problem. Pickpockets frequently used this system. They usually gave a false name in court and quickly found a surety. The thief paid his bondsman a fee plus enough money to cover the forfeiture of bail and returned to work in a matter of hours.[64]

The continued growth and increasing sophistication of professional crime helped to perpetuate the detective system in America. The average patrolman after 1840 did not have the opportunities to develop the skills necessary for detective work. Furthermore, all the principals involved—the constable, the victim of a property crime, and the thief —retained their interest in the old arrangements. Citizens continued to pay rewards for the recovery of their belongings; policemen accustomed to the old ways of conducting their work maintained their contacts with professional criminals. Merchants and ordinary city dwellers supported the idea of a preventive police after 1840, but they saw little reason to forsake the opportunity to recover their property through the customary channels.[65] Consequently, there was a tension between public attitudes and private practices.

Some constables responded to this tension by taking the last logical step in their development as entrepreneurs. They became private policemen. In June 1845, Gil Hays,

once a member of New York's constabulary, established an
"Independent Police." According to a news account of this
event, Hays and several other former officers intended to
"open an office for the arrest of burglars and the prevention
of pickpockets."[66] Hays decided to go into business within
a month of the city's finally adopting the 1844 reform bill
after a year-long struggle. His failure to secure a reappointment under the new system possibly precipitated his decision, but the juxtaposition of the two events may have been
coincidental. Where changes in the old policing structure
proceeded more slowly, other men with detective experience
also set up agencies (and usually called themselves Independent Police). These organizations appeared in St. Louis
(1846), Baltimore (1847), and Philadelphia (1848).[67]

From these origins in the 1840s, private policing grew
into a thriving enterprise. At first, the men engaged in this
trade were former officers who had either retired or who
found themselves politically unacceptable to an incumbent
administration. In the mid-1850s a slightly different individual emerged—entrepreneurs who had either minimal
police experience, or none at all. They styled themselves
"private policemen," "preventive police," "counterfeit
detector," or otherwise claimed to operate a "police
office."[68] Allan Pinkerton, beginning in Chicago in the early
1850s, was the most successful and probably the most
efficient of this new type—although he had a penchant for
publicity and a talent for self-glorification.[69] Other, less
scrupulous, individuals developed unsavory reputations for
manufacturing evidence of marital infidelities in divorce
cases and for their anti-labor activities.[70]

Even though some private detectives developed unenvi-
able reputations, the appearance of these entrepreneurs did
have an effect on the development of a reliable preventive
police. Private enterprise siphoned off some of the best talent
available to the new departments and provided citizens with
an alternative means of recovering property. This latter point
was particularly important in the attempts to institutionalize
the preventive model in America. Because prevention was a
new idea in American policing, it had not had sufficient time

to demonstrate its virtues by the 1850s. Moreover, this approach to law enforcement had its greatest impact on such problems as suppression of gangs and curtailment of street crime. While progress in these areas was certainly desirable, property crimes constituted a peculiarly sensitive issue which the preventive policing concept had to confront.

During the 1850s property crimes not only continued; they spread geographically as cities expanded, and they appeared to increase in number.[71] Officials sought to deal with this trend by increasing the number of patrolmen. As the cost of this response spiraled, public support declined and was replaced by a demand for economy. Opponents of larger law enforcement agencies justified their position on the grounds of efficiency, tying the issue to continuing property losses. An editor complained, for example, that "in spite of the large police force employed by the city, the burglars seem to have a first rate time of it."[72] In Chicago, another newspaper put the matter even more clearly, asserting that "if it be not the business of our police to detect crime, as well as to arrest criminals . . . , the people . . . will soon come to the conclusion that the services of that body . . . had better be dispensed with."[73]

The proponents of preventive policing faced a dilemma by the mid-1850s. If they continued their strict adherence to the preventive theory, and the trend in property crimes continued, public support for the new departments would be eroded. Private policing might then become a major alternative for victims of theft. But if the advocates of prevention compromised by incorporating detection into the structure of each department, they would have to accept the risk that corruption, and public outcries against it, would recur.

This dilemma was most serious in Chicago, where politics and private policing combined nearly to destroy the concept of prevention. The Democrats, relying heavily upon the foreign-born population for support, did not want any reforms in law enforcement which would antagonize their followers. The nativists and temperance advocates, who dominated the emerging Republican party, wanted changes in the city's peace-keeping arrangements in order to control the rowdy Irish. When Levi Boone won the mayoral campaign of 1855 on the Law and Order ticket and pushed through a reorganization of the police, the battle was joined. Public safety, and how best to achieve it, became a major issue and remained so for the next six years.

Unfortunately for the Republicans, Chicago held annual elections at this time. The Democrats swept back into power in 1856. Their solution to the crime problem (as distinct from disorder) de-emphasized public law enforcement. The previous year, Alderman William S. Church had proposed that the mayor have authority to appoint persons "who may be employed as private watchmen, policemen, and giving them the same powers as city policemen in the regular service." This idea failed, but in 1856 the Democrats added a similarly worded amendment to an ordinance reforming the department.[74]

In the usual housecleaning following a party's return to power, the Democrats had also eliminated Cyrus P. Bradley, the city's first chief of police, by abolishing his position. During his year in office, Bradley had gathered some of his friends on the force into a special unit which worked to detect crime. These men, eight in number, resigned with Bradley. The rabidly Republican *Tribune* commented that "now, when our citizens are robbed, they must pay the private police to catch the robbers and receive the property." Within a month Bradley and some of his companions founded their own agency, and, suddenly, the *Tribune* became a devoted advocate of private policing. The newspaper began to sing Bradley's praises and to give prime space to his exploits. At the same time, it launched a bitter campaign against the regular officers.[75]

By the middle of 1856 both political parties had reached the same conclusion—that a publicly paid police controlled by their opponents could not protect the city. With neither the Republicans nor the Democrats interested in building a strong department, it quickly degenerated. Within a year Mayor John Wentworth could express the opinion that "our citizens have ceased to look to the public police for protection, for the detection of culprits, or the recovery of stolen property. It cannot be relied upon for the preservation of order."[76]

Wentworth tried to save the Chicago police in 1857. Shortly after offering his assessment of their reputation, he personally led the posse which cleaned out the Sands, an area on the north side of the Chicago River's main branch which had become the center of disorder in the city. Then he launched a campaign against gamblers and prostitutes. These raids made little impact on those arrested; they were often back at work within a matter of hours. But Wentworth had selected his targets with care. His officers received considerable publicity for their efforts and recovered some of their standing as protectors of the community.[77]

Unfortunately, Wentworth did not attack the main problem undermining public confidence. During the spring of 1857, Chicago experienced a wave of property crimes. From February to March the *Tribune* reported thirteen burglaries. In May these offenses occurred at the rate of one a day; and in the first three weeks of June forty-one were recorded. Wentworth tried and failed to halt this outbreak by increasing the number of patrolmen.[78]

As the thefts continued, the *Tribune* began to lose its patience with Wentworth and his police, in spite of their Republican affiliations. Joseph Medill, the paper's editor, decided to examine conditions himself, and made a tour of the city one night in the company of two friends. In a surprisingly mild report, Medill concluded that "the patrolmen were doing their duty" but in preventing burglaries "they amount to nothing at all." His analysis of the situation struck at the crux of the problem: "This is not the fault of the men but of the system. The present police force is no doubt as good and efficient a body of men as is needed for the preservation of order . . . but for the purposes of catching adroit and experienced rogues, they are useless, and it is unreasonable to expect them to be otherwise."[79]

Medill offered three solutions to the crime wave: citizens' night patrols, another increase in the number of officers, or the creation of a detective detachment. The editor favored the last choice, but subsequent events revealed he had definite prejudices about the composition of such a squad. Although the city did employ one or two detectives between 1857 and 1861, the appointees were never very acceptable unless the men happened to belong to Bradley's private organization. In 1858, for example, Mayor John Haines hired Issac H. Williams (a member of Bradley's firm), and Medill praised the selection. But the editor continued to attack the police in general for failure to apprehend criminals.[80] In effect Medill had developed a modified idea of preventive policing, but he refused to believe anyone but Bradley could implement it adequately.

Nevertheless, the fortunes of public law enforcement had reached a turning point. By late 1858 the *Tribune* was arguing that "private police will do much, but the city government . . . will do even more."[81] The Bradley-type sleuths began to lose support when their numerous abuses came to light. They had at times thwarted the regular officers, had taken money from criminals in exchange for letting them go, and had used the premises of some merchants to run houses of prostitution. Private detectives also turned many customers against them for charging enormous fees.[82] As these excesses increased, opinion swung back to support for a city-run department. According to one newspaper, "the only legitimate or proper detectives are those created and sustained by the laws." Recognizing the problems of the old constabulary system, this editorial suggested that "it is the duty of the people . . . to correct their [detectives'] inefficiency."[83] Thus the key to the further development of detective details lay in imposing restraints on the methods which appalled public opinion.

The altered circumstances for receipt of rewards made the idea of accepting detective work as a formal part of policing more acceptable to those who were familiar with the faults of the old stool pigeon system. Court decisions, and the various local regulations governing the disposition of extra compensation, established some legal and administrative controls over this problem. Furthermore, not every constable-detective had become a private policeman. Some officers in every department had continued to work on the solution of property crimes. Public distaste for this activity had caused them to adopt certain subterfuges. "Detailed duty" had become a common euphemism for detective operations. Experience had shown that at least some of these men were willing to conform to the strictures regarding rewards.[84] Thus, while corruption remained a constant threat, there was some basis for feeling that the detective would be successfully incorporated into the new police.

Hoping that the worst problems of the old stool pigeon system had been modified, the cities responded to the rising public demand for more adequate means for dealing with property crimes. Boston, always in the lead in this particular aspect of policing, organized the first detective force in 1846. New York followed suit in 1857, Philadelphia in 1859, and Chicago in 1861.[85] Staffing the new detachments was not difficult. Cyrus P. Bradley of Chicago typified the selection process. He accepted an offer to return to the regular police as general superintendent in 1861. Ordered to establish a detective bureau, Bradley hired several of his former employees from his private police business. Thus the first officially approved detectives in Chicago and elsewhere were invariably men with considerable experience in dealing with the underworld.[86]

Some detectives turned these developments to their own advantage. The old stool pigeon partnership between constable and thief had given each a share of the victim's reward offer. But with the emergence of regulations dealing with such compensation, the detectives had legal access to the total sum. Secure in the knowledge that they would receive remuneration for their efforts, detectives could approach the criminal on a new basis. They could now demand that the thief match or exceed the amount of the reward or face arrest. Thus the detectives altered an earlier form of corruption from cooperation to exploitation in order to give themselves a larger share of the spoils.

As detectives became less dependent on thieves in securing rewards, the nature of the stool pigeon system, and the meaning of the phrase itself, changed. In the past, officers had given some criminals the freedom to pursue their trades in exchange for information or cooperation in returning stolen goods. In the 1850s a new technique appeared: detectives began to pay their informants. The police now became a source of income for some thieves (most probably petty criminals and hangers-on in the underworld). This practice helped to destroy the old relationship between criminals and lawmen. The difference may be seen in attitudes. Before the 1850s, "stool pigeon" had been an expression of ill-repute among the general public; after this change it became a term of contempt in the underworld as well.[87]

Thus the detective became an established member of the police. Integrating his functions into the new departments did give officials some control over his behavior, and their displeasure could result in his dismissal. But unfortunately for the good reputation of the departments in the nineteenth century, they needed the detective's services more than he needed their approval. The police were caught between two challengers to their legitimacy. On the one hand, the professional criminal continued to plague the public, thereby generating a demand that he be controlled; on the other hand, the private detective offered an alternative solution to thefts, thus pressuring the police to maintain their own detective corps if they did not want to jeopardize their fragile reputation for efficiency in this particular area of crime control.

Creating detective bureaus was, in effect, a capitulation to the private interests involved in the conflict between the duties of a public employee and the instincts of a private entrepreneur. Their peculiar position in the police departments defeated any efforts to discipline them. Chicago, for example, abolished its detective detail in 1864 after another investigation of scandalous conduct; New York's press exposed some noisome habits among these officers in 1866; and Boston eliminated its detectives in 1864. In each case, the police could not get along without them for very long, and the detectives were quickly reinstated.[88] Without effective checks on their behavior, the old corrupt habits of these officers continued unabated. In effect, police officials tolerated corruption among the detectives in exchange for their services in pursuing criminals who figured prominently in the public's mind as a major source of trouble. This surrender was perhaps necessary in order to achieve the larger goal of preserving crime prevention as the basis for maintaining social order, but, at the same time, criminal behavior had played an important role in shaping the structure and policies of the new police.

Three   Street Crime: Philadelphia as a Case Study

Thomas Welsh, down on his luck, was about to stumble onto a fortune. A clerk in the Philadelphia offices of Jay Cooke and Company, at Third and Chestnut, had spilled the contents of a bag of gold coins he had been counting. While he and the other clerks scurried about on the floor, the shabbily dressed Welsh walked in. Everyone assumed the stranger had business in the rear of the office, but when he departed hastily, someone noticed another sack containing $5,000 had disappeared with him. When pursuit proved useless, the clerks notified the police. Headquarters sent patrolmen to watch all the railroad depots and other exit points of the city, and a search began. Several hours later a prosperous-looking fellow walked into a jewelry store only five blocks from the scene of the crime. He bought a ring, paying for it with a twenty-dollar gold piece. Another customer in the store, having heard of the robbery, became suspicious because of the mode of payment. He took the liberty of hefting the gentleman's valise, and thinking it rather heavy, called for the police. After his arrest, Welsh made no attempt to deny the theft, "but said he thought that he needed the money as much as Cooke & Co."[1]

This robbery typified crime in American cities during the nineteenth century. Opportunity and inclination proved time and again to be the combination which resulted in thefts and assaults. This does not mean that each criminal incident had no larger context. Some thieves, such as Welsh, stole because they either needed or wanted money. For others larceny constituted part of a life-style—a group of rowdies might deprive a passing stranger of his cash in order to buy themselves liquor or amusement. Physical violence often derived from racial prejudice. Rivalries between various gangs also accounted for a large number of assault cases. And deep hostilities among volunteer fire companies produced a long series of battles which enlivened urban life. Crime was therefore both rational and random: rational because individuals had sufficient reasons, at least in their own minds, to commit these acts; and random because opportunities to steal or to assault someone depended upon time and circumstance.

Random crime therefore posed an entirely different challenge to public order than did the professional thief. But randomness did not imply complete unpredictability. A city's social and physical geography influenced the incidence of crime; some urban areas were more prone to some kinds of offenses than others. While time and circumstances might explain why a particular offense occurred where it did, patterns did exist. An understanding of these generalized configurations in criminal behavior is crucial to any examination of the attempt to apply preventive policing to American cities.[2]

While no city can be completely representative of patterns in street crime, Philadelphia underwent several important changes from approximately 1840 to 1870 which were shared by other northern metropolises. Its population grew rapidly; it experienced an urban transit revolution which created a modern metropolitan arrangement of affluent suburbs surrounding poorer immigrant and working-class neighborhoods; its downtown emerged as a distinct area; and it was an important city in the development of industrialization. The social tensions and crimes which these changes produced were fairly typical of those in other large cities at a time when rising concern over safety in the streets prompted the widespread adoption of crime prevention as the theoretical basis for police reform.

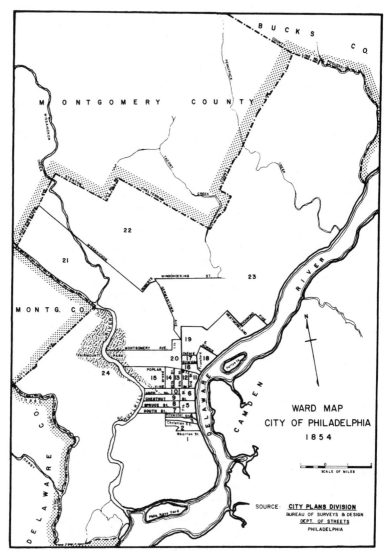

Map 1   Philadelphia Wards, 1854

In 1840 the Delaware and Schuylkill rivers and Vine and South streets formed Philadelphia's political boundaries. The business section centered along the Delaware from Walnut to Arch with Second Street as the west boundary. This concentration was only relative. Many merchants maintained warehouses and stores outside this area. Because Philadelphia was still a walking city, her upper classes resided close to their places of work. Few wealthy citizens lived west of Broad or in the various districts surrounding the city. Hence there was no commercial nexus in the modern sense because of the mixture of residences and businesses. Industries located beyond the political confines of Philadelphia, especially in Spring Garden, Kensington, and Southwark. The working classes lived in housing clustered around these factories. An incipient slum existed along South Street, from the Delaware to Seventh, and from Pine (within the city limits) to Fitzwater (in Southwark). This area served as the entry point for immigrants and as the home of Philadelphia's Negroes. These spatial patterns meant that the low-income groups, as well as the least desirable housing, were on the fringe of the settled section.[3]

During the next three decades the residential patterns underwent drastic changes (see Map 1). With the advent of the omnibus, the upper classes began to leave the central city for the suburbs. Sidney George Fisher, a local Philadelphian, noted in 1847 that "the taste for country life is increasing here very rapidly. New and tasteful houses are built every year. The neighborhood of Germantown is most desirable."[4] Led by the wealthier citizens, people began moving in large numbers toward the northwest and across the Schuylkill into West Philadelphia. The main thrust of this migration was up Ridge Avenue, though many residents also bought new houses within the city, west of Broad. The slum district along South Street remained the worst section of the city and expanded slowly toward Broad. By 1870 these population movements reversed the character of the suburbs and city. The outlying districts now contained the best, not the worst, housing.[5]

Philadelphia's downtown grew steadily as the well-to-do
citizens moved outward. Shopkeepers either took over abandoned houses or demolished them to make room for imposing new commercial buildings. These conversions occurred
most rapidly on Chestnut Street, but the other major east-
west avenues (Walnut, Market, and Arch) were not far
behind. Some of the north-south streets also developed major
concentrations of businesses. Third, from Walnut to Willow,
and Eighth and Ninth from Walnut to Vine were especially
noteworthy for their fine stores. By the mid-1860s the area
bounded by Third, Eighth, Market, and Walnut had emerged
as the center of the downtown district. The merchants on
these streets served the upper and middle classes. South
Street became the major shopping thoroughfare for low-
income families. A miscellaneous collection of stores offering
a vast assortment of cheap wares lined this artery running
through the heart of the slums. By 1870 these business
changes had produced a distinctive downtown which had
specialized along socioeconomic lines.[6]

Philadelphia's property crime patterns closely followed
residential and business shifts (see Maps 2-8).[7] The emerging
downtown, from the Delaware River to Broad and from Vine
to South (wards 5 and 6 after 1854) had a persistent concentration of these offenses. Sneak thieves, till-tappers, and
window smashers victimized merchants in that area.[8] A
nineteenth-century store offered many opportunities for
grand and petty larceny. Shopowners sometimes aided
criminals by placing merchandise on the sidewalk fronting
their stores during business hours. Daring sneak thieves
simply walked off with whatever they could carry. In the
days before cash registers, the merchant kept his money in a
drawer under the counter. A group of boys could send the
smallest of their number to raid the till while they occupied
the owner's attention. Or a customer might ask for something
which he knew was in the back of the store, and while the
clerk searched for it, the thief reached over the counter and
emptied the cash compartment. There were numerous variations on till-tapping, which seems to have been a favorite
endeavor among juveniles.

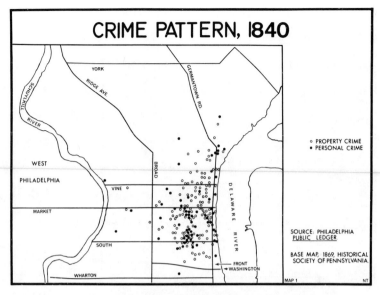

Map 2   Crime Pattern in Philadelphia, 1840

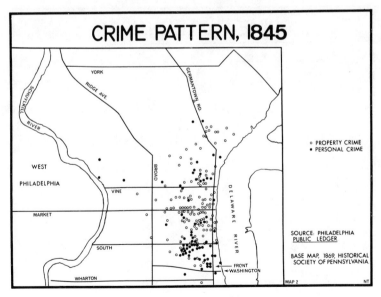

Map 3   Crime Pattern in Philadelphia, 1845

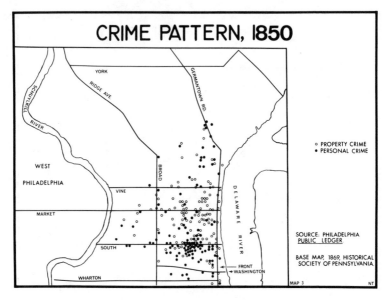

Map 4   **Crime Pattern in Philadelphia, 1850**

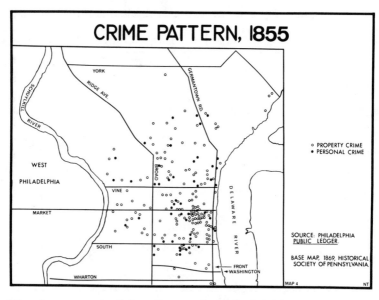

Map 5   **Crime Pattern in Philadelphia, 1855**

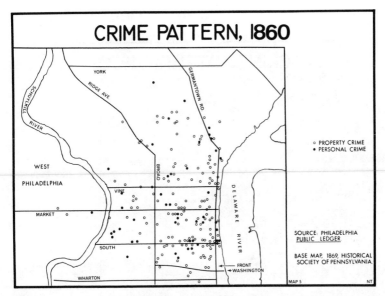

Map 6   Crime Pattern in Philadelphia, 1860

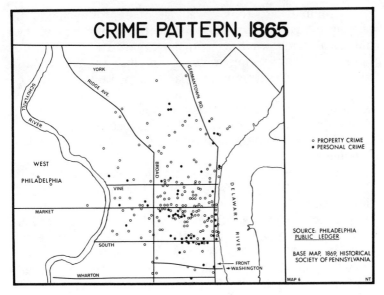

Map 7   Crime Pattern in Philadelphia, 1865

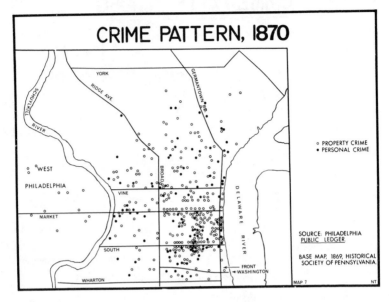

Map 8   **Crime Pattern in Philadelphia, 1870**

Criminals also took advantage of improvements in displaying goods. In the 1820s merchants began to replace their old, small shop windows with large bulk panes.[9] A handy brick or stone and nimble hands combined to make window smashing a prevalent form of larceny by 1840, and this offense continued to plague store owners for many years. Because of the noise involved in this particular crime, its practitioners soon turned to various glass-cutting instruments (which also reduced the chances of getting cut on jagged glass fragments).

As the residential areas of Philadelphia expanded, so did the incidence of thefts from houses. The heaviest concentration of these property losses occurred where the upper- and middle-income groups settled, especially in the northwestern part of the metropolis. The entryway thief was very prevalent. He owed his success to the custom of leaving coats, hats, umbrellas, cloaks, and similar wearing apparel hanging on a rack just inside the doorway of a house. The criminal had only to step inside briefly, grab whatever was within reach, and depart. Bolder sneaks, posing as servicemen or repairmen, entered homes and stole any watches, pieces of jewelry, and clothing which were lying loose. Juveniles were especially persistent depredators. New, unoccupied houses were a favorite target. They broke into many such residences and stripped away the plumbing fixtures to secure the brass and lead. When elaborate doorknobs and knockers became popular, youthful thieves developed the ability to rip those objects quickly and quietly from their fastenings. Even the family wash disappeared frequently, as did any miscellaneous household items carelessly left in view. The cash loss in most of these thefts was low, but the incidents still annoyed the victims.

Although highway robberies often included an assault on the victim, these offenses constituted another form of property crime because the assailant sought money, not a fight. The thefts occurred throughout the city and suburbs, though the perpetrators seem to have favored side streets and the less densely settled areas. Juveniles and young men, especially those wandering about in small groups, committed many of these outrages. Two social customs aided the thieves. At a time when only rudimentary checking and credit systems existed, many urban residents carried large amounts of money with them while shopping or conducting business, and merchants employed messenger boys to carry funds to the banks. These couriers and well-dressed pedestrians offered tempting targets to robbers. Secondly, since watches were expensive and scarce before the Civil War, the habit developed of asking strangers for the time. Criminals used this convention to their advantage. When a man pulled out his watch in order to answer a query as to the hour, the thief grabbed it and ran. Or, if the watch happened to be attached to a chain, he pulled the victim off balance by jerking the timepiece toward him and then quieted the fellow with a blow on the head. Both methods usually proved successful.

Some of the wide variety of articles stolen by Philadelphia's criminals seem of little value. But a market did exist for these goods. The city's numerous pawnbrokers and junk dealers purchased most of these pilfered items for a fraction of their value, and asked few questions about ownership. Because these shopkeepers were so willing to buy miscellaneous merchandise, the petty thieves always had a way to convert their day's work into ready cash. A part of the mercantile structure of the city therefore helped provide incentive for these particular offenses.[10]

Crime against persons exhibited a rather stable pattern between 1840 and 1870. The center of assaults was located in the heart of the lower-class section of Philadelphia, around Seventh and Lombard. From that point these acts spread along South Street, and toward Market by way of Fifth, Sixth, and Seventh. Water and Front streets, running parallel to the Delaware River, provided the setting for numerous attacks on people. Residents living in the area from South to Christian, between the Delaware and Broad (wards 3 and 4 after 1854), witnessed or experienced many assaults. The working-class districts of Kensington and Northern Liberties (wards 11, 12, 16, and 17 after 1854) also had a persistent pattern of these offenses. In general this type of offense did not follow population movements during these years. Though there were exceptions, especially in 1870, assaults remained concentrated in the oldest sections of Philadelphia.

Customs of a different sort than those involving property crimes produced the opportunities for violence which occurred so frequently during these years. A city's streets were centers of social life in the nineteenth century. The habit of wandering the avenues seeking relief from a day's labors provided many victims to small groups of rowdies prowling about. Unprovoked assaults marred practically every evening on the city's south side and in the less densely settled areas to the north. The victim might be an adolescent, a lonely stroller, a man (or woman) suddenly slashed by a knife as he brushed past a gathering of juveniles, or—especially along South Street—a Negro. Racial antagonism kept the area in turmoil for years. Philadelphia experienced five major anti-Negro riots between 1829 and 1849. In the intervals between major battles, white and black youths constantly attacked one another. Raids and reprisals became commonplace and kept tensions high until the mid-1850s. Though the antagonism behind these assaults seems to have declined somewhat by 1860, it flared occasionally after that date, as in 1871, when a minor race riot erupted.[11]

The adolescent habit of forming street gangs posed one of the most serious threats to personal safety. Precise data on these organizations are rare. Contemporary sources complained of their disorders but devoted little attention to their structure and functions. But although any analysis of the role these bands played in mid-nineteenth-century urban society must therefore remain tentative, gangs did constitute a major problem in the older cities, and descriptions of their activities do reveal some general patterns.

The working-class districts bordering Philadelphia (especially Southwark and Moyamensing) were the stamping grounds of these organizations (see Map 9). Within the city, the low-income wards adjacent to the districts contained much of the raw material for gang membership. In 1840, those ages which tended to form these associations (ten to fourteen and fifteen to nineteen) comprised 3.6 and 4.4 percent of the total city population. Cedar Ward, bounded by Seventh, Spruce, the Schuylkill River, and South, had 12.9 and 9.6 percent respectively in those age categories. Other wards also had percentages which were higher than the average, but none had so many of these groups operating along its edges. Standard socioeconomic factors therefore help explain the distribution of gangs.[12]

Within this broader context, four different kinds of gangs emerge: street corner, theft, violent, and combat. No sharp distinctions existed between these categories; some adolescent associations occasionally drifted from one class to another. The typology is useful in that it describes the basic group behaviors which both irritated and alarmed many citizens of Philadelphia. The precise number of gangs in each division is impossible to know. Between 1840 and 1870 the *Public Ledger* mentioned forty-eight of these bands by name, but in most cases no such identification was made. A survey

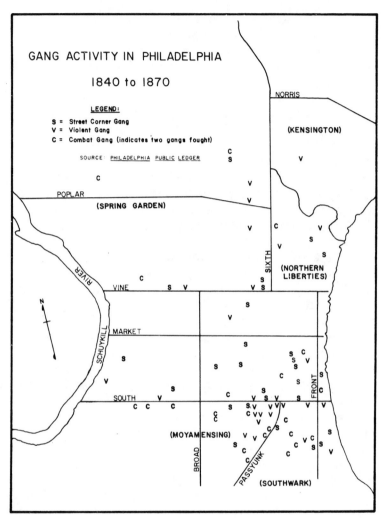

GANG ACTIVITY IN PHILADELPHIA

1840 to 1870

LEGEND:

S = Street Corner Gang
V = Violent Gang
C = Combat Gang (indicates two gangs fought)

SOURCE: PHILADELPHIA PUBLIC LEDGER

Map 9   **Gang Activity in Philadelphia, 1840-1870**

of all the incidents involving these organizations resulted in the distribution shown in Table 1. Undoubtedly there was some duplication in this study because of the difficulty of identifying the groups, and ten associations were counted twice because they indulged in two separate types of activity.

Table 1   **Gangs Grouped According to Type**

Decade	Combat	Violent	Theft	Street corner
1840-1850	39	22	1	21
1851-1860	12	10	6	11
1861-1870	4	3	2	6
Totals	55	35	9	38

Source: *Public Ledger*.

Even so, at a conservative estimate one hundred gangs existed for varying lengths of time during the period. Most groups lasted no more than three years, but there were exceptions. The Schuylkill Rangers held the longevity record with twenty-six years, followed by the Buffers (ten), the Forty Thieves (nine), and the Snakers (seven).[13]

Many city residents complained about youths who congregated at street intersections. The practice, referred to as corner lounging, played an essential role in the social life of adolescents. As one such lounger pointed out, young men naturally sought friends, and in the nineteenth century there were few places for them to meet with their peers except in the public avenues. He also claimed this custom had redeeming traits: the crowds of juveniles helped pull fire engines, and the older teenagers were among the first to volunteer in wartime. This lounger concluded his defense by suggesting that if Philadelphians wanted to stop the habit they should provide meeting halls "where we could talk ourselves, and not have an orator or preacher to do the talking."[14]

In the 1850s, responding to demands that they pursue socially acceptable goals, some of these groups rented rooms, bought a few books, and called themselves library companies. The press attacked this development because the juveniles still escaped adult supervision. The clubs, according to the *Ledger*, provided excuses for boys to gather to play cards, get drunk, "and indulge in language of the most demoralizing character."[15] Later, when police raids in one section of the city denied them their favorite corners, a few enterprising youths built a series of underground dugouts in which they carried on their usual activities. When officers descended on this complex because of neighborhood complaints, one of the boys explained that they had made hideouts "because they were not allowed to stand on the corners, and had no place to go."[16] The social impulse behind lounging obviously proved hard to curtail.

The degree of cohesion among these juveniles probably depended on the inclinations of individuals and the amount of group pressure exerted on each member. One editor, searching for the causes of disorder, complained that "a young man who déclines indulgence in irregularities should not be rated by his young associates as a 'muff' or a 'milk-sop.' There is more of this sort of social tyranny among certain classes of young men than their elders are aware of."[17] Judging from complaints, profane verbal abuse of pedestrians was the most frequent breach of public decency. This activity did not require an elaborate organization to sustain it. Pelting the local citizenry with rocks and snowballs also occurred regularly. These assaults, while annoying, did not pose a serious threat to social order. But this conduct did suggest greater cohesion because a number of boys participated as a unit attacking a target. Some groups established an identity by adopting names, but this move did not necessarily imply an increased propensity for violence. The Chesapeakes and the Darts, for example, never appeared in any connection except as mildly bothersome street corner gangs.[18]

Some juvenile thieves operated in gangs, had special hiding places, and, in at least one instance, had their own slang language. These groups acted more systematically than most young petty criminals. They concentrated on temporarily vacant rented houses or those homes whose owners had retired to the countryside during the hot summer months. Once inside, they stripped metal fixtures from the walls and ripped open partitions to remove the lead and copper plumbing. They emptied pantries, toted away liquor, and smashed everything they could not carry. The destruction ended when water from the burst pipes inundated the house.[19]

Those juvenile groups which had acquired an identity not necessarily tied to a particular street corner developed the more dangerous characteristic of actively seeking victims to assault. These violent gangs chose a variety of targets: lonely pedestrians, police officers, younger adolescents (who might or might not belong to a rival organization), and isolated members of competing ethnic or racial populations.[20] Fists, slung shots, clubs, knives, and pistols were the favorite weapons in these attacks. The slung shot emerged as the mark of the rowdy because of its widespread use. This contraption was a ball of lead, weighing about half a pound, with a hole in its center through which a buckskin thong was passed. The thong was attached to a strong piece of cord about eighteen inches long. The entire weapon could be concealed in the palm of the hand. "Thus armed," noted a contemporary reporter, "the ruffian gets into the middle of a crowd and lays about him, . . . 'clearing' a space where he can show off and receive the homage of the younger members of the club."[21] Brass knuckles, which first appeared in the 1850s, completed the gangs' arsenal.[22]

The structure of violent gangs remains problematic. Their dominant characteristic—actively seeking victims—meant that most of these groups roamed the streets rather than defending a particular spot. Of the fifteen associations which could be positively identified, only the Privateers guarded a special street corner.[23] The others prowled at will in the districts, making few forays into the city proper.[24]

Street warfare between rival gangs, especially in the 1840s, formed one of the basic themes of city life during the middle decades of the nineteenth century. These clashes generally occurred in the evenings and, in the absence of an effective police force, lasted as long as the participants felt like fighting. But the ferocity of these encounters was not uniform. Some had an almost ritual quality in which few persons were hurt; other battles resulted in serious injuries and deaths. The variations in intensity and casualties were due to differing conflict situations. The least deadly fights involved disputes over control of a locale. Combat in these situations was probably between inhabitants of the same community. Lower-class adolescents in Moyamensing and Southwark frequently gathered in open lots to fight with fists, bricks, and stones. These encounters appear to have been a source of recreation for the boys in the districts. By 1850 one such piece of ground had become known as the "Battle Ground" (located at South and Schuylkill Third in the far west fringe of Moyamensing). Rival groups fought at this spot while "crowds of men" stood on the sidelines and cheered their favorites.[25] Within this general context of conflict, there were a few identifiable gangs which competed for control of particular street corners. The Rangers and the Bulldogs usually struggled over possession of the intersection at Penn and Front (near the Delaware River). The Buffers and the Shifflers contested the use of Fourth and Washington.[26] In these fights, according to reporter George Foster, the participants "took good care not to hurt one another; and . . . these affairs were mostly quite harmless."[27] A neighborhood's windows and quietude suffered most from these clashes.

The most dangerous battles were manifestations of basic ethnic, religious, and political conflicts. Reflecting national trends after 1830, Philadelphians had divided over such issues as temperance reform, Bible reading in public schools, and the rights of immigrants.[28] Southwark's and Moyamensing's diverse population of Protestant Americans and Orangemen and Irish and German Catholics represented opposing views on these questions. Until the 1840s, both districts had been heavily Democratic, but at the beginning of that decade the temperance movement and nativism splintered the old party coalitions. As a consequence, the American Republicans (nativists) in Southwark won the 1843 local elections and dominated that area's public offices for the remainder of the decade.[29] Political divisions therefore represented fundamental differences among the various groups in urban society.

The antagonisms generated by these divisive issues transformed a venerable institution, the volunteer fire company, from an important defender of public safety into one of the principal dangers to social order. The volunteers had been a product of necessity in the eighteenth century, when fire posed one of the greatest hazards to urban life. Beginning in the early nineteenth century, the previously good-natured contests to be first to a blaze, and first to a hydrant, slowly shifted into determined battles between claimants to those honors. Fights developed en route to a conflagration as competitors sought to prevent their rivals from arriving first. At the scene of a fire partisans of one or another organization slashed hoses and fought for possession of the best hydrants.[30] Firefighters therefore had a tradition of conflict separate from the social tensions of the 1840s and 1850s.

Changes in the membership of fire companies ensured that they would become centers of offense and defense for proponents of the issues convulsing society. Beginning in the 1830s, the social elite which had controlled these organizations began to lose interest in active participation because of the new demands on fire fighters. As the city increased in size and blazes became more frequent, the upper and middle classes discovered that they could no longer devote time to both the public safety and their own careers. As some of their number said in a public statement: "In a larger community, . . . there is a tendency to a division of labor, so that we all have our occupations and pursuits, which we cannot drop unless in cases of great emergency. Hence, almost from the necessity of the case, the volunteer fire department has passed from the men of the town into those of minors."[31]

Their altered character resulted in a greater combativeness among the volunteers. Community loyalties formed one basis for trouble. Many firemen in each of the several companies came from the same neighborhood. This gave cohesion to an outfit, but it also made these organizations competitive with others formed along similar lines. The internal structure of the companies also changed. Volunteers built hose and engine houses which became social centers where young men, who had few places to spend their leisure time, met friends, drank, and played cards.[32] Persons of like political, ethnic, and religious outlooks therefore had viable organizations through which to express their antagonisms toward individuals and groups of opposing beliefs.

Firemen fought with increasing frequency from the mid-1830s to the 1850s. The thirst for combat reached the point where many blazes were set deliberately to provoke a riot. As a company charged along a street in the direction of a fire, its enemy either collided with it or lay in ambush. The opponent's engine was the supreme prize in these affairs, and several valuable pieces of equipment were severely damaged or destroyed as a result of a battle. In other cases companies waited until after a fire had been extinguished to begin a riot. The encounters lasted for varying lengths of time; most confrontations were brief, but others went on for hours, covered several city blocks in the course of the engagement, and occasionally continued the next day or evening.[33]

The groups which attached themselves to fire companies constituted the most dangerous adolescent bands in Philadelphia. These were the combat gangs in their purest form. The Rats illustrate the evolution of this type. They first appeared in the press as an unusually aggressive street corner group which waged at least four fights with rivals in 1845.[34] All these struggles occurred within a block of the corner of Christian and Second (Southwark). Unlike most such gangs involved in these contests, the Rats moved beyond the initial stage of development. Led by Edward Paul, they emerged as a major power in Southwark.[35] Paul's ardent loyalty to the Weccacoe Engine Company probably explains the transformation from street corner band to combat gang. Many of Paul's followers also belonged to that organization. The Engine Company adhered to the principles of nativism and American Republican politics. Its arch rival, the Weccacoe Hose, containing both native-born citizens and Irish immigrants, was decidedly Democratic. The Hose Company numbered among its supporters a group called the Bouncers. Beginning in 1846 the Rats became locked in a continuous struggle with the Bouncers, and their battles constituted a part of the larger contest between the belligerent volunteer fire associations.[36] Since the companies attended fires all over Southwark and Moyamensing, the gang brawls no longer had any geographic limits. Fights developed whenever and wherever the opportunity offered itself.

Another combat gang, the Killers, were the most feared group in the metropolitan area. The author of a fictional romance described this band's composition:

They were divided into three classes—beardless apprentice boys who after a hard day's work were turned loose upon the street at night, be their masters or bosses. Young men of nineteen and twenty, who fond of excitement, had assumed the name and joined the gang for the mere fun of the thing, and who would either fight for a man or knock him down, just to keep their hand in; and fellows with countenances that reminded of the brute and devil well intermingled. These last were the smallest in number, but the most ferocious of the three.[37]

The "brute" element, according to this account, provided the gang's leadership. Its members infiltrated the Moyamensing Hose Company during the 1840s, and that organization developed a reputation for disorder which few other volunteer firemen could match.[38] By 1846 the reputation of both associations was such that few rivals dared to attend fires in Moyamensing.[39]

Irish Catholic in background, the Killers and the Moyas (the volunteer firemen) actively sought conflict with competing ethnic groups and native Americans. In 1849 the Killers led the mob which attacked the Negro-owned California House. The resulting race riot was one of the city's worst uprisings.[40] That same year, the gang twice attacked the nativist Shiffler Hose Company of Southwark. During the second assault, the Killers captured the Shiffler's carriage. After dragging the prize into Moyamensing, the Killers ceremoniously hacked it to pieces and distributed the remains to an admiring crowd as mementos. In April 1850, the Killers set a blaze in order to draw the Shifflers into an ambush. But when the gang returned to the conflagration with a mob estimated at five hundred persons, they found the Shifflers waiting with their own ambush. A volley of musketry drove the Killers off in disorder.[41] The Moyamensing Hose also ran into trouble in April. They arrived at a fire in an Irish Protestant area known as Buena Vista. The Franklin Hose, already on the scene, abandoned the blaze to attack newcomers. Spectators provided the Franklins (whose members came from this neighborhood) with guns, and battle raged for an hour before mutual exhaustion ended the struggle.[42] These setbacks did not deter the Killers or their cohorts in the Hose Company. These volunteers especially were known throughout the next two decades for their ferocity.

This type of violence occurred in a completely different context than a simple question of sovereignty over a street corner. Both the gangs and the volunteers reflected the political, religious, and ethnic loyalties of their communities. There was a certain tolerance, even admiration, for these activities. The crowd which watched the destruction of the Shiffler Hose carriage encouraged the Killers with cries of "Go it, Moyamensing!" During the riot in Buena Vista an eyewitness reported that "the whole spirit of the neighborhood . . . seemed to be in sympathy with the conflict."[43] The volunteers and their adolescent auxillaries acted out the hostilities which existed among different segments of Philadelphia's inhabitants. The combat gang functioned as a defense unit for its own population in an urban society which was in the process of evolving other, more acceptable, means of social control.[44]

Gang activity provided an additional dimension to the generally stable pattern of violent crime. On the one hand, certain changes in the physical structure of the city as a whole helped create conditions in which violent behavior patterns could emerge. To some extent businessmen seeking new sites for their stores and factories in the inner city undermined neighborhood stability. Old, as well as new, residents in these areas had to live in properties which might soon become commercial or industrial sites. The sense of impermanence generated by this circumstance may have weakened the fabric of neighborhood controls over potentially violent persons or situations. Thus some of the assaults which occurred in the older areas of Philadelphia could be attributed to the degree of social disorganization existing there. Yet the presence of the combat gangs indicates that disorganization did not reach the point where neighborhoods became totally incapable of sustaining any viable local institutions. Rapid population and physical changes made these groups all the more important to those people who had to live in deteriorated areas of the city. Gangs afforded protection to the remnants of their ethnic group who remained behind. In performing that role, gangs contributed to a significant degree to the level of violence.[45]

Street crimes thus occurred in bewildering variety and derived from complex motives. Ethnic, religious, and political hostilities, mixed with the individual offender's desire for personal gain or revenge, explained much about these offenses without making them any more controllable. The patterns of street crime created more problems than professional crime did. Because property offenses tended to have a different spatial distribution than crimes against persons, each required different treatment. While the difficulties which dissimilar remedies implied were considerable, the task of dealing with various types of offenses was not altogether hopeless. The general locations of some crimes were fairly predictable. Violence broke out in certain areas more often than in others. Burglars preferred targets in the business district or the suburbs rather than in the slums. Robbers were more apt to work in the evening in locales favoring surprise. Policing had to become more flexible in order to cope with these disparate patterns. A city government needed a police which could be constantly adapted to changing neighborhood conditions as well as to continuing urban growth.

The new police departments seemed to fit all these requirements. Their structure, with its emphasis on local control, meant that they would recruit men from the neighborhoods who represented a city's various ethnic, religious, and political factions. Presumably, these men would be able to tailor their behavior to local sensitivities while still obeying their general responsibility to maintain order. They would also be knowledgable about their neighborhoods' particular crime problems; that information would alert them to the special needs of each locale in the city. These advantages existed only as expectations, however. It remained to be seen whether a preventive police could in fact control street crime.

Four   Organizing for Crime Prevention

The laws which reformed the police could not guarantee that the new departments would be effective in preventing crimes. Success or failure in achieving that goal depended, in part, upon how well inexperienced administrators organized their agencies to conform to the idea of crime prevention. The structure of the reformed police provided the theoretical tools for success. For the first time, all the men responsible for law enforcement worked together in a single bureaucracy, allowing officials to establish common rules for conduct and discipline. Ideally, patrolmen would now conform to higher performance standards than had been typical of the watch or the constables. Secondly, the larger number of men available meant that the new police would be more pervasive than their predecessors. Administrators could therefore manage a city's space more effectively, extending protection to more persons and property than had been possible in the past.

Since the early police administrators shared the general populace's ignorance of how crime prevention worked, they had to grope their way along as they created these first bureaucracies. Unable to draw upon experience, they sought to solve obvious problems. If the new police hoped to convince the public of their efficiency, for example, they would have to alter their personal behavior drastically. Patrolmen would have diverse backgrounds and habits. Most of them probably liked at least an occasional drink; profanity came easily; smoking a cigar seemed second nature. They dressed as their inclinations and incomes dictated. Pride and prejudice, kindness and brutality, figured in their actions and attitudes. No disciplinary tradition existed to mold these men, which meant that departmental administrators had to evolve techniques to induce each man to accept a common standard of conduct. Each patrolman would be required to surrender a portion of his individuality in order to achieve the goal of an effective preventive police.

Existing police tradition complicated the task of winning public acceptance of the new departments. The watch's inability to control criminals before 1840 had accustomed urbanites to police inefficiency. Watchmen had no effective street patrol techniques, and as a group they displayed little ability to subdue rowdies or to capture thieves. Therefore prior experience colored public expectations regarding a reformed police. No evidence yet existed that crime prevention would work. In order to combat this situation, city officials had to make maximum effective use of the hordes of patrolmen they now commanded. An intelligent distribution of these men to cope with the geography of crime therefore became a major concern.

Politics was yet another threat to the new police. The structure of the departments, with the emphasis on local controls, institutionalized political considerations in policing. But political partisanship was antithetical to the effective application of crime prevention theory for several reasons. First, urban bosses who had begun to emerge in the 1840s and 1850s needed appointive positions to reward friends and to extend their influence. The new police departments offered a potentially large source of patronage, but faithful party workers would not necessarily be the best men for those jobs. They might adopt biases in law enforcement which would undermine public confidence in police impartiality. Secondly, favoritism toward friends and harassment of political enemies were a strong possibility. If officials preached the necessity for a common standard of conduct, but displayed undue leniency or severity toward individual patrolmen because of their political affiliations, they would disrupt discipline among their officers. This would seriously damage a major tenet of crime prevention, thereby reducing police effectiveness. Finally, frequent local elections introduced the problem of instability. Patrolmen on the beat one day might be replaced the next. Such a situation could produce sudden shifts in enforcement policies which would confuse and irritate the general public. That would reduce public confidence in the police. Department administrators had to devise strategies and techniques which would modify or repress the dangers inherent in a politically controlled police.

These disciplinary, geographical, and political problems proved difficult to overcome. Different circumstances in each city dictated how wide or narrow the gap between theory and reality would be. That police departments did develop similarities from one place to another testifies to the persistence with which city officials tried to apply the *idea* of prevention to their peculiar local conditions.

Military analogies strongly influenced the architects of the new police. The theory of crime prevention, with its emphasis on centralized control, pervasiveness, and visibility, implied a close correlation with military modes of behavior. (The British police, drawing heavily upon their army for disciplinary models, may also have influenced American practice.) Military chains of command established clear lines of authority and defined responsibilities. Theoretically, such an arrangement ensured obedience to orders and guaranteed that general policy objectives would be enforced. These supposed advantages led to the universal adoption of military models as the basic structure of American policing. In fact, one of the more remarkable things about reform was the total absence of any significant debate over the appropriateness of such models for the internal organization of the new departments.[1]

Widespread agreement also existed on the question of what kinds of men would make good officers. Potential recruits should possess such qualities as "courage, moderation, intelligence and great *discretion.*" They should be men who would exercise their powers "promptly, decidedly, and in a polite and gentlemanly way." The allusion to a gentleman was deliberate. Upper-class behavioral prototypes dominated the thinking of the men who wrote departmental regulations. Patrolmen must not disgrace themselves by smoking or by using profanity in public, "as both habits are indicative of contempt for the opinions of some of our best citizens (to say nothing of right or wrong) which ill comports with their official positions."[2] These general requirements emphasized that the new police would help maintain order by their own examples of personal decorum. Such behavior would also be important in gaining public approval. The average citizen would be more inclined to accept a police whose members acted according to the rules of polite society.

A gentlemanly demeanor, however, would not always be the most effective way to enforce the law. At times, physical force might be required. In the opinion of some commentators, the possibilities for violence in police work required that only "powerful, resolute, active men" should receive appointments to the departments.[3] Physically imposing officers would "command respect from others," and thereby awe the disorderly classes into quiet obedience to the laws.[4]

Perhaps recognizing that most applicants to the police would be more familiar with the rough and tumble ways of street life than with the polished manners of the drawing room, departmental administrators sought to define behavioral patterns for their men in explicit terms. Rule books were basic to this effort. All these guides, which attempted to translate the theory of crime prevention into terms the average officer could understand and implement, had remarkably similar formats and language.[5] Each contained a general statement that "the principal object to be attained is the prevention of crime, and to this end, every effort of the Police is to be directed."[6] The guides warned patrolmen that "the absence of crime will be considered the best proof of ... efficiency ... and when in any district or beat offenses frequently occur, there will be good reason to suppose that there is negligence ... on the part of policemen in charge."[7] Following such admonitions, the rulebooks detailed the particular responsibilities of each officer and defined his powers by quoting from pertinent laws regarding his right of arrest, forcible entry, and other matters.

These general provisions had one major problem: officials had no way to supervise each patrolman on his beat directly. But some control was necessary if administrators hoped to accustom their men to the practice of crime prevention. Their solution was to require every policeman to keep a written record of everything that happened during his tour of duty. Philadelphia Mayor Robert Vaux, for example, ordered his officers to note the time needed to walk their beats, to record any violations of the law which occurred, to mark down the number of doors found unlocked, and to provide information about the locations of corner loungers and disorderly houses. New York and Chicago had similar regulations designed to instill institutional goals in their officers.[8]

In addition to establishing these general regulations, the rulebooks also tried to shape personal conduct. Officers were warned to speak correctly and politely to strangers and women, to refrain from loitering in taverns and on street corners, and to abstain from smoking in public. Hoping to eliminate some of the more obnoxious habits of their recruits, police administrators prohibited drinking or sleeping while on duty. Some regulations went even further. When Chicago's police commissioners took charge of the department in 1861, they issued orders which prohibited mustaches, prescribed the proper style for beards, and required that all patrolmen eat with forks.[9] On the delicate matter of physical force, the rules forbade using any more violence than was "*absolutely necessary.*"[10] In sum, police officials sought to create gentlemen whose behavior would earn the respect and admiration of the public.

Military drill also contributed to the growth of an organizational identity. New York's recruits began to receive training in 1853. Philadelphia started in 1854 under the Marshall's Police, but a controversy over its necessity as an instrument of discipline seems to have delayed regular drilling until the late 1850s. Other cities did not institute parade practice until the early 1860s, when the impact of the Civil War may have made the idea more acceptable to the men. St. Louis introduced drill for its patrolmen in 1861; Boston began in 1863. By requiring individuals to function as parts of large units, city officials advanced another step in their campaign to create unanimity of purpose in the various departments.[11]

The "show-up"—identifying habitual criminals to as many officers as possible—was another innovation which helped establish group goals over individual achievement. This technique may have begun informally among the police themselves. New York detective William Bell frequently "spotted" thieves to his colleagues so that they would recognize these people in the future. But the procedure quickly became an official part of police work in several cities. Boston's Marshall Francis Tukey instituted it in 1851; Philadelphia had adopted it by 1861.[12] Rogues' galleries constituted a variation of this idea. The departments in each city began compiling photographic exhibits of professional criminals which every man on the force would examine at his leisure. New York began its collection in 1857; Philadelphia and Chicago started in 1858; and Boston followed suit in 1861.[13] Neither the show-up nor the rogues' gallery would have had any use under the old system of policing, when only a few constables knew the identities of criminals. But with the adoption of these measures, the thieves' vulnerability increased as a far larger number of officers became familiar with them. These techniques therefore emphasized the new, collective nature of law enforcement.

These rules and new techniques represented an important advance over the procedures of the watch and constabulary. But they did not go far enough. To establish the presence of a preventive police on the streets, city officials needed to make their new officers visible to the public. According to the theory of crime prevention, a patrolman's presence ensured the peace by inhibiting potential lawbreakers. For many years, however, individual policemen looked, and sometimes acted, like everyone else. They had nothing about them which indicated their authority. Furthermore, personalized dress accentuated an officer's individuality and undermined the efforts to impose group behavior standards on the police. For these reasons, a uniform was absolutely vital to the creation of a more effective police.

The need for some visible symbol of authority had been obvious for years. For example, when a group of medical students disturbed Philadelphia's Chestnut Street Theater in the winter of 1840, Patrolman Bramble remonstrated with them and "informed them that he was an officer and would be obliged to interfere unless they conducted themselves in a more orderly manner." The students persisted, and a near riot occurred.[14] Some years later, when a New York policeman attempted to arrest a thief, a band of rowdies attacked and severely beat him. No one came to his assistance because he "was not generally recognized" as a patrolman.[15] Such fights appeared to be typical brawls, and private citizens refused aid because they "did not know [an officer] was acting in an official capacity."[16]

No initial agreement existed that distinctive dress, or some other symbol, would eliminate the identification problem. Many observers objected to such an idea on philosophical grounds. One Philadelphia councilman called any sort of uniform a "badge of servitude."[17] An editor questioned whether "any man, claiming the proud title of an American freeman, . . . will lay aside his ordinary dress as an American citizen [to] strut about the streets of Chicago decked out in the livery furnished at the public expense."[18] Also, in the general reaction against the stool pigeon system after 1840, some people believed that *all* patrolmen should both prevent and detect crime (thereby making no distinctions between two essentially different functions). In this latter view, a uniform would hinder an officer's detective responsibilities by making him too visible.[19]

But even the critics acknowledged the value of some symbol of authority. "There can be no doubt that it may have a tendency to deter some from breaches of the peace and disorderly conduct, by an early recognition of an officer," observed the *Public Ledger,* "and we doubt not that the officers will be treated with due respect in the discharge of their duty by all good citizens."[20] Realizing the utility of an easily identifiable police as a means of curbing rowdies, many people supported the adoption of uniforms. Then, too, in an age which distrusted power, a special outfit might ensure that patrolmen would be "very shy of infringing upon the rights of orderly citizens."[21] Finally—from a very practical viewpoint—the uniform would simplify the problems of someone looking for help.[22]

Distinctive dress also made possible greater departmental control over the men. A lieutenant checking the officers on their beats did not have to walk beside them; he could easily observe a uniformed man's performance from a distance. Uniforms also made the command of a large body of patrolmen during a riot much easier. In the midst of a fight, the authorities could readily identify friend and foe.

None of these advantages guaranteed that a uniformed police would appear on the streets. Mayors, councilmen, editors, and the public might desire this reform, but the patrolmen's opposition effectively blocked the idea for years. The officers justified their resistance in several ways. For instance, when one man failed to apprehend several small boys who robbed a fruit stand, he explained that "they discovered him by the large silver . . . badge that he wore."[23] Others refused to wear any distinguishing dress "because it designates their business, and is called by them a 'livery.'" Another officer regarded a uniform as repugnant to his theory of citizenship: "I hereby present my resignation, as an American citizen— not wishing to wear anything derogatory to my feelings as an American."[24] Confronted by these antagonisms, politicians showed considerable timidity in pushing through this innovation.

Police administrators tried various devices for distinguishing officers. New York began with a leather badge in 1845. Philadelphia experimented with a silver star which was so large that the sun's reflection from it made a patrolman visible from some distance.[25] Policemen often hid these emblems by pinning them under their coat collars. This practice conformed to the letter of the law and made the individual officer the judge of when to reveal his identity. This subterfuge became so common that A. D. Chaloner, a private citizen interested in the problem, suggested that the men wear a bright red, turn-down collar so that "when about to make an arrest [the patrolmen] elevates the collar of his coat . . . showing his character."[26] Despite Chaloner's suggestion, badges remained the only symbols of authority in every department.[27]

The first major breakthrough on this problem came in New York in 1853. Most of the city's police, nearing the end of their four-year terms under an 1849 law, looked forward to reappointment under a rule guaranteeing tenure during good behavior. The city's police commissioners seized this opportune moment to announce that they would not rehire any man who refused to wear a uniform. The patrolmen held protest meetings and denounced the requirement, but in the end the majority put job security above principle and grudgingly accepted the regulation.[28]

Progress in Philadelphia was much slower. In November 1853, the Police Board voted to uniform the Marshall's Police, and the marshall announced that he would dismiss any officer who refused to obey the order. The men grumbled, and the lieutenants hired an attorney to test the issue in court. In spite of this opposition, the rule stood, and the patrolmen appeared in uniform on February 1, 1854. But the men's antipathy to the idea eventually triumphed. The marshall did not enforce the regulation, and "a seemingly fixed determination on the part of the officers not to conform" defeated the board within a month.[29]

None of the other police forces of the metropolitan area had become involved in the uniform controversy. But following consolidation in 1854 the Philadelphia councils decided that all officers should wear a plain black coat, a glazed hat, and a badge. Mayor Conrad, perhaps remembering the Marshall's Police experiment, only insisted on the hat.[30] Even that proved too much. As opposition mounted, Conrad tried to encourage compliance by appearing in the new headgear in public. And he ordered that only the patrolmen in the first four wards should follow suit. His conciliatory efforts failed. Fifteen officers resigned outright, and the men's hostility triumphed again.[31] Robert Vaux, elected mayor in 1856, issued orders requiring the police to wear their badges, but he made no mention of hats.[32]

Mayor Alexander Henry, beginning his first term in 1858, had more determination and skill than his predecessors. The Reserve Corps, which Vaux had created to act as a riot squad, contained the most physically imposing men in the department. They took great pride in their special police role. Henry decided to take advantage of this attitude. A uniform, he might have argued, would make the corps even more distinctive. He prescribed a single-breasted blue frock coat, pants, and a cap (patent leather cover). The corps appeared in the new outfit in November 1858. In contrast to all previous experience, "there appears to be no opposition to wearing the uniform."[33] Henry probably hoped to induce the ordinary patrolmen to accept the "livery" by this example, but they resisted for another two years.

On August 3, 1860, a commission examining the Philadelphia police issued a report favoring a uniform. Henry moved quickly to implement the recommendation. On August 11 he ordered the patrolmen to outfit themselves with blue frock coats, dark gray pants (soon changed to blue), and a blue cloth hat adorned by a silver wreath in which the officer's number would appear. Some men continued to resist, but Henry adopted stringent rules to force compliance, he did not back down, and the controversy over uniforms finally ended.[34]

Boston's police adopted uniforms by 1858 with little fuss. In this city the men seemed unconcerned over the issue, and many had voluntarily worn distinctive dress for some time.[35] Chicago procrastinated for a few years. During his term as mayor in 1858, John Wentworth refused to allow his officers to wear any uniform. Instead they carried leather badges which he personally designed. While Wentworth was temporarily out of office in 1859, the city administration experimented with a blue cloth cap and silver badge. Wentworth returned to power in 1860 and abolished those innovations. Finally, when the Illinois legislature created the police board in 1861 to run the department, the commissioners promptly ordered the force to appear in outfits similar to those adopted elsewhere. As in Boston, the men seem not to have raised any great commotion.[36]

All these changes could not have become effective without some cooperation from the police themselves. Merely imposing orders which required drastic changes in behavior would not work. Experience soon proved that those affected by the new rules did not intend to submit without some persuasion. When New York's police officials issued their first complete rule book in 1848, "it was received with amazement and alarm by the men."[37] Reading about regulations might cause consternation; actually obeying orders could occasion outright resistance, even in trivial matters. When a Philadelphia lieutenant ordered his men to stand during roll call, they refused, claiming such treatment was "tyrannical, and not fit for Americans."[38] The men in charge of the new departments had to offset these objections by providing job benefits which would make patrolmen willing to forego some of their individuality.

Officials also had to cope with the expectations of the men who sought positions on the new police. Among the many reasons why candidates beseiged mayors' offices seeking appointments was the prospect of obtaining a lucrative job. The constables, after all, had made a very good living working the old stool pigeon system. But public indignation had made departmental officials wary of monetary rewards, and the new rules either banned such gifts completely or placed severe restrictions upon them. These bans and controls could adversely affect police morale. As a Philadelphia reporter put it, paraphrasing an experienced officer he had interviewed, "before, . . . there was an inducement to lose sleep; now there is none, hence the apathy on the part of the officers." An editor might denounce such feelings, warning that "those who cannot attend to the duties for which they are handsomely paid, without receiving an additional bribe, are unfit to be entrusted with office," but in practical terms previous attractions to police work had to be replaced by new ones.[39]

The outraged editor noted one important technique for both inducing men to obey orders and making police work attractive. Officers earned salaries which made them some of the highest-paid workers in every city. During the 1850s and 1860s patrolmen commonly received between $600 and $700 a year, with officers getting slightly more. These wages compared favorably with the annual earnings of such skilled craftsmen as carpenters, bricklayers, and stonecutters.[40] Moreover, police salaries tended to rise during the remainder of the century (although there were numerous fluctuations). By the 1870s, a survey of seventeen cities showed that patrolmen earned anywhere from $821 to $1,500 per year. By the eighties, $1,000 to $1,200 seems to have been fairly common.[41] Thus a man who joined a department assured himself of a relatively high social status based on his income alone.

A patrolman who wanted to supplement his salary could do so in various ways. After completing a tour of duty, he might accept an opportunity to stand guard at a theater or amusement center, or he might maintain order at meetings, balls, and other social events. The pay for such extracurricular activities varied. One source indicated an officer could expect anywhere from two to forty dollars for his labors, depending upon the circumstances and generosity of his temporary employers.[42] While the frequency of such opportunities is unknown, the fact that they did exist may have been an important consideration for many officers who expected police work to provide them with additional financial rewards.

City officials also enhanced the attractiveness of police work by providing sickness, accident, and death benefits for officers. New York established The Police Life and Health Insurance Fund in 1857, while other cities founded similar organizations during the 1860s. The initial payments in these associations were rather small. New York, for example, paid a $150 annuity to disabled policemen. But the trend during the remainder of the nineteenth century was toward greater generosity. By the 1880s, St. Louis gave superannuated patrolmen a $450 yearly pension, and a New York officer could retire at half pay. Such government-guaranteed benefits were unheard of in other areas of employment. The development of these programs further eased the burden of conforming to regulations.[43]

Despite these inducements, the effort to regulate conduct did not exactly meet with resounding success. Many officers continued to follow behavior patterns to which they had been accustomed as private citizens. Profanity punctuated their speech; in dealing with the general public they acted with as much rudeness or civility as their personal inclinations dictated. Many men drank on duty.[44] And, as Chicago patrolman Michael Quirk admitted, "occasionally when I get tired I sit down on a box or something; sometimes fall asleep, but not often; other policemen are in the habit of doing the same."[45] Absenteeism, which plagued some departments, may have been one way by which many officers indicated their displeasure over the attempt to impose discipline upon them. In Philadelphia, for example, 114 men out of a total strength of 650 reported sick in a single day.[46]

Attempts to handle police misconduct varied from city to city. Mayors often acted as the final judges in deciding disciplinary cases. If a police commission ran a department, the commissioners sat as a court to pass sentence on errant officers. And in some cases, the chief of police (or superintendent) had control over matters of discipline. Some cities tried all three approaches, or variations, to this problem.[47] Regardless of the apparatus adopted, which varied for local political reasons rather than because one form was more effective than another, the intent was always the same: to impose discipline upon those officers who could not, or would not, obey regulations.

Reports of disciplinary proceedings appeared frequently in the press, beginning almost at the same time that the preventive police came into existence in each city and continuing throughout the remainder of the century. In most cases, patrolmen were punished for offenses which violated the public image of the police. Philadelphia's police manual directed lieutenants to suspend any officers who failed to make an arrest whenever a crime occurred on their beats. While this may seem an impossible demand, it was occasionally enforced. The motives in such cases may have been less to spur the men to their duty than to convince the public that the police were earnestly attempting to prevent crime.[48]

Concern over the image of the police did not extend to cases involving brutality. Physical violence had quickly become a normal part of police work.[49] As long as officers beat up lower-class criminals, the public seems to have been willing to condone their efforts. Outcries against police violence usually occurred only when the victim happened to belong to the more respectable classes. This tolerance may explain why clubbing, a frequent practice, was so infrequently a subject for disciplinary proceedings, and why punishment for this offense was often less than for other infractions of police regulations. Suspensions and dismissals occurred most often for behavior which rendered a man unfit to carry out his assignments. Drunkenness and sleeping on duty seem to have been the major causes for disciplinary actions. Neither activity comported well with official attempts to portray the police as a vigorous, efficient shield against crime.[50]

While continuing to struggle with the deficiencies of individual officers, police administrators had to consider another major problem: how to conquer their cities' geography. Only partially victorious in disciplinary matters, administrators had to move ahead simultaneously with their efforts to protect residents and property more adequately than the old police had. The public would judge the new police on the basis of their effectiveness, as well as their personal behavior. Thus the implementation of the idea that a pervasive police presence would suppress random street crime became just as crucial as the struggle over discipline. Here again the legitimacy of the new police was at stake.

The police never achieved complete pervasiveness for a variety of reasons. Urbanization was a major problem which administrators obviously could not control. Cities grew at extraordinary rates. Between 1860 and 1890, Philadelphia, which acquired new residents at a more leisurely rate than many cities, doubled its population. During those same years Chicago experienced a tenfold increase. These increments vastly expanded the physical size of each city, and the many thousands of new homes and businesses implicit in this growth placed a heavy burden on the police, who were expected to guard the entire metropolitan area. Surburbanization posed another challenge. As the population within the cities moved outward, criminals followed. The police had to be alert to these shifts and adopt tactics which would take them into account. Public parsimony complicated an already difficult situation. Almost as soon as the new police departments appeared, their expense became a matter of concern and criticism.[51] City councilmen responded to this fiscal conservatism by frequently debating reductions in the police. As a result, the strength of the departments fluctuated markedly over time, although the trend was slowly upward. Philadelphia maintained a fairly respectable ratio of patrolmen to population; in 1860 it stood at 1:870; by 1880 it had improved to 1:705. Chicago, however, had a rather dismal ratio of 1:1,950 in 1860, and 1:1,390 in 1880 (the latter figure changed to 1:1,823 two years later because of a council demand for new economies in law enforcement). The differences may be attributable to the characters of the two cities. Philadelphians had a strong tradition of community controls and a self-image based on public order; Chicagoans prided themselves on their individualism and their reputation as a wide-open town. While these differences might explain why Philadelphia had a larger police force than Chicago did (1,200 men vs. 362 in 1880), the fact remains that both departments found it extremely difficult to provide adequate protection to the public with the men available to them.

Coping with urbanization and suburbanization within the confines imposed by demands for effective, but economical, law enforcement meant that police administrators had to distribute available patrolmen in the most efficient way possible. Efficiency, however, was an elusive quality. To attain that goal city officials had to weigh such things as an area's reputation for disorder, and they had to make value judgments as to whether business districts warranted more protection than certain residential neighborhoods (such as suburban developments).

Philadelphia's early juggling with the problems of man-power distribution illustrates the difficulties in balancing these varied considerations. Shortly after metropolitan con-solidation in 1854, the new city councils approved a plan to establish fourteen police precincts. Most of the precincts contained two wards, although some of the outskirts of Philadelphia were coterminous with a single ward. The allot-ment of officers among these precincts indicates that depart-ment officials had decided to concentrate protection in the central city (police districts 2 through 8, covering wards 3 through 14). That area received 81.7 percent of the available policemen. Although no records survive to establish precisely why this arrangement was chosen, a glance at the crime pat-terns map for 1850 indicates that police administrators probably distributed their men in this fashion because most street crimes had occurred in that general area. Furthermore, this distribution allowed them to cover the business district fairly well.[52]

This arrangement came under attack before the year ended. In October the *Public Ledger,* staunch proponent of a preventive police, claimed that arrests for vagrancy and drunkenness had increased, but that thieves "flourished with the same impunity as formerly."[53] Burglaries began to plague the 24th ward in November. Hoping to compensate for previ-ously inadequate protection in that suburban area, the mayor transferred thirty-one more officers to temporary duty there. But his decision to send reinforcements only underscored the apparent error in concentrating too many men in the cen-tral city, thereby exposing outlying areas to opportunistic criminals.[54]

These circumstances led to some extraordinary criticism of the new police. Commenting on the mayor's transfers, the *Ledger* claimed that the number of men in certain precincts "have been found to be too great for the purpose of main-taining good order." Apparently, too much pervasiveness was undesirable—the police had suddenly become inefficient. The reason readily suggested itself: "This difficulty of di-viding the men is owing, we think, to the larger force now in commission."[55] *Efficient* pervasiveness now replaced saturation pervasiveness as the principal rationale for the distribution of manpower. Too many policemen were a detriment to effective law enforcement.

Responding to this kind of criticism, the city councils haggled over administrative reforms of the police late the next year. Eventually a new ordinance expanded the number of precincts to sixteen and reduced the number of officers and patrolmen from 820 to 650. The new plan became effective in the spring of 1856. Under the new arrangements nine of the precincts contained two wards. Of the seven which were coterminous with a ward, five were located in suburban areas; the other two were in the downtown (wards 5 and 6), perhaps indicating that the councilmen from those wards had sufficient political influence to demand total control over police appointments. While only minor precinct boundary changes occurred, major shifts took place in manpower allotments. The sharp reduction in the department's authorized strength caused administrators to become more efficient. Precincts 2 through 8 received 59.3 percent of the available patrolmen, indicating that police officials still regarded that part of Philadelphia as the major source of disorder. Older suburban areas, close to the original city boundaries, seem to have enjoyed an increased priority for protection, but the newer suburbs (wards 21 through 25) did not. In sum, the 1856 reorganization distributed the police more evenly over the metropolitan area, but at the cost of a loss in pervasiveness in the most disorderly precincts.[56]

In contrast to Philadelphia, Chicago's police administrators originally used the city's geography as the basis for distributing the force. Since the river divided Chicago into three parts, officials simply created three corresponding police districts. This practice continued until after the war, when population growth in all sections of the city made smaller precincts necessary for efficient departmental management. As in Philadelphia, administrators initially had biases within this general framework. Commenting on those prejudices, a local editor noted that "the central portions of the city are the most frequented by dangerous characters, [and therefore] the police are chiefly concentrated in the business districts, leaving the outskirts without any protection."[57] This distribution provoked complaints from residential areas, causing some embarrassment to officials. When, for example, citizens in the western portion of the city demanded protection from "low thieves and burglars," the superintendent had to admit that current arrangements left him no men "to detail to patrol that portion of the city."[58]

Departmental records for the years from 1875 to 1885 indicate that Chicago's police officials responded to citizens' complaints by adopting administrative tactics similar to those used in Philadelphia. During the first four years of that decade the department suffered a steady erosion of its manpower due to pressures stemming from the national economic depression. The loss, from 565 to 409 policemen, represented a 27.6 percent decline. But administrators distributed these reductions so evenly among the precincts that only one district experienced a loss greater than one percent in its share of the city's police force. Better times returned slowly after 1878, and comparatively flush times arrived in 1884 after the city council authorized a major increase (44.9 percent) in departmental strength. Police officials did not, however, use this opportunity to experiment with saturation patrolling in crime-prone areas. Instead, every precinct received reinforcements, and none gained more than 2.8 percent in its share of the total available manpower. By the end of the decade some precincts had increased their absolute strength, but the percentage changes in every case of loss or gain were minor. The average decline in these ten years averaged 3.1 percent; the average gain measured only 1.9 percent. Philadelphia's compromise between the demands for efficiency and pervasiveness in 1856 appears to have become administrative dogma in the postwar era.[59]

Certain other administrative decisions, necessary either for reasons of bureaucratic order or for their supposed value in preventing crime, further vitiated pervasiveness. Criminals, it was widely believed, were most active at night. To combat that threat, police officials continued the tradition of the watch by assigning most of their patrolmen to night duty. Only a third or a fourth of the police worked during the day.

Chicago, for instance, had only eighty-three men walking a day-beat in 1884. Platooning further reduced the number of officers on the streets. Morning, afternoon, evening, and night shifts were necessary as a means of resting the men, but this practice further diluted available strength.[60]

These circumstances, combined with a persistent shortage of men, diffused the police presence at its critical level, the beat. The theory of crime prevention, with its emphasis on pervasiveness, became something of an impossibility in practice. While few statistics survive to provide complete information concerning the size of beats, extant evidence indicates they were large. By 1883 the average night beat in Chicago measured one-half by one-quarter miles; day beats were three times as large. An officer walking that distance, checking doors, alleys, and miscellaneous problems, could not hope to cover his beat more than twice in his tour of duty.[61] Long absences therefore became one of the chief characteristics of patrolmen's beats.

Individual patrolmen carried a disproportionately heavy burden of responsibility for upholding the theory of crime prevention because of the compromises police officials had to make. When available, statistics show that their workload reflected this situation. In the years from 1875 to 1882, for instance, the number of arrests per patrolman in Chicago climbed steadily from 38.9 to 87.5. While incomplete data make conclusive generalizations impossible, the evidence also suggests that the size of the police force had little to do with the total number of arrests.[62] Unable to establish a pervasive influence in urban neighborhoods, police officials had to rely upon the discretion of individual patrolmen to protect city residents.[63]

Police administrators did very little to relieve the burdens of their patrolmen. When they did act, it was usually to deal with special problems or particular fears. Guarding port facilities posed one serious challenge. Harbors offered innumerable opportunities for theft, and the business community, sensitive about their city's reputation for waterfront pilferage, could make things unpleasant for police officials who neglected their interests. In response to such considerations, Boston, New York, and Philadelphia created harbor police detachments within their departments during the 1850s.[64] Traffic control was another difficult challenge which drew off available manpower. In Chicago, where the river's several bridges could become traffic bottlenecks during peak business hours, the problem could become particularly acute. By the 1860s, fully 10 percent of the police (17 out of 150) had to be used on the bridges alone, while another three men were posted at key street crossings.[65]

The fear of riots prompted officials to take several steps for their suppression. Platooning, for example, established a ready reserve in each station house for dealing with major disorders. Especially large headquarters detachments provided additional aid. Philadelphia had a group called the Reserve Corps, consisting of the most powerfully built men on the force. But these special squads would be of little use unless they could be quickly concentrated wherever trouble occurred. The telegraph solved this problem. New York's police installed telegraphic communications in the early 1850s, Boston did so in 1855, and Philadelphia had done so by 1858.[66] These systems only connected station houses with their central headquarters. Technology would be used, in the words of one commentator, to ensure that "common breaches of the peace have no opportunity to grow up into great public disorders as they are likely to do from license and neglect."[67] New York's spectacular Draft Riots in 1863 demonstrated the importance of communications in police work, but officials failed to grasp the possibilities of technological control over patrolmen on the beat for several more years.[68]

During most of the nineteenth century the average patrolman walking a beat remained extremely isolated. His best hope of obtaining help in a hurry lay in rapping his nightstick on the pavement; otherwise he had to walk (or run) to his station house. If he had a prisoner, the patrolman had to escort him back to the precinct house, abandoning his beat for as long as the trip took. These flaws prevented a more thorough application of crime prevention theory to actual street conditions, and they created a large gap between promise and practice which police administrators seemed unable to bridge.

One solution to this difficulty developed in Chicago during the early part of 1880. While attending a picnic, Mayor Carter Harrison, Sr., and Austin J. Doyle, the secretary of the police department, discussed the lack of communication between patrolmen and their precinct houses. Perhaps influenced by the fact that the fire department had recently installed a system of alarm boxes telegraphically connected to centrally located fire stations, the two men decided that a similar arrangement might solve the police department's problem. Doyle asked the superintendent of the Fire Alarm Telegraph to look into the matter, and he quickly devised a similar plan for the police.[69]

The superintendent, a Professor Barrett, proposed a system of call boxes, two or more on each beat, which would be connected to each precinct house by telegraph lines. Each box would be enclosed to protect it from the weather; it would be locked to prevent vandalism or false alarms by pranksters; and it would be capable of sending eleven different signals: police wagon, thieves, forgers, riot, drunkard, murder, accident, violation of city ordinance, fighting, test of line, and fire. A wagon-mounted patrol of four or five men would be stationed at each precinct house, ready to respond to any of the alarms.[70]

Barrett's system, the first of its kind in the nation, made it possible for police officials to use a flexible approach to the problems of administering a city's space. Call boxes enabled them to refine the idea of pervasiveness by introducing variations which had seemed impossible before 1880. Early experiments with the new system indicated their awareness of their opportunities. Since insufficient funds precluded the immediate installation of call boxes in every precinct, Chicago's police officials decided to begin in the West Twelfth Street precinct. At the time, that area was one of the toughest in the city. In such a district the police needed to maintain as constant a presence as possible. The call boxes contributed to that goal because a patrolman no longer had to leave his beat to obtain help or escort prisoners to the station house;

he merely called for the wagon patrol to pick up an offender and continued his rounds.[71]

Crimes in middle-class neighborhoods occurred less frequently, but were more noticeable to local residents because they represented atypical behavior in these areas. Since the number of offenses was fewer, police officials usually assigned fewer patrolmen to such districts. To maintain the required presence in the entire precinct, patrolmen had to walk enlarged beats. This created the paradox that those citizens who were most likely to seek police aid had less chance of finding help. Chicago's West Lake Street precinct, for instance, had been "most miserably cared for, and some of the most startling crimes have occurred within its borders. This was wrong, for the district is fairly filled with some fine residences and the thousands of tax-paying citizens received no equivalent for their money, at least in police care and watchfulness."[72] Call boxes allowed police administrators to devise a different kind of pervasiveness for such areas. When West Lake Street became the second precinct to receive the new system in February 1881, police officials announced that virtually all beats would be abandoned. The district's residents, supplied with keys to the boxes and given the opportunity (at their cost) of installing an alarm in their own homes or businesses, would notify the police of any disturbances. Administrators apparently made this decision on the basis of experiments in the West Twelfth Street precinct which showed that a patrol wagon could reach the scene of disorders within five minutes of a call.[73] In this manner, ordinary citizens would provide the element of pervasiveness.

Call boxes had another characteristic which endeared them to police officials: they tightened discipline. Patrolmen had to report in to their precincts once an hour. This new regulation, as Captain John Bonfield noted with some satisfaction, "keeps them out of some hole, and compels them to do their duty."[74] Since the patrolmen realized that technology threatened to change long-established habits by bringing them under closer control by their officers, they resisted this innovation for several years. Their methods of obstructing the implementation of this intrusion into their lives could not have been very effective, however, because police officials continued to install the system as fast as money became available. By the end of 1881 over half the stations had been fully equipped; at the end of 1884 all but one had the call boxes.[75]

The rapid, even enthusiastic, adoption of the call boxes occurred not only because they offered greater flexibility and control over patrolmen, but also because the technology seemed so efficient. With this new system, the police superintendent proudly proclaimed, "our present Police Department could perform the same duties as two thousand patrolmen."[76] The economy in police expenditures implicit in that assertion probably made a powerful impression on cost-conscious politicians and their constituents. Technology became a substitute for adequate manpower. Arrests statistics show how rapidly, and to what extent, Chicago's police developed a dependency upon this tool. In 1881 the patrol wagon service accounted for only 6 percent of the total arrests; by 1885 that figure had reached 44 percent.[77]

Chicago's success with signal boxes inspired other cities to adopt similar systems during the eighties. But there were major exceptions. Boston, New York, and Philadelphia police officials moved slowly, if at all, toward implementing the innovation. In Boston political bickering and the initial cost of the system postponed the introduction of call boxes until the end of the century. New York's police experimented with a version of Chicago's apparatus in 1884, but for reasons which remain obscure, nothing further was done about the idea until the 1890s. Philadelphia's councils authorized the installation of call boxes in 1884, but on such a limited scale that only two precincts had them the following year. Mayor William Smith explained that a lack of funds prevented a more extensive adoption, but Philadelphia's fairly high ratio of policemen to population may have had something to do with the lack of progress. The city simply was not growing fast enough to make technological help seem imperative in police work.[78]

The public's desire for efficiency and economy severely hindered police administrators' efforts to conquer urban geography. A similar conflict between legitimate police goals and the narrow concerns of special interests hindered the attempt to stabilize the working force in each department. At a time when experience was a patrolman's only guide in performing his duties, some form of indefinite tenure seemed the best way to ensure that each man would receive the "education . . . which time and practice would naturally give a man."[79] Professional politicians initially regarded this idea with considerable distaste. The police department was one of the largest sources of patronage available, and any concept of tenure threatened to reduce their power. Convincing these politicians to limit their interference proved difficult.

The nature of urban politics helped bring about change. Faced with the uncertainties of elections, party leaders sought ways to guarantee that some of their friends kept their positions as patrolmen. On April 11, 1849, for example, New York's legislature amended the police act for New York City so that the head of the department held the same two-year tenure as the mayor, while other officers received four-year appointments. Maryland's assembly adopted a similar procedure in 1860, when it approved of five-year contracts for policemen.[80] Staggered terms increased police stability and gave officers more time to learn their business.

These laws combined with the uncertainties of political life to introduce bipartisanship as another stabilizing influence in police departments. In New York shifting political fortunes at the ward level gradually convinced Democrats and their opponents to share the wealth. The Democrats, for example, won the city's 2nd ward in 1846 and 1848, but the Whigs dominated that area in 1847 and in 1849. Twenty-eight of the thirty policemen assigned to this ward in 1846 received reappointments two years later. A similarly high percentage of Whig patrolmen who joined the force in 1847 obtained new contracts in 1849. By 1870 this kind of balancing act had produced an informal agreement that the Democrats would share police commissionerships with the Republicans, and that each commissioner would control a certain number of appointments to the department. This arrangement remained intact throughout the remainder of the century.[81]

Although bipartisanship served politicans well, it did not satisfy the needs of the police. Political interference did not cease, and experienced men might still be capriciously dismissed. Only tenure during good behavior could eliminate political meddling, or so it was widely believed. But lawmakers would not accept that idea unless they became convinced that public support for the police would suffer irreparable damage without it, or unless they perceived some possible political advantage in it. In these circumstances, tenure during good behavior did not gain universal acceptance. New York adopted it in 1853 only because an aroused public felt that an inexperienced police was failing to provide even minimal protection. Bitter intraparty feuding among Illinois Republicans explains why Chicago police obtained greater job security in 1861. John Wentworth, Chicago's mayor from 1857 to 1858, returned to a second term in 1860. His flamboyant style and ambition clashed with other powerful personalities in his party, and after a convoluted sequence of events his enemies deprived him of control over the police by creating a board of commissioners to run the department. The Republican-dominated state legislature, probably hoping to retain control of the police after the transition to this new form of departmental governance, authorized tenure during good behavior.[82]

A unique situation stifled concern over capricious dismissals in Philadelphia. Throughout the 1850s the police had experienced wholesale turnovers as nativists won or lost election contests with Democrats. Rapid personnel changes had prompted a demand for tenure rules, but no agreement had been reached by 1858, when Alexander Henry became mayor. Henry's reputation for rectitude, and his behavior in selecting men for the police, squelched the cry for tenure during good behavior. The new mayor sought good candidates for patrolmen and even defied his own party to build a strong department. In one case a Protestant Irishman and a native American jockeyed for a lieutenancy and the latter won. When the Irishman's friends discovered court records showing their opponent had been imprisoned for riot, Henry immediately dismissed the former convict, much to the amazement of party hacks.[83]

A popular mayor, Henry remained in office until 1866 and managed to achieve his purpose of building a reputable police department. But by the time he stepped down, Philadelphia had become almost a one-party city. The Democrats, in disarray from charges of disloyalty during the war, had never recovered their former strength. Instead, a few Democratic ward leaders sold out their party for a few patronage plums. William S. Stockley solidified Republican dominance upon his election as mayor in 1871. Nearly total control of the city's political life meant that Stockley and his machine had no need for bipartisanship to stabilize their influence with the police. Nor did they need to pay much attention to the occasional demands for changes in tenure rules. Consequently Philadelphia's reformers remained ineffectual throughout the remainder of the century. Only in 1881, when they managed to elect Samuel G. King as mayor, did they have an opportunity to remove politics from police appointments. King adopted a policy of tenure during good behavior, but his successor in 1884 quickly returned to the old ways.[84]

Philadelphia's failure to adopt formal rules for tenure during good behavior should have resulted in a much more volatile personnel policy according to contemporary wisdom on the subject. Such was not the case, however. An analysis of John Flinn's history of the Chicago police and Howard Sprogle's book on the Philadelphia department reveals that most officers in both cities had served five or more years by 1887, indicating a degree of continuity among policemen which was important in stabilizing each department (see Table 2).

The Chicago statistics are somewhat misleading because of the large increase in the force in 1884. Deleting that addition as a fortuitous occurrence, 41.1 percent of the Chicago police had less than five years experience. That figure is remarkably close to Philadelphia's. The similarities in the first

Table 2   **Length of Patrolmen's Experience, 1887**

	Chicago		Philadelphia	
Years	No.	%	No.	%
0-4	649*	52.34	642	41.93
5-9	114	9.19	264	17.24
10-14	159	12.82	327	21.36
15-19	109	8.79	215	14.04
20-24	34	2.74	35	2.29
25-29	8	.01	32	2.09
30-	5		16	1.05
N. I.	162	13.06		
Totals	1,240	98.95	1,531	100.00

*Force increased by 236 men in 1884.

Source: John J. Flinn, *History of the Chicago Police from the Earliest Settlement of the Community to the Present Time* (Chicago: W. B. Conkey, 1887); Howard O. Sprogle, *History of the Philadelphia Police* (Philadelphia: n.p., 1887).

category are all the more striking because of the different political developments in each city. Perhaps this indicates that the 40 percent represents a kind of "index of instability"—and a very considerable one—for nineteenth-century police departments. But about 60 percent of all the men were experienced officers, at least in the postwar period. The existence of this latter group may indicate that professional politicians in Philadelphia and elsewhere conceded the need for a significant body of patrolmen who knew their jobs well.

While the idea of indefinite tenure enjoyed only mixed success, other developments stabilized personnel changes and helped keep experienced men in every department. Among the more important innovations was the introduction of the rule that no man could be discharged except for cause. This regulation implied judicial proceedings to determine guilt, and by the late nineteenth century such hearings had become fairly common.[85] These procedures could be abused, and no doubt were from time to time, but the need to maintain departmental morale and to preserve the reputation of the police with the general public helped curb excesses.

But the politicians refused to surrender control over many crucial aspects of departmental affairs. Politics, for example, still dominated personnel policies. A man had to have the right friends to obtain an appointment to the police. Promotions and choice assignments depended upon his maintaining good relations with his sponsors.[86] In this regard, favoritism could cost a department some of its manpower for patrol duty. During the depression in 1877, Chicago's police force declined 12.9 percent, but the number of patrolmen dropped 15.6 percent. When better times two years later permitted additions to the force, the total size of the department expanded 5.1 percent while the number of ordinary officers increased only 2.2 percent. Politicians seem to have protected administrators during hard times and added to their numbers wherever possible.[87] Ward leaders also used their influence to frustrate punishment for breaches of regulations. This kind of interference protected incompetent officers and weakened discipline.[88]

Political meddling in internal affairs was fairly common. But the extent to which politicians could interfere with officers on the beat is problematical and probably varied from city to city. Differing administrative practices confused the situation. Philadelphia's police officials seem to have made permanent assignments to a precinct; transfers were used for political rewards or punishments. In these circumstances patrolmen could become familiar with the political situation along their beats. The evidence for this conclusion is tenuous, however.[89] Precinct and ward boundaries in Chicago could not by law coincide until 1881. Furthermore, administrators frequently rotated men among the districts.[90] This may have prevented patrolmen from developing an extensive knowledge of any but the most prominent politicians or their friends. Practical considerations compounded any efforts to interfere with arrest decisions. A patrolman simply could not ask a man his political views in the midst of a brawl. Nor could an officer believe everyone who claimed to have powerful friends.

Confronted by these problems, and well aware that many of their more rowdy partisans expected protection from the police, politicians had to find some way to help their errant followers. Their solution was to control the pre-cinct station houses and the police courts (which were often located in the same building). The men in command of these places owed their positions to party bosses, and they could be relied upon to discharge any prisoner who could substan-tiate his claims to protection. If departmental rules denied such powers to precinct commanders, police justices could dismiss complaints against faithful party workers.[91] The normally mundane nature of administering criminal justice at the precinct level helped obscure the extent of this type of political interference in policing. Petty crimes did not attract much newspaper attention, and the large number of these of-fenses handled in summary fashion made it difficult for any but the most knowledgeable observers to identify those per-sons who were discharged because of their political influence. In sum, politics remained an intimate part of policing throughout the nineteenth century.

Police administrators had only mixed success in solving the organizational problems of preventive policing. A decen-tralized bureaucratic system susceptible to the whims of democratic politics frustrated anything more than muddled solutions to most problems. The struggle over police disci-pline reveals how principles frequently became compromised by political realities. Not every indolent or incompetent patrolman disappeared from the ranks as a result of disci-plinary proceedings. Officials often failed to enforce the rules, or they did so capriciously. Political favoritism or per-secution disrupted the impact of regulations, although to what extent this undermined police morale is very difficult to determine.[92] On the other hand, by establishing conduct norms police administrators could at least define deviant acti-vities. By referring to those codes they could justify punitive action against offenders. The regulations identified proper group behavior and therefore helped create the foundations of institutional unanimity. These rules would, in time, contri-bute to more effective law enforcement than had been characteristic of policing prior to 1840.

The inability to conquer urban geography was perhaps the most important failing of the new police. But this failure cannot be attributed to a lack of effort on their part. It was due instead to the parochialism of city residents who could not reconcile their desire for a preventive police with their demand for inexpensive government. When Mayor Wentworth tried to reduce the number of Chicago patrolmen in 1858, for example, he found that "it gave great dissatisfaction, as the people of no portion of the city were willing to have the protection they received . . . lessened."[93] Citizens quickly complained whenever the police did not suppress disorder. These complaints came not only from the better residential sections, but also from less reputable areas. In 1856, petitioners living in the vicinity of Tenth and South streets, near the heart of Philadelphia's south side slum, asked the mayor to preserve order there. Some years later the residents of old Spring Garden, a north side suburb, made a similar request.[94] In sum, taxpayers insisted on economy, but not at the expense of superficial protection for their particular neighborhoods.

Considering the size of beats and the lack of men to patrol them adequately, some complaints were inevitable. But the persistent inability of the police to cover every neighborhood to the extent demanded by its residents opened the door to alternative means of adequate protection. Spontaneous "law enforcement" was one such solution, as when some Philadelphia boardinghouse residents drove off a group of rowdies who attacked their building. Remarking on this incident, an editor concluded that "the residents of the neighborhood are compelled to take the protection of their lives and property into their own hands" because the police visited the area "at but rare intervals."[95]

Resort to self-help represented only an infrequent extreme. A more typical response was to hire private police. According to Philadelphia Mayor Daniel Fox, "applications are continually being made to this office for the appointment of officers to be employed and paid by citizens residing in particular neighborhoods, to guard their immediate localities."[96] These auxiliaries had the same authority as regular patrolmen within the boundaries specified by their employers.[97] Residential watchmen were only one type of private police. The demand for localized protection presented many entrepreneurs with an opportunity to open law enforcement agencies. In Chicago, for example, G. T. Moore established the Merchant's Police. Moore charged his customers fifty cents a week and instructed his men to protect only those stores which subscribed to his service. Such organization as Moore's had an important advantage over the city's police: they could maintain a higher degree of pervasiveness. As Moore proudly noted, "We take small beats, so that we are able to visit the alleys and streets four or five times an hour, and once each hour we try each subscriber's door."[98] Better police protection therefore went to those willing to pay for it. Money spent in this manner apparently seemed a better investment than money expended in taxes.

The use of private police in residential and business districts indicated that city officials had not uniformly succeeded in establishing a convincing police presence on the streets. Many residents obviously felt the need for greater protection. That attitude did not, however, completely undermine public support for preventive policing. Not everyone, after all, could afford to hire their own personal watchmen; most people had to rely upon the new police if for no other reason than because it constituted their only source of protection, whatever its deficiencies. Technology may have helped ease the problems of pervasiveness, although the available evidence makes any conclusive argument on that score impossible.

On the more positive side, police administrators managed to establish some form of job security for most of their men. Whether this came about by legal or informal means, it made possible a greater degree of stability than most people realized at the time. This allowed men to build careers as police officers in spite of changing political situations. George W. Walling, appointed a New York patrolman on December 22, 1847, became superintendent of police before finally retiring in 1885. Chicagoan Cyrus P. Bradley began as a constable in 1849, served as a detective in Levi Boone's administration (1855), as captain under Mayor Wentworth (1857), and as chief of police from 1861 to 1863. Charles

D. Grant became a Philadelphia patrolman in 1859 and served continuously, rising to the rank of lieutenant, until he died in 1884. Other men had similarly long tenures beginning in the 1850s and extending into the late nineteenth century. At a time when the street was an officer's only school, and experience his only guide, the opportunity for a long career was an important achievement in creating an effective police.[99]

The successful struggle to uniform the police was an equally important achievement. Failure would have undermined police visibility, an essential element in the theory of crime prevention. By uniforming their officers, administrators managed to establish symbols of centralized authority in the neighborhoods. They also advanced another step in their constant battle to make individual patrolmen conform to institutional goals. The men could take pride in their appearance, especially after the Civil War accustomed many more people to uniforms. Policemen were now more likely to regard themselves as members of a vital public agency, and they would begin to act accordingly.

While these were important victories, it remains true that the practical problems of administering police departments made any resemblance between the theory and the practice of crime prevention tenuous at best. The principles of republicanism combined with public demands for economy to frustrate any serious attempt to test adequately the idea that deviant behavior could be prevented. Crime control, for all practical purposes, would depend less upon centralized direction of the police than upon the performance of individual patrolmen walking their beats.

Five   **The Patrolman on the Street**

The efforts to establish departmental discipline revealed a laudable concern for police group behavior. Rules and regulations were a necessary step in the creation of an effective agency of social control, but the interest administrators displayed in solving internal difficulties did not carry over to the equally vital area of the patrolman's problems on his beat, where two questions required solution before he could perform his duties. The first problem concerned who should be subject to arrest. At first glance the answer to that seemed obvious: patrolmen should apprehend those persons whose behavior violated state and city laws. The new police had not been created to deal with *all* criminals, however; just some of them. This meant that specific groups had to be identified as the proper objects of police attention. The second question involved the correct methods for effecting an arrest. For the first time America's major cities had large numbers of men committed to the idea of daily enforcing the law and preventing disorder, but only those men who had previously served as constables or watchmen had any experience with the delicate matter of depriving a citizen of his freedom. How would the new policemen react when confronted with a situation requiring their official intervention? What constraints would influence their behavior? As the fledgling patrolmen took to their beats, no one knew the answer to these and other problems.

Police officials provided a partial answer to the first question. Turning to the theory of crime prevention for help, they ordered the patrolman to arrest any person he had "just cause to suspect" was about to commit a crime. This wording revealed the ordinary policeman's crucial role in implementing crime prevention. No matter how effectively administrators might enforce discipline, no matter how efficiently they distributed their men, the ultimate effectiveness of the new police depended upon how well the officer on his beat translated theory into practice. Administrators could only warn their subordinates that "police officers must judge from all the circumstances of the case, what the intention of the party is"; a patrolman's innate sense of discretion would have to do the rest.[1]

But vague official injunctions to arrest persons found in suspicious circumstances needed refining if they were to provide adequate guidelines for patrolmen. Officers had to have more precise ideas concerning normal and abnormal behavior if they were to be effective. Police administrators, caught in the turmoil of politics, did not pay much attention to the difficult problem of more carefully defining deviance. Since police recruits were drawn from the neighborhoods they would patrol, popular attitudes, not official strictures, would shape each officer's definition of suspicious actions.

The public feared or disliked many groups, but it generally concentrated on social rank as a guide for condemning or accepting specific individuals. This tendency was a legacy of the eighteenth century's deference to the upper class. The regard for the "better sort" carried over into the nineteenth century in a much attenuated, but nevertheless significant, attitude that gentlemen should not be inconvenienced too much because of some minor mistake. In 1826, when a New York watchman arrested a man who refused to move away from a crowd, and he complained of maltreatment to the city council, the officer defended himself by saying that "no person came forward to inform him what his standing in society was."[2] Presumably the watchman would not have arrested someone who could claim gentleman status.

Respectability shielded even those persons who had in fact violated the law, regardless of whether the offense was a minor one like drunkenness or a crime such as fraud. The more conservative newspapers refused to print the names of gentlemanly drunks, though they readily did so for those of the lower class.[3] Wayward sons who had systematically written forged checks on the bank accounts of family friends need not fear prosecution; they were only committing youthful errors.[4] A sympathetic judge might suspend sentence for a member of the upper class, even for larceny, "on account of the respectability of his family."[5] This does not mean that all the privileged escaped arrest; rather, it indicates that social attitudes protected them, that they were less subject to police scrutiny, and that, if caught, they received more consideration than less fortunate people.[6]

Patrolmen needed some way to distinguish social standing at a glance. Those Americans who tried to define for the police whom to arrest placed great faith on dress as an indication of sociability. A well-appointed suit of clothes showed that a person recognized the value of "the habit of order, of system, and of having a time for everything." Contrariwise, "the man, woman, or child who feels habitually worse dressed than their neighbors will be apt to shrink from society and behave awkwardly and strangely in it." These people would not have "that comfortable feeling of being allied and equal to the better part of the social world," and would as a consequence adopt attitudes and conduct contrary to the public welfare. It followed that anyone who dressed in a slovenly manner posed a potential danger to the community, and that the police ought to watch them carefully.[7] Thus, by adopting appearance as a guide, officers could quickly identify those who might threaten society's well-being and keep them under control.

Society considered the idler even more dangerous than the badly dressed person. American cities usually contained a class of people contemporaries identified by the phrase "floating population." Even before industrialization became a major factor in the economy, commercial cities had a problem with laboring people who, through economic changes, found "that the skill or art, on which they depend for subsistence, has become useless."[8] Instead of moving on to places where they could find work, some stayed in the city, forming a pool of unemployed, "congregating in particular localities, where they lived among companions and friends in similar circumstances and of similar habits."[9] Others traveled from city to city in search of work, and by mid-century they were a common feature of urban life.[10]

The term "floating" appeared as early as 1812, but more important than the first use of the word or phrase was the attitude society adopted toward these unfortunate people.[11] The public regarded them as dangerous because they violated the work ethic, one of the canons of nineteenth-century society. Popular opinion held that "every idler is a public enemy" because "every man, rich or poor, ought to have some great absorbing purpose, . . . to which his main energies are devoted. Not enjoyment but *duty,* daily duty, must be the aim of every life."[12] The logical step, enunciated by one journal editor, was to approve police surveillance over this class of citizens:

> As a general thing, an idle, able-bodied poor man, has no right to complain, if the eye of the police follows him wherever he roams or rests. His very idleness is an offense against all social laws. He wrongs somebody, and only wants a faint impulse to push him into a league with burglars and incendiaries.[13]

The young and the intemperate constituted the final groups whom general opinion regarded as fit subjects for police control. Laws against drunkenness, dating back to the seventeenth century, attempted to preserve public decorum by prohibiting the abuses committed by those under the influence of alcohol. Juveniles posed a persistent challenge to order. Their gang battles and assaults on pedestrians were a constant source of danger to ordinary citizens. The adolescent thieves and beggars annoyed and dismayed urban dwellers.[14]

The children and drunks shared a common niche in the public mind. They seemed to endanger the whole social fabric by their lawlessness. At a time when there were few asylums or institutions designed to care for these two groups, the public turned to the police as the best way to regulate their conduct. The patrolman symbolized society's authority over the individual, and, in theory, he was the best equipped to impress the young and to remove the obnoxious drunk from view.

The slovenly in appearance, the idle, the young, and the intemperate formed the basic groups which society defined as deviant in the nineteenth century. Other prejudices only reinforced suspicion of anyone in these four categories. Nativism, for example, intensified the implicit distrust of slovenliness, idleness, and inebriety. Attitudes toward juveniles, drunks, the ill-clad, and the floating population were extremely complex, ranging from sympathetic efforts to help to suppression. But however any one segment of public opinion responded to them, all agreed that they posed a problem for society. This feeling that certain persons had departed from accepted norms of conduct formed the rationale for giving the police the responsibility of controlling their behavior. Unfortunately, the popular identification of problem groups did not include specific means for handling individual cases. Having defined their concern, the public left that task to the patrolman on the beat.

Police acceptance of these general guidelines meant that most arrests would be for misdemeanors rather than for felonies.[15] This result conformed to the general interpretation of crime prevention theory. Since popular opinion held that certain kinds of behavior eventually caused serious crimes, it was important to curb minor offenses before they led to more consequential ones. Early statistics for Philadelphia indicate this bias in arrest practices (see Table 3). The large number of arrests for disorderly conduct and drunkenness reveal how much public opinion emphasized those offenses as causes of crime. Those two categories dominated annual police reports, as the data for Chicago in Table 4 show.

Case histories of arrests for drunkenness indicate that officers worked to achieve two goals vis-à-vis the individual

Table 3   **Arrests in Philadelphia, 1858**

Type of arrest	No.	%
Misdemeanors		
Breach of peace and disorderly conduct	11,443	
Drunkenness	4,453	
Gambling	33	
Violations	640	
Vagrancy	1,352	
Unspecified	1,225	
Felonies		
Arson	49	
Assault and battery	1,761	
Counterfeiting	153	
Larceny	1,001	
Murder	20	
Picking pockets	79	
Riot	332	
Robbery	93	
Totals		
Misdemeanors	19,146	84.64
Felonies	3,488	15.36
All arrests	22,634	100.00

Source:*Public Ledger*, Jan. 21, 1859

drunk. First, the police sought to maintain order, as public opinion demanded. The general rule, as a New York captain expressed it, was that "where there is a violation of public decency, as for instance a man staggering up against parties, he must be arrested."[16] William Bell fulfilled this role when he apprehended two inebriated men he had observed insulting pedestrians and crowding women off the sidewalk.[17] But patrolmen also provided services to intoxicated citizens who were not being obnoxious to anyone in particular. A man too drunk to remember his name or address might spend the night in a cell instead of lying in the street.[18] If he could recall where he lived, the policeman might escort him safely home.[19] Someone who drank too much while in the wrong

Table 4   **Arrests in Chicago, 1872-1885**

| | | Arrests for drunk and disorderly | |
Year	Total arrests	No.	%
1872	21,931*	13,781	62.84
1873	27,995*	15,993	57.13
1874	24,899*	13,882	55.75
1875	19,206+	10,724	55.84
1876	27,291	13,280	48.66
1877	28,035	13,178	47.01
1878	27,208	12,600	46.31
1879	27,338	12,604	46.10
1880	28,480	14,294	50.19
1881	31,713	15,971	50.36
1882	32,800	18,036	54.99
1883	37,187	21,415	57.99
1884	39,434	23,080	58.53
1885	40,998	25,407	61.97
Totals	413,515	224,245	54.23

*Year ending March 31.

+Beginning in 1875, the reporting period ended December 31 of each year.

Source: Chicago, *Annual Messages of the Mayors* (Chicago: The City Council of Chicago, 1872-1885.)

company might have his money saved by an alert officer who would take him into custody as a means of discouraging a potential robbery.[20]

Arrests for drunkenness and other misdemeanors also served dual purposes for police organizations. Preventive policing measured success differently from its predecessor. The recovery of stolen property had been the principal gauge of achievement for the constables. After initial expectations that patrolmen could perform that task collapsed, the new departments reassigned property recoveries to the detectives. This decision deprived ordinary policemen of a major source of prestige and left administrators with the problem of how best to evaluate an officer's competence. To remedy this situation, officials defined other goals for their men. Ideally, the best patrolman was one whose beat was totally free of crime. If an offense did occur, however, an officer's superiors demanded that he capture the guilty party without fail. Arrests thus became an important indicator of a man's efficiency.

Patrolmen responded to these conditions by arresting persons who committed minor offenses. The large number of intoxicated urbanites an officer encountered practically every day made it possible for him to meet the quantitative standards used to measure his performance. By regularly apprehending a few tipsy citizens, a policeman showed that he was a productive employee. Officers kept records of their arrests and used these data as justification for their continued employment and as a source of prestige.[21] The more arrests a man made, the higher his status was. Individual achievement, measured in terms of quantity, thus conformed to group goals.

Secondly, misdemeanor arrests served departmental needs. Simply by referring to these statistics, administrators could demonstrate that their subordinates were doing their jobs, thereby justifying their department's existence. As Chicago Police Commissioner Mark Sheridan pointed out, "The force was efficient; they had made 28,000 arrests during the past year."[22]

The size of the new departments provided the police with an opportunity to regulate the public conduct of large numbers of idlers and juveniles. In practical terms this meant that patrolmen intruded into the previously undisputed domains of these people—the street corners. By 1850 these two groups had become so standard a feature of the intersections that one editor could unequivocally assert that "it is only the idle and disorderly who congregate all day about the corners, riotously acting and using obscene and disgusting language."[23] Popular opinion held that one of the best ways to ensure tranquillity was to disperse those assemblages. Philadelphia's first police manual therefore instructed officers to clear the sidewalks, the corners, and doors of public halls, taverns, and engine houses.[24]

The manual advised patrolmen that they should first civilly request idlers and youths to move on. If they did not disperse, the officers should arrest the offenders. Since a policeman normally traveled his beat alone and could not therefore apprehend everyone, he usually tried to break up these gatherings by taking one or two persons into custody. Even with assistance at hand, these encounters did not result in mass arrests. Patrolmen chose to seize only those who appeared to exercise some leadership over these groups. By removing the most intransigent, the officers probably hoped to discourage the remainder.[25]

The efforts to suppress this form of behavior were seldom successful. Unless the police made a concerted effort to clear the corners, their occupants usually returned as soon as the patrolman moved on. An officer's diligence in this matter probably depended upon a neighborhood's attitude toward the problem. When the citizens of an area complained, or a particular intersection developed an excessively rough reputation, the police moved to quash activity at that corner. But enforcement remained sporadic throughout the century. This state of affairs was due to the nature of urban society at the time. With a constantly shifting population, old trouble spots might disappear while new ones developed elsewhere. Under these conditions, patrolmen could only respond as the need arose. They could never be sure where the next problem corner would be.[26]

In order to better regulate the activities of individuals (as opposed to groups), the police made use of a person's clothing as an indicator of his intentions, taking into custody "parties who have a hang-dog look or are very seedy in their appearance."[27] These people had not always committed a crime. The police arrested them "simply on general principles."[28] This reliance on personal attire had its hazards. Detective Bell, observing a prisoner caught in a theft, remarked that "from his appearance he is the the last person I should have drop[p]ed on for a thief."[29] Philadelphia Patrolman Taney found a man standing in the doorway of a store which was later robbed. At the trial of this suspect, Taney excused his failure to arrest the man by explaining that the robber dressed well and had a genteel demeanor, so he "did not suppose anything wrong was intended."[30] In spite of such occasional mistakes, the police continued to rely on clothes to determine who posed a threat to society.

A person's behavior, and the circumstances in which an officer found him, formed another basis for arrest. Departmental manuals directed patrolmen to be aware of unusual variations in neighborhood routine and to note the presence of strangers.[31] Policemen operated under generous instructions to "arrest all persons found under suspicious circumstances."[32] Officers used these orders as a tool in their campaigns to clear the street corners of idlers and juveniles. Charges of disorderly conduct, assault, and interfering with an officer often resulted from situations in which someone had refused a patrolman's command to disperse.[33]

In addition to providing a handy means of regulating public behavior, investigations begun because an officer's suspicions had been aroused also constituted an effective weapon against the random nature of crime in an urban setting. Policemen often arrested men whom they saw standing in the shadows on a street, or looking into store windows long after closing hours, or carrying bundles in commercial and residential areas after dark.[34] In this manner, numerous thieves found themselves in court the next day. Experience had taught patrolmen that behavior of these kinds often presaged a robbery or burglar. Some officers might occasionally assume a more active role in these arrests. A Chicago policeman, observing "a suspicious looking trio passing along the street at a late hour," secured the aid of some fellow patrolmen and disguised himself as a drunk. Staggering down the sidewalk in sight of the three men, he conspicuously examined his wallet under a lantern. Then he wandered off into an alley. The trio followed, whereupon the officer suddenly wheeled and grabbed one of them. The others escaped, but the prisoner turned out to be a "notorious character," thereby justifying the entrapment.[35]

Notoriety, especially when applied to professional thieves, was a standard justification for taking someone into custody even before most cities reformed their police establishments. News accounts of an arrest often contained variations on the phrase "this [suspect] seems well known to the police."[36] Officers developed a familiarity with career criminals in two ways : by observing their behavior, and by cultivating a good memory.   According to the great French thief-taker E. F. Vidocq, "there is something in the habits of every man which reveals his profession."[37] American lawmen, who probably had no knowledge of Vidocq's opinions, proved by their actions that they agreed with him. Detective Bell frequently noted the presence of pickpockets in his district simply by their demeanor. A Chicago officer saved a country visitor some discomfiture by arresting a young companion whose conduct indicated he was a confidence man.[38] To supplement his observations on behavior, a patrolman also relied on his memory. Individuals arrested on suspicion were "spotted" before they were released.[39] In this way the police stigmatized certain people who then became objects of special scrutiny whenever an officer saw them wandering about the city. Patrolmen thus conditioned themselves to expect deviant acts. A Chicago detective, for example, took two convicted burglars, just freed from prison, into custody "chiefly for the purpose of showing them up to the police." He apparently did not consider the possibility that these men might want to abandon their criminal careers.[40]

The police also interpreted vagrancy statutes liberally as a means of regulating the conduct of professional thieves. One such law, passed in St. Louis in 1847, proved instrumental in ridding that city of several members of the "blackleg gentry" (gamblers) whose "fine clothes, [and] gold chains" did not prevent them from being branded as vagabonds.[41] Chicago's council passed an ordinance in 1858 authorizing the arrest of "all persons who, for the purpose of gaming, travel about or go from place to place; and all persons upon whom shall be found any instrument . . . used for the commission of burglary, larceny, or for picking locks or pockets."[42] Other cities had similar acts which officers used to punish criminals who could not be convicted of a more serious offense.[43] The legality of these arrests did not go unchallenged. In 1873 a Chicago gambler sued a patrolman for taking him into custody on a vagrancy charge. The de-

fendant attempted to justify himself, in an appeal to the
Illinois Supreme Court, by submitting as evidence "what
he had been told by other police officers concerning the
habits and conduct" of the complainant. The court refused
to allow that defense.[44] In spite of this decision, the police
continued to arrest notorious characters for vagrancy.[45]

Although the courts might rule that arrests based on reputation constituted a misuse of vagrancy acts, they sanc-
tioned harassment of notorious individuals under professional
thieves codes. These latter statutes emerged after the development of straw bail, and they may have been an attempt to
nullify that ploy. The Pennsylvania legislature passed such a
law in 1862.[46] (There is some indication that the Philadelphia police employed such a charge even before 1862.)[47]
Two pickpockets immediately appealed their conviction on
the grounds that the new act violated their right to trial by
jury. The state's supreme court upheld the statute, arguing
that "vagrants, including rogues . . . , and those who frequent public places for unlawful purposes, are liable to summary conviction and punishment, notwithstanding anything
in the Constitution, for they were [liable to such treatment]
before the Constitution was adopted."[48] Three years later a
Philadelphia judge explicitly approved the basis for these
arrests by ruling that "reputation is sufficient to justify
their commitment when found in places prohibited by the
law."[49]

A reformed police also had more success in suppressing
riots than its predecessors. Prior to the 1850s, a skillful leader
could occasionally quell disorder using a combination of the
militia and lawmen. Philadelphia's mayor had managed such a
feat in the 1834 race tumult. But officials usually did not
have enough men available to stop these battles, and the militia rarely arrived until after the worst was over. Many minor
confrontations swelled into major clashes because the police
could not adequately patrol all the territory in a city like
New York or Philadelphia. The first crucial problem in mob
control, then, involved increasing the number of officers. The
enlargement of the departments contributed to a reduction
in the incidence of rioting by making it more likely that a

patrolman would be close at hand when gangs or firemen collided.

The presence of a policeman curtailed disorders only if he acted promptly. When a fight started, he could seize those persons most responsible for the hostilities. Then, if the affair had not escalated too quickly, the other combatants would disperse without further trouble.[50] But preventive arrests had limited effectiveness. This method of crowd control could not quell a riot which had already begun. In these situations, the officer needed help. Initially, he could obtain aid only by returning to his station house as rapidly as possible to report the situation to his superior. The precinct commander might decide to handle the problem with his own men, or, more probably, he would call for assistance from other districts. This process took time, and in the interval a small battle might grow into a sizable conflict. Only after the telegraph was widely adopted during the 1850s could officials concentrate large numbers of men at the point of trouble more quickly.

Once the police had a communications apparatus and sufficient strength, it was only a matter of time until officials learned how to manipulate this new weapon against rioters. The insistence on departmental discipline helped by teaching patrolmen how to work together. With more trained men available, their commanders could afford to adopt precautionary measures to deal with anticipated trouble. They could withhold a reserve at key locations if rumors indicated that a riot might occur.[51] Unexpected disorder complicated matters because of the somewhat clumsy telegraph system. Precincts had to call central headquarters for help; they had no direct wire links to nearby stations. But once enough patrolmen had been gathered, they usually proved more than a match for the rioters. Although there were some spectacular exceptions such as the New York Draft Riots in 1863, urban rioting became far less common after 1860 than it had been before that date.[52]

A patrolman's having to seek aid at his station house to suppress a disturbance underscores the characteristic isolation of every officer in the mid-nineteenth century. Before the call box went into effect in the 1880s, a policeman could contact his precinct headquarters only by walking there. In order to summon men from their beats, lieutenants had to send out their sergeants or roundsmen to bring them in personally. The size of most patrol areas (usually a mile or more) further increased an officer's solitude. Except in emergencies, he had to rely on his own abilities to preserve order.

When the new patrolmen first began walking their beats, they entered an environment prone to violence. The legacy of the old watch system posed one problem in this regard. Watchmen had become a public joke long before the 1840s. Those guardians of public safety had frequently slept at their posts, had often been drunk on duty, and had usually run from trouble. They had been favorite targets of rowdies looking for fun, and any watchman courageous enough to oppose them had done so at his peril. Thus the people whom popular opinion regarded as fit subjects for police supervision had developed hostile views of previous lawmen. The violence of the decades after 1830 further complicated matters. Volunteer firemen and gang members who appreciated only physical superiority would not be inclined to respect a patrolman's authority without some test of strength. Many other urban residents had developed a habit of settling their personal arguments by whatever means they thought necessary, from fists and clubs to knives and guns. These people had to learn to rely upon the new police to arbitrate individual as well as neighborhood disputes before officers could claim control over their beats.

An officer's isolation, and the disorderly population's expectations, made every arrest a challenge for the patrolman as well as his prisoner. The policeman had to escort his captive to the station house unaided, and that could mean a considerable walk. This situation made escape a tempting possibility and provided plenty of opportunities. The trip to precinct headquarters often became a physical contest for supremacy.

Little information exists about the actual events prior to an assault on an officer, and the frequency of such attacks remains problematic. But newspaper accounts chronicling the injuries of patrolmen making arrests formed one of the staple stories in the daily press. A prisoner might turn on the arresting lawman and attempt to knock him down; a man's friends frequently banded together and attacked the patrolman in order to free their comrade; a captive sometimes drew a knife or pistol and tried to kill the officer; mobs, which usually coalesced at the scene of a difficult arrest, assaulted policemen; a lawman entering a home to settle a domestic dispute might suddenly find himself the object of abuse. Even if the patrolman successfully brought his prisoner in, he faced other dangers. A gang which had seen one of its members locked up might ambush the offending officer; the prisoner, once freed, sometimes went looking for the man who had caused him so much trouble. And finally, unprovoked assaults occurred from time to time, reaching an apparent peak in the late 1840s and early 1850s.[53]

Some policemen's behavior complicated an already dangerous situation. One of the most frequent complaints against officers was their arrogant insistence on a respectful acknowledgment of their authority. If their commands did not receive prompt attention, patrolmen were quick to make an arrest. Considering their isolation from aid, this behavior could antagonize a potentially helpful bystander and escalate a rather simple matter into a serious confrontation. The general resistance among policemen to the adoption of a uniform also contributed to their problems. A peremptory command to move on or to stop fighting, coming from an otherwise ordinary-looking individual, could reasonably be resisted, from the viewpoint of the average citizen, because he had no way of knowing if the man had the authority to order him around. Offenders frequently excused an assault on an officer by claiming they did not recognize him as a patrolman. Finally, the police complicated arrests by neglecting to search prisoners. There was a remarkable number of incidents in which lawmen sustained injuries when a prisoner suddenly pulled a knife, a blackjack, or even a pistol. Many assaults could have been avoided if the officer had examined a man's pockets before beginning the long walk to the station.[54]

If patrolmen had worn uniforms, and adopted a more congenial manner and better search procedures, they would still have faced a dangerous problem. In the late 1840s the police became a target for firearms. No systematic conspiracy existed to shoot law officers; there was no need for any such plan because in the 1840s residents of cities began to use firearms on a wide scale for the first time.

The use of deadly weapons in this country has been largely ignored.[55] But there is no doubt that the rationale for owning and using guns forms an early and persistent theme in American society. In 1798, an anonymous writer, referring to the Bill of Rights as his justification, argued that "when the privileges of the people are attacked; or when standing armies are introduced or greatly increased," citizens should arm themselves in self-defense.[56] In 1844 the chief justice of the Pennsylvania Supreme Court offered the opinion that "a man has a right to keep whatever arms he pleases in his house. . . . *This is a freeman's privilege.*"[57]

The increasing use of these weapons apparently began with the political struggles of the 1830s. During election campaigns opposing parties sometimes stored muskets and other small arms in their headquarters. If a mob of political enemies forced them to take refuge in those places, the beseiged were apt to resort to shooting their attackers in defending the building. Battles between rowdies participating in parades precipitated the next stage in the use of firearms. After one such confrontation in 1844, New York's Whig newspapers advised their followers "to go armed to every political meeting or procession which takes place."[58] As a result, one journal reported that "the gunshops and hardware stores, where firearms are to be found, have had a most extraordinary increase of business."[59] In Philadelphia the Nativist Riot of 1844 had similar consequences. Sidney George Fisher, a local Philadelphian, remarked upon the use of guns and concluded: "We have never had anything like it before, but now that firearms have been once used & become familiar to the minds of the mob we may expect to see them employed on all occasions."[60]

Fisher's prediction came very close to the truth. Before the riot, knives, fists, and clubs had been the standard weapons in street fights and various assaults. Pistols had not been common, though there were scattered accounts which indicated that such weapons were beginning to appear.[61] The incidence of firearms use increased significantly following the May riot. In July 1844, the *Public Ledger* noted that "for several months past, but more particularly within the last two or three weeks, frequent discharges of firearms have been heard in every quarter of the city and country." The editor asked plaintively: "What does it mean?"[62] It meant that for the first time, on a massive scale, ordinary citizens—juveniles and adults—had begun to carry and use pistols to settle disputes.

Rioting and political factionalism did not provide the only incentives for arming. Simultaneously with those developments, the "better elements" in society also became interested in owning pistols because of the numerous assaults on individuals and an apparent increase in the number of burglaries. As a result, "many people have concluded that the only safety is in every man looking out for himself. . . At a party up town the other evening, it was discovered that four-fifths of the gentlemen present were armed with pistols."[63] Following a rash of robberies in 1857, George Templeton Strong reported that "most of my friends are investing in revolvers and carry them about at night."[64] An alarmed citizen of Chicago offered a reward of fifty dollars "for the first thief shot, while caught in the act of stealing."[65] Fear of crime at a period when the police were beginning to learn their jobs therefore spurred people who had little knowledge of or use for firearms to acquire them for self-defense.

Police attempts to control rowdies, juveniles, and thieves naturally resulted in confrontations with armed adversaries. Deliberate attacks on officers began to occur in the late 1840s.[66] These assaults culminated, in Philadelphia, with the fatal shooting of a watchman by some volunteer firemen in May 1850.[67] This death caused a furor, and the city launched an unsuccessful investigation into the incident. The use of firearms complicated the problem of controlling disorderly individuals and groups. Not every rowdy carried a gun, but so many did that a patrolman had to consider that possibility in any arrests he might make. This potential threat to an officer's personal safety placed severe limits on his behavior.

If a policeman looked to his superiors or to the public for support on the question of firearms, he saw only confusion. Popular attitudes divided between those who feared that patrolmen would abuse their powers if allowed to carry guns and those who regarded criminals as a greater danger. One side held that the authority of the law "is equal to being thrice armed;"[68] the other view was that "policemen do not use their pistols enough."[69] Judicial doctrine was about as muddled. According to a Baltimore criminal court judge, "deadly weapons should not be used except in cases of high felony, where it is necessary to secure the arrest of the guilty party."[70] But the jurist neglected to define "necessary," thereby leaving the issue unresolved. When Philadelphia reorganized its police in 1854, the mayor told the men to buy guns. But the following year the Select Council conducted a spirited debate which revealed that many councilmen distrusted armed officers.[71] New York's and Boston's officials seemed to have avoided the problem altogether.[72] Lacking any consistent guidelines, patrolmen began acting as their own judges as to when to use pistols in making an arrest.

As private citizens many of the men probably owned guns prior to joining a police department. But before 1849, officers did not normally carry their weapons while on duty.[73] Thereafter, the patrolmen's use of firearms became increasingly common. There were many variations in this general trend.[74] In Philadelphia, Officer Folby attempted to arrest two sailors for disorderly conduct "when they turned on him and inflicted a severe beating." Nearly overpowered, Folby "was in the act of drawing his revolver as a last resort" just as help arrived. Patrolman John Roan displayed less restraint. Roan stopped a suspicious-looking Negro and demanded to see the contents of a bag the man was carrying. As Roan examined the sack, the Negro moved off a short distance and began to throw rocks at the lawman. Roan retaliated by shooting him dead.[75] Chicago patrolman Casper Lower's milder response to a problem cost him his life. When he tried to arrest Patrick Cunningham, Cunningham grabbed hold of a tree and refused to move. Lower pulled his pistol, thought better of that, and instead used his cane to persuade the man to proceed to the station house. In the ensuing fight Cunningham mortally wounded Lower with a knife.[76] As these examples indicate, throughout the nineteenth century each officer made his own decision whether to employ firearms, and acted accordingly.

The same freedom of judgment existed regarding "necessary" physical force in making an arrest. Patrolmen often dragged, struck, or otherwise abused their prisoners while taking them to the station house. Sometimes an offender never reached a cell: a Philadelphia officer beat a drunken woman so badly that she died, and an intoxicated lawman shot a bystander who objected to his treatment of a captive. There were many similar incidents.[77] Once in jail, a prisoner's behavior might prompt a policeman to quiet him with a rubber hose or some well-placed kicks.[78] This brutality even produced refinements. Langdon Moore reported the use of a "sweat box" (a specially designed narrow and uncomfortable cell) in New York during the 1860s.[79] To prevent telltale marks, one officer wrapped his black jack in a handkerchief before hitting a captive.[80] And in a flagrant case of maltreatment, an unoffending carpenter died from a beating by a sergeant whose sleep he had interrupted.[81]

Some public officials, though they might condemn such abuses, nevertheless regarded violence as a necessary part of police work. Philadelphia's Mayor Vaux, for example, personally led his patrolmen against the Schuylkill Rangers. He approvingly described his tactics in encounters with the Rangers as more "muscular than intellectual."[82] In 1853, Captain George Walling used similar methods on New York's Honeymoon Gang. Walling claimed that "in a few weeks, by dint of some pretty hard 'licks' judiciously administered," that group ceased to exist.[83] In addition to these personal examples, the authorities also contributed to the widespread use of force by the nature of some appointments. A number of volunteer firemen and rowdies were among those who became policemen.[84] Their backgrounds conditioned these men to meet violence with violence. The practice of selecting nominees for the department who had connections with the disreputable elements they policed continued throughout the middle decades of the century.

This policy in effect legalized hitherto objectionable behavior for those who became officers. The influence of these men is impossible to determine. But there are indications that their presence contributed to street violence until the police established their supremacy over the disorderly elements in the population. Assaults in the pre-Civil War decade appear to have remained as high numerically as in the 1840s. The maps in Chapter 3 show a decline in these attacks from 1850 to 1860, but the incidents involving patrolmen increased. The downward trend may therefore be due to a shift to legal violence. At the time, the public accepted this development as necessary to achieving order. Although there were some complaints that "force is too readily resorted to when milder means would prove more effectual," such criticisms did not become significant until the 1870s.[85] In the critical decade of the 1850s, when the police fought to demonstrate their mastery over the "dangerous classes," respectable opinion supported their tactics.

The nineteenth-century patrolman carried a heavy burden of responsibility for effective crime prevention. Yet he found himself in an amorphous situation. His police superiors and the general public armed him with only vague notions of how to perform his job; then they placed him in an isolated environment where people were predisposed to ignore or to challenge his authority. In these circumstances, a patrolman had to establish some basis for maintaining order. Experience became his only reliable guide. Boston's Police Chief Edward Savage, after offering a few words of advice to novice officers, admitted this when he concluded: "I might say more, but should I, you would still have to go out and *learn* your duty."[86]

Learning proved to be a complicated business. A policeman first had to develop his basic skills: how to judge a man's intentions by by his actions and dress; how to suppress potential trouble; how to get a prisoner to the station house; and how to break up riots. Each of these tools required a certain amount of practice before an officer became proficient in their use. By the 1870s patrolmen were demonstrating that they had mastered the rudiments of their jobs.

At times, the police achieved their suzerainty "by dint of some pretty hard 'licks,'" as Captain Walling recalled. But violence alone did not distinguish the new officers from those of the past. Two Chicago patrolmen, Bowden and O'Connor, illustrated that the difference lay in a combination of force and perseverance. In March 1873, these two men arrested Paddy Connors, "one of the most notorious roughs" in their precinct, as he abused a citizen. Seven or eight of Connors' friends followed the policemen as they started toward the station house with their prisoner. They "threatened the officers with immediate death if they did not release their prisoner, and exhibited their revolvers to show that they had the weapons to carry out their threat." Instead of bowing to superior numbers, as most watchmen had done, O'Connor drew his own pistol and told the rowdies to disperse. This admonition established a stalemate until Connors called on his friends to rescue him instantly. They tried. In the ensuing fight, Connors slipped away, but the patrolmen promptly recaptured him. Disheartened, the gang retreated.[87] Such persistence, rare before 1840, had become a standard feature of police work by the 1870s.

Bowden and O'Connor used discretion, the other fundamental attribute of the new patrolman, in not firing on their assailants. Unhindered by any consensus regarding arrest tactics, policemen acted according to their interpretation of how best to preserve the city's tranquillity. They used their own judgment to determine whether or not to handle a problem with words, with a club or pistol, or by taking someone into custody. Such a decision depended upon an officer's personality, the nature of any given situation, and the participants' response to his presence. Like the two Chicago lawmen, not every patrolman chose to apply force in every case.[88] As one citizen observed, "there are some officers . . . who are more conciliatory than others."[89] Two Philadelphia policemen, for instance, drew criticism from the press when they separated two combatants, "mildly asking them to desist," instead of immediately arresting them.[90]

A patrolman's authority served as a needed check on disorder, and his use of discretion in applying that power resulted in a growing dependence on the police to regulate the tensions of urban society. George Walling indicated the success of this development in his bemused observation that "people fly to the police upon the very slightest provocation. . . . All nervous and excitable persons apparently look upon the force as having been organized for their own personal benefit." He had in mind trivial incidents which citizens thought officers should handle: harnassing a jumpy horse; arresting wives who stole from their husbands; and even chastising someone who had burned a fish.[91] These trifling examples reveal the extent to which many people by the 1870s depended upon the patrolman to assist them. By settling such miniscule disputes every day, he helped to curtail the turmoil of urban society.[92]

In the process of contributing to a reduction in social disorder, the police became aware of themselves as a unique group in urban society. They developed an emotional sense of cohesion which had the appearance of an emerging professionalism, but which lacked its substance. Superficially the police displayed many characteristics common to a profession.[93] They provided a crucial service to the public based upon specialized knowledge which the average citizen did not want to acquire through his own efforts. But the way the police evolved made the difference between a group consciousness based upon emotion and one rooted in professional training.

That distinction originated on the streets. Departmental officials could not play the role of masters initiating apprentices into the mysteries of a profession because their formal knowledge of police work was limited to an acquaintance with the theoretical outlines of crime prevention. Rulebooks transmitted that information to the patrolmen. But no administrative machinery (police academies, for example) existed to tutor officers in the implementation of bureaucratic goals. Essentially, apprentice officers had to learn their jobs by practical experience. The first group of policemen in each city therefore developed the initial data on the nature of their work. They enriched their knowledge by comparing anecdotes in casual discussions at station houses. New officers acquired that information by participating in those conversations and by briefly helping an experienced patrolman before moving on to their own beats. Over time, actual solutions to disorder problems, transmitted to other policemen by these informal means, were transformed into a shared body of folklore. Constantly reinforced by repetition and the addition of more incidents, that lore became the basis of group consciousness.

Since initial experiences would become the central core of police folk wisdom, the nature of those incidents is crucial to understanding patrolmen's attitudes and behavior during the nineteenth century. While many encounters with urban residents were trivial and sometimes amusing, many others were not. Latent or overt hostility frequently characterized confrontations between officers and unruly citizens. That hostility often moved swiftly from verbal abuse to physical assaults. Violence was a consistent theme in the early days of preventive policing, and therefore became part of station house folklore. As a result, the threat of death or injury was basic to the emerging emotionalism of police work.

Fatal injuries sustained in the line of duty strongly reinforced group consciousness by underscoring the violent nature of policing. When New York patrolman Thomas Walker died of gunshot wounds in 1865, a large contingent of fellow officers attended his funeral in an impressive display of group solidarity. Seven years later New York's police had collected enough money to erect a statue of a patrolman on the cemetery plot reserved for members of the force.[94] This fund indicated that the police were perhaps developing a commitment to their work which equaled or transcended loyalty to other important institutions such as the family or church.

The police responded to the tensions associated with the prospect of violence by developing a strong sense of rectitude. A Philadelphia detective revealed this attitude in his assertion that the public did not understand police business.[95] This feeling often produced an arrogance which offended ordinary citizens. "To indulge in any familiarity with a patrolman is worse than treason," complained one observer; "to pass without lifting your hat, or in some way acknowledging your sense of his importance, might be dangerous."[96] In these circumstances, verbal abuse became a serious affront to an officer's individual and group identity which he could not allow to pass unchallenged. His response was often violent. "There is no remedy for insulting language," one New York captain testified, "but personal chastisement."[97] From a policeman's point of view, preemptive force became a defense against the threat of violence.

While experience may have taught a patrolman the value of force, the general public became increasingly concerned over what it regarded as a callousness which made policemen "careless of injuring . . . others."[98] But because violence had proven its usefulness, officers responded to criticism by rallying to their own defense. When Philadelphia patrolmen Thomas Hussey and Andrew Irons used force to quell a small riot in 1869, irate citizens swore out complaints charging the two men with assault with intent to kill. After both the mayor and the district attorney refused to interfere in this affair, the officers from Hussey and Irons' district raised bail for them and twenty of the men resigned in disgust over the failure of city officials to defend the police.[99] Some years later, during a probe of police misconduct during a gambling raid, Detective Philip Reilly refused to criticize his immediate superior on the grounds that "he is a brother officer."[100]

The public failed to realize that their officers' working conditions were very different from those of their much admired British cousins. American policemen developed behavior patterns based upon the emotional tensions of contact with latent and frequently overt violence. Instead of perceiving that difference, the American public disparaged the efforts their police made to control disorder. Criticism, however, only strengthened group consciousness and made the police hostile toward those whom they were supposed to protect. Efforts to remove politics from policing in the late nineteenth century by introducing such measures as civil service therefore missed an essential problem. The police would not become more amenable to greater control over their behavior until the general public understood the nature of police work in an American context and took steps to help combat the causes of violence. Until that occurred, the patrolmen would continue to rely upon their experiences on the streets to guide them.

Six   **Policing Sin**

There was not much doubt, the *Chicago Tribune* asserted in 1865, "as to the proximate incitements to theft and violence . . . , [namely] drinking, gambling and prostitution."[1] That statement summarized popular wisdom on the basic causes of crime in the nineteenth century. All three activities had one common characteristic: they led to personal excess. Drawing upon a socioreligious heritage which stressed the individual's responsibility for his actions, many people believed that society's primary duty was to suppress those conditions which could undermine a man or woman's self-control. The liquor problem received the greatest amount of attention at the time, often to the neglect of crime's other "causes." Although relegated to secondary positions in the pantheon of evil, gambling and prostitution proved equally difficult to control.

Prostitution and gambling enjoyed no overt public acceptance, but both had enormous implicit support. Young men and old, whether in business or politics, high society or low, shook their heads in disapproval of prostitution at the same time that they mentally checked whether they had sufficient funds for an evening of sinful pleasure. This male-dominated society allowed itself the luxury of occasional sexual dalliances on the grounds that a man's transgressions against the sanctity and purity of family life were far less serious than a woman's.[2] Gambling, according to its critics, destroyed a family's economic security and drove the bread-

winner to crime as a way to sustain his misplaced passion.[3]
Betting, however, appealed to the democratic instincts of the
era. Any man had an equal opportunity to acquire a fortune
and the social status which went with it.

The indirect acceptance of these vices was also based
upon the urban population's need for organized recreation.
Prior to the rise of more legitimate forms of popular entertainment, such as organized sports, cities offered their residents very little with which to amuse themselves. Prostitution
and gambling supplied a partial solution to this problem.
Illicit sex and the tensions of betting diverted men from their
ordinary concerns.

A long-standing popularity, stretching back into the colonial era, provided the basis for the enormous prosperity of
both prostitution and gambling in the nineteenth century.
The tremendous rates of urbanization after 1830 vastly expanded the clientele for vice. As the number of customers increased, so did the incomes which prostitutes and gamblers
could earn. The people engaged in these occupations introduced new ideas and organizational concepts into their work
to satisfy their patrons' demands for entertainment and to
maximize their own profits. In effect, the rise in the demand
for women and betting transformed these professions into
major businesses of considerable complexity.

As vice became more lucrative and better organized,
some members of this urban subculture became more con-
scious of the need to stabilize relations with legitimate society. There were at all times large numbers of whores and
gamblers who pursued highly individualistic careers, moving
from one place to another as necessity or circumstance dictated. But many others felt that their continued prosperity
depended upon their ability to maintain themselves at relatively fixed locations for long periods of time even though
such permanency made them vulnerable to periodic fits of
public outrage and to police harassment. Prompted by these
disruptive threats, this group within the vice world developed
a variety of ways to protect themselves from the hazards of
their work.

The development of these protective strategies coincided with the rise of preventive policing. Those Americans who regarded vice as the proximate cause of crime looked upon the new police as their most useful tool in the battle for public order. Theoretically the new departments would suppress vice and its corollary, crime, for the first time, but this expectation would prove frustratingly difficult to fulfill for a variety of reasons. In the first place, the police had no authority to prevent citizens from determining their own modes of entertainment. Since the victims of vice chose to entangle themselves, few complainants existed to help prosecute violations of the law. Furthermore, prostitution and gambling occurred on private property, which was protected by legal tradition. Policemen had to be careful not to violate some laws in order to enforce others. When these complications were combined with the defense tactics of certain vice entrepreneurs, the police were left with few options in their attempts to devise effective policies for controlling these activities. These difficulties raised a basic question of whether the American version of crime prevention could cope with so complex a problem as vice.

Prostitution experienced few changes in its methods. Its business structure varied from the lone entrepreneur to the intercity vice organization, while its participants earned livings which ranged "from gilded luxury to squalid poverty."[4] The manner of acquiring customers formed the basic occupational distinctions. At the top were those prostitutes whose patrons came to them; at the bottom were the streetwalkers, who had to seek clients. Many gradations existed within each of these major groups.[5]

Various women with no known ties to organized vice occupied the lowest rungs of prostitution's occupational ladder. Juvenile whores were the most pathetic of this group. Children abandoned, lost, or disowned by their parents quickly learned how to survive on the streets. The girls among them discovered the value of sex among certain classes of citizens, and prostitution among minors developed by at least the 1820s.[6] Some practiced this trade exclusively, while others combined it with the sale of pencils, apples, and other small articles. New York Detective Bell arrested one fifteen-year-old who had established a steady demand for her favors among coal barge operators.[7] In the downtown areas, female vendors did a considerable business with the merchants since enclosed offices provided the necessary measure of privacy.[8]

There is no evidence that these promiscuous adolescents constituted a class of women who moved on to permanent careers as prostitutes once they reached maturity. Older whores usually came to their jobs in a variety of other ways. Loneliness was a major problem for the thousands of single women who flocked to cities in the nineteenth century. Their quest for companionship provided the catalyst to seduction, one of the more common routes to a life of prostitution. Cities did not yet offer sufficient organized public diversions which would appeal to young women seeking relief from a day's labors. Saloons and gambling houses were too masculine. Dance halls, which offered an amusement in addition to drinking, were a principal attraction to females looking for excitement and new friends. These places may have appeared in the late 1820s; at any rate, by the 1840s, if not earlier, they had become notorious as disorderly houses which young women patronized in large numbers.[9] These establishments provided the setting for "bad company," where girls could meet men quite willing to seduce them on the promise of marriage.

Men accomplished seductions in two ways: by consent and by force. Many women succumbed to the entreaties of erstwhile suitors only to discover that their confidence had been abused. Some females might find themselves locked in a room where they would be obliged to submit to their captors. One such unfortunate was raped by a "merchant of standing" two or three times a week for more than a month before she managed to escape. Others who barely missed similar treatment indicate that such experiences may have been infrequent, but not unusual.[10] Regardless of the circumstances, girls who had been misused in these ways could not expect much sympathy from friends, family, or an understanding public. Women occupied a special place in American society; the community expected them to maintain the family, the basic unit of social order.[11] Punishment for violating this trust came swiftly and fell completely on the seduced. The victim became an outcast whom, one writer noted, "society fears, and justly, to bring in contact with private families."[12] Denied the comfort of those closest to her, a woman in this situation frequently "went on the town."[13]

Societal condemnation of seduced females is not the only reason why so many women became prostitutes. Young single women who migrated to America's burgeoning cities were also victims of the strains appearing in old social values as a result of urbanization and industrialization. Cities provided a slowly widening range of jobs to these women, but the majority centered in domestic service and in unskilled factory work, neither of which paid very well. Thus, women could find some opportunities outside their traditional roles as wives and mothers, but their chances of sustaining themselves in circumstances other than honest penury were rather dim. Prostitution was the only kind of work which offered women high wages. It is likely that many women chose prostitution as a way to stave off poverty or to maintain a comfortable life style.[14]

Although contemporaries often assumed that a woman started in the best brothels and gradually sank to the worst type of streetwalker, there is no conclusive evidence for such a tidy capsule history. That interpretation better served the interests of morality than of truth since it taught the "inevitability" of degradation and destitution for those women who dared defy accepted standards of behavior. In fact, a new recruit could conceivably begin at any level, depending upon the circumstances which brought her to this career.

Streetwalkers were the most numerous type of prostitute. A girl whose seducer had abandoned her might simply begin patrolling the avenues, using a rented room as her business headquarters. But there were distinctions. In 1869, reporter Edward Crapsey divided streetwalkers into three types. The best gave every appearance of respectability. Only the hour of the evening, their lack of an escort, and (to a careful observer) their reappearance at regular intervals on the same routes indicated their character. The second class of streetwalkers, slightly bolder in manner, usually looked directly at a potential customer and sometimes engaged him in conversation. No pretense of gentility distinguished the last order of these women. Their speech was coarse and to the point, their prices the lowest, and their quarters were dives (or "cribs" in contemporary parlance).

Crapsey also asserted that each class had "its metes and bounds laid down by an unwritten code of its own enactment, which is rarely violated."[15] It is impossible to discover such a neat division of territory in the extant records of Philadelphia and Chicago. In the former city women persistently patrolled around Washington Square on the southeast side of town and in an area bounded by Arch, Wood, Eighth, and Eleventh streets on the northeast. Both localities shared two features: each bordered on the central business district, and each had easy access to a major concentration of boardinghouses located along Market Street from Sixth to near Twelfth. Prostitutes thus had access to customers and accommodations to entertain them.[16]

Chicago's streetwalkers apparently concentrated in the central business district where they did a brisk business among the patrons of this area's theaters, restaurants, saloons, and gambling houses. A large community of single men who lived in rooming houses located between Madison and Van Buren, east of Clark Street, also furnished many customers. Commercial buildings which had apartments on their top floors provided the facilities for entertaining these men.[17]

Streetwalking was not a complex business. Prostitutes patrolled certain localities, found their own customers, and made their own arrangements with them. Ancillary expenses, such as rent, were minimal. This structure, combined with the lack of any amenities like music, liquor, or comfortable surroundings, meant that the women could not charge much. While the exact prices can only be estimated, they probably did not exceed three dollars. Fifty cents may have been common among the lowest order of streetwalkers.[18] There-

fore, although such monetary returns may have been sufficiently attractive to individual prostitutes, streetwalking
probably did not figure prominently in the rise of organized
vice. The number of women involved and the independent
nature of their business operations insulated them from more
centralizing tendencies.[19] A few pimps may have exercised
control over some of these prostitutes, but contemporary
commentators do not mention any.[20]

Parlor houses required more sophisticated organization.
These places offered more than female companionship; they
also provided many amenities to induce their customers to
spend more money. But a persuasive ambiance implied large
investments in furniture and other facilities. And since elegant paraphernalia had to be housed appropriately to become
effective, such brothels could not be located in tawdry urban
areas. They had to be along or close to major streets conveni-
ent to the central business district to attract their customers.
That meant higher rents than streetwalkers paid. Hence, parlor houses always charged more. In order to justify higher
prices, the inmates had to be more attractive than their street
sisters. Obtaining "higher-quality" females required a rational
recruiting system run by a competent staff. In sum, the business structure of parlor houses was far more elaborate than
that of streetwalking.

The short careers of most prostitutes complicated the
problem of finding attractive personnel for parlor houses. An
overwhelming majority of these women did not last for more
than four years. Furthermore, women may have moved from
one house to another several times. One observer claimed
that the inmates in some places changed completely every
two or three months. This rapid turnover made necessary
continuous recruitment.[21]

Available evidence suggests that the madames of individual parlor houses competed with one another in acquiring
new inmates. Recruitment did not become a highly specialized function prior to 1885, although there are some indications that it was becoming so by the late 1870s. Sometimes, acquiring new women required little effort. Madames

simply enticed recruits right off the street by talking with them.[22] Procurers working outside of the brothels usually frequented places where they could find large numbers of young women. Dance halls and intelligence offices (privately run employment agencies) always had a good stock of fresh faces. Experienced prostitutes, acting as female procurers, visited the waiting rooms of intelligence offices and attempted to persuade likely prospects to accompany them to brothels.[23] Male procurers recruited in dance halls and sometimes tried to pick up women at railroad stations.[24] In all these cases, the people involved worked from a particular parlor house.

There are some indications, but no conclusive evidence, that madames began to rely upon recruiters outside their parlor houses after 1860. Unscrupulous employment office operators may have been one source of aid, since they were in an excellent position to direct young women to "openings" in houses of ill-fame.[25] Some other types of small businessmen who had wide contact with the public might also help obtain women. John McLaughlin, the owner of a notorious saloon in Chicago, had a reputation as a procurer by the early seventies.[26] Interurban recruiting, which might imply more elaborate organization of prostitution, also appeared at least by the 1870s.[27] But the details of these transactions, again, are too scanty for firm conclusions. In one case involving a new recruit in Philadelphia, the man in question owned brothels in both New York and the Quaker City.[28] This may prove more about one individual's enterprising nature than about the existence of an incipient interurban white slave trade, but it may also reveal the beginnings of the much more highly organized recruiting of prostitutes after 1885.

Many women became prostitutes willingly; but brothel madames had to be prepared to deal with those who did not. If all else failed, a new recruit could be drugged by placing something in her drink or by applying chloroform. This technique has obscure origins, but was in use before 1840.[29] In a letter to a friend, one Chicago madame described her success with this method:

I am happy to inform you that so far our plan has worked to a charm. the girl cried some, but the doc give [sic] her the stuff you left, and yesterday afternoon while under the influence "Scoty" accomplished his purpose—This morning she said she wanted to leave the house, and return to her parents, but another dose of the stuff fixed her and I think she will soon come down. She is admired by everyone who visits here and if we can only keep the matter dark for about two weeks by that time the old folks will give up looking for her and she will make a big stake for us both. Keep mum, for I have just heard the old man is in town. I will keep her dosed[.] Come as soon as you can.[30]

As this letter indicates, rape was occasionally used as part of the recruiting process. Madames used either procurers or favored customers to accomplish these assaults and relied upon public condemnation of unchaste women to keep the girls under control afterwards.

Distinctions existed among parlor houses just as they did in streetwalking. Houses of assignation were generally the highest-class brothels. Some of these places served the needs of adulterously inclined men and women of elite society; others catered to an upper-class clientele which sought the company of prostitutes. Discretion and decorum characterized these houses more than any other type of bordello. The best parlor houses occupied the next rank. Drawing their customers from the wealthy, these brothels contained luxurious furnishings and offered visitors their choice from among three to ten women. The inmates paid the proprietor a weekly rent ranging from ten to sixteen dollars (exclusive of extras). Slightly below these houses were those catering to the middle classes. Clerks, skilled mechanics, and strangers to the city usually patronized these places. The women boarded for sums of from six to ten dollars a week. Family-run brothels complete the list. Husband and wife teams, sometimes immigrants (especially Irish and German), charged their prostitutes half their earnings. Customers paid prices varying from three to fifty dollars in these places, depending upon the class of the house and the services asked.[31]

A measure of geographic segregation existed among the parlor houses, although Philadelphia's best bordellos seem to have been well scattered around the city. Before 1860 the middle range of brothels in the Quaker City, containing two to nine women, were located approximately between Walnut and Spruce, to the west of Ninth Street. The lowest-grade places were to the south of this area, down to South Street. These latter houses had become well established at least by 1840. As the central business district developed along Market Street, and South Street emerged as a lower-class shopping thoroughfare in the late 1860s, these already existing dispositions were reinforced.[32] A few bordellos situated in the northern part of the city along Wood Street close to the Delaware River, and also near Eleventh, presaged that section's growth into the principal red light area in the latter part of the nineteenth century.[33]

Each of Chicago's three divisions had its share of brothels, but the south side always contained the majority. The worst houses originally located just north of the river in an area known as the Sands. When the authorities destroyed the dives in the Sands during a raid in 1857, most of the whores who lived there moved to the south side, occupying several blocks bounded by Van Buren, Twelfth, Wells, and State streets. The best bordellos situated themselves on State and along Van Buren between Third and Fourth avenues; on Ontario and Ohio west of Wells (north side); and near Halsted and Madison (west). Even so great a disaster as the Chicago fire could not alter this basic distribution. Although some expansion occurred after 1871, the heart of the elite vice district remained unchanged in its geographic borders.[34]

Reliable data on the income of prostitutes are rare, and are incomplete when they do exist. But the evidence indicates that this was a profitable business for all concerned. During her brief career, the individual prostitute earned very high wages, an impossibility in any other occupation open to her. Women in the best houses at mid-century possibly had gross earnings of about sixty dollars a week. The

madame's fees (a one-dollar service charge per customer plus
a boarding assessment ranging up to sixteen dollars) left a
courtesan with a net income of approximately thirty-two
dollars. Even assuming that madames doubled their service
charge for each customer by 1890, a woman could still make
about twenty dollars a week.[35] The lowest-class whores, even
at fifty cents a man, obtained more money in one day than
more virtuous females earned in a week.[36] Such sums far exceeded the wages of even the most skilled male workers
during the nineteenth century.[37] Proprietresses of brothels
had rather impressive incomes. The operator of a first-class
house in New York during the 1850s grossed over $20,000 a
year. While their expenses were probably high, their net earnings allowed many madames to acquire comfortable fortunes.[38]

The aggregate income from prostitution can only be
estimated. From the evidence available it would seem that
New York and Chicago's best parlor houses were million-
dollar-a-year businesses.[39] But without adequate data on the
total number of prostitutes and their prices over time, the
amount of money earned in all facets of vice remains problematical. At mid-century its income possibly ranged from 3
to 3.5 million dollars.[40] This figure does not include profits
from the sale of liquor in brothels, nor does it take into consideration either the wide range in prices which prostitutes
charged or the distinctions between the best and worst parlor
houses and streetwalkers. The appraisal is therefore probably
low.

Unfortunately for its practitioners, this rather large business was illegal. Some persons who studied prostitution concluded that it ought to be regulated for health and other
reasons. Backed by a portion of the medical community and
other interested observers, various legislatures attempted to
license prostitution during the 1860s and 1870s. This effort
succeeded briefly only in St. Louis (1872–1874). Elsewhere,
the reform idea failed completely. Opponents of the proposal charged that such a move would legitimize immorality,
and their views prevailed.[41] In the meantime, people involved
in prostitution found themselves in a vulnerable position.

Public opinion condemned them; politicians could not overtly sympathize with their situation because prostitutes had no political power—women could not vote. But the courtesans did have money, a commodity of considerable appeal. Some of these women would use that means of influence to protect their businesses.[42]

Both brothels and streetwalkers had been common in cities for many decades before rapid urbanization transformed prostitution into a major enterprise. Its practitioners usually elaborated upon previous experience to meet the increased demand for their services, although recruiting techniques did change somewhat under the pressures of expansion. In contrast to this kind of development, gambling underwent major changes in its personnel and organization. With the exception of lotteries, which were legal until after 1830, most gambling was informal and extremely decentralized in the eighteenth and early nineteenth centuries. Westward expansion, which created opportunities for the rise of professional gamblers, produced the first important shift in the growth of organized gambling. Then, as the nation's population began to urbanize, these early professionals followed their customers to the cities. After 1840 faro, policy, and horse racing combined to make betting one of the era's largest and most lucrative businesses.[43]

Prior to the 1840s professional gamblers plied their trade primarily on steamboats and in cities located along the Great Lakes and the Ohio and Mississippi rivers. Poker and three-card monte (a card version of the shell game) were the mainstays of this period, being ideally suited to gambling along transportation routes. A few decks, or a set of monte-cards, could be easily stored and quickly produced. Various subterfuges, such as secret markings, helped to ensure victory. The games did not last very long. Several hands could be played in the course of a single sitting, thereby increasing the amount of money a gambler could win. When the betting slowed, partners pretending to be strangers could usually entice the unwary into a ruinous wager.[44] The steamboat trade gradually declined in importance after 1840. This may have been due to the mounting hostility of the gambling public, which had become disenchanted with the tricks and cheating of the blacklegs, but the decline might also be attributed to the gamblers' discovery of an even more lucrative source of income in the burgeoning cities.

The sporting fraternity introduced the urban populace to faro. This became the single most popular card game in the United States by the 1840s because of the widespread belief that it offered the bettor the fairest odds. That illusion derived from the way faro was played. The equipment for this game included a green cloth embossed with a complete set of cards and a deck placed in a dealing box which had a slit just wide enough to allow passage for a single card. Presumably, this mechanical device ensured that the dealer could not manipulate the deck to his advantage. Participants purchased betting checks from the dealer and the game began. Basic play was very simple. After the bettors had placed their checks on cards of their choice upon the cloth, the dealer drew a card, called a "winner," from the box, and paid anyone who had bet on it. Next he dealt a card, denoted a "loser," for himself, and collected the checks of those who had wagered on it. The "turn" completed, players could reconsider their bets. Honestly dealt, the percentage against the bettor was less than in any other game at the time. But gamblers had several ways to improve their own chances, and by mid-century the dealing box had become one of the surest ways to cheat the public.[45]

Devotees of "bucking the tiger" (the popular phrase for faro playing) gambled in "hells" of varying quality. Most faro games had a symbiotic relationship with a saloon. Gamblers set up shop either in a corner or on the second floor, and the nature of the game they dealt seems to have been roughly related to the character of the host business. Low dives offered the public small-change betting in which the only real question was how rapidly the dealer could cheat the customer. More reputable saloons had higher-stake games which were supposedly more honest. Elite faro houses, operating in their own buildings, provided their guests with the finest wines and liquors, a well-stocked buffet, and free dinners in addition to nearly unlimited wagers.[46]

Faro's popularity encouraged many gamblers to abandon their footloose lifestyles for more permanent commitments. As they settled down, these blacklegs transformed their occupations. They found that permanency implied ties to the local community which required a more businesslike approach to their affairs. Gamblers, for example, now became employers. An average faro bank operated with four persons: the dealer, two assistants (to record the progress of the games and to watch for cheating among the customers), and a doorkeeper. In addition to these men, a successful bank needed several "ropers" who scoured hotel lobbies, restaurants, and saloons for visitors willing to "buck the tiger." Depending upon the success of any particular house, staffs ranged from four or five to nearly thirty—including a cook and waiters. The number of faro houses varied over time; there were fewer such resorts in the antebellum period than in the years after 1860. New York had ten "first-class houses" in 1849 and about one hundred less reputable places. In the years after 1860 the number fluctuated between ninety and one hundred and fifty. Chicago's three hells in 1849 grew to about thirty elegant houses by the 1870s; there was an unknown quantity of lesser resorts. With no way to obtain accurate figures, contemporary observers estimated that between 1,500 and 3,000 persons in New York depended upon gambling houses for their livelihoods by 1870. A faro dealer earned at least twenty-five and sometimes as much as one hundred dollars a week depending upon his skill. The average wage may have been thirty to forty dollars. On the basis of admittedly sketchy evidence, New York's gambling houses poured between $37,000 and $75,000 a week into the local economy. Such figures made gambling a major employer in the nineteenth century.[47]

The location of the gambler's hell represented another tie to the local community. To be successful, a faro house had to attract a large number of players. Gamblers therefore sought sites central to the major hotels, railroad depots, and entertainment areas in the emerging downtowns of American cities. In Chicago the principal houses were located along

Randolph from State Street to Clark, and along Clark from Randolph to Monroe. New York's most important resorts were on lower Broadway, from approximately the 400 to the 800 block, and along adjacent side streets such as West Twenty-fourth, East Eighth, and Park Place. In Philadelphia the area bounded by Sansom, Eleventh, Fourth, and Market contained the largest number of first-class houses. These locations commanded high rents, and the blacklegs paid them to some of every city's most reputable citizens. While keeping the building owners happy, the gamblers also helped other local businessmen. Saloonkeepers, restauranteurs, and hack drivers were among those whose custom increased because of nearby hells. Gambling therefore had a subsidiary economic impact on the surrounding neighborhoods.[48]

Southerners persisted in running houses throughout the nineteenth century, but they were increasingly supplanted by the Irish. The turning point in this process came in the 1860s. While the Civil War might have had some impact on the change, the Irish began to intrude into gambling for more prosaic reasons. They had been in cities long enough to produce a second generation of ambitious individuals who were acculturated to gambling and regarded it as a legitimate avenue to success.[49] Some Irishmen followed the extravagant lifestyle of the Southern blackleg, but others introduced a much more sedate behavior pattern and carefully invested their profits in crime, horses, and politics. These men exercised more influence in their society than Southern gamblers had, and they foreshadowed the development of the twentieth-century criminal businessman.[50]

Faro represented only one branch of the profitable gambling business. Policy was another. This form of betting first appeared in England as an offshoot of lotteries. It appeared in America before the Revolution and had become an important part of lotteries by 1800. During the 1830s policy increased in importance as it began to develop its own subculture. Dream books appeared to advise the superstitious how to translate dreams into winning numbers; special names such as "magic gig" and the "washerwoman's gig" developed for certain types of combinations. The price of a bet declined steadily. By 1845 it had reached a low of three cents among Philadelphia Negroes.[51]

Such small wagers might seem inconsequential, but the structure of policy guaranteed profits. Lottery drawings occurred twice daily, and the winning numbers were telegraphed to interested parties.[52] These instantaneous results, by nineteenth-century standards, helped establish a feverish atmosphere proper for continuous betting. Dealers accepted wagers up to the minute of the drawing. Secondly, policy was a neighborhood game. The number of shops ranged from six hundred to one thousand in New York and Philadelphia. Anyone desiring to play had no trouble finding a dealer. The shops were located in the inner wards of the city where clerks, shopgirls, and other likely customers concentrated. Although this was primarily a poor man's game, bettors came from practically all ages, nationalities, and classes. The combination of the drawing system and the local character of policy ensured a large volume of business. By the early 1850s the daily income from New York's shops averaged between six and eight thousand dollars.[53]

Dealers did not rely solely on street trade to sustain that volume of business. Each shop had perhaps a minimum of three employees: a clerk to record bets made by walk-in customers, and two canvassers who visited cigar, clothing, shoe, and other manufacturing establishments whose workers might not have the time to patronize their local policy dealer. Larger shops had more employees. Thus a minimum of 1,800 persons earned their livings from policy. The number could easily have exceeded 3,000 in New York and Philadelphia. These people's wages depended upon their functions and abilities. Clerks may have merely received a weekly stipend, but there is no evidence regarding their pay scales. Canvassers received one-eighth of their daily sales in the 1850s; this increased to 20 percent in the seventies. An above-average agent could sell an estimated $100 worth of policy slips a day, earning a commission of $12.50. Less persuasive canvassers may have made only about $30 a week, but even that was far more than an ordinary worker made.[54]

Before 1860 policy dealers depended upon the results of lottery drawings to determine winning bets. As long as lotteries were legal and widespread, policy remained decentralized because it could rely upon local city, state, and private organizations' drawings. After 1830, when many states began to outlaw lotteries, policy became vulnerable to more centralization. Individual dealers now had to rely increasingly upon those few states which still permitted drawings. As that number shrank, the ability to control the information vital to policy increased.

This situation eventually attracted the attention of gambling entrepreneurs in New York City. A group of fourteen men, some legitimate businessmen, others professional gamblers, organized C. H. Murray and Company to gain control over policy in New York and elsewhere in 1861. This syndicate had two important assets. First, their association held monopoly rights to conduct drawings in all states where lotteries were still legal. Any policy dealer who wanted telegraphic information on the results of drawings would have to deal with Murray and Company. Secondly, this group adopted the organizational format of a legitimate business corporation. Its members purchased stock for $8,000 a share. The capital acquired in this manner could be used to insure individual policy shops against disastrous losses. A large number of bettors wagering on a particular gig which just happened to turn up in a drawing could wipe out a dealer. To protect themselves from the threat of such misfortunes, most shops had wealthy silent partners. If Murray and Company could provide more insurance than local backers, dealers in New York and other cities would be tempted to abandon former loyalties in favor of greater security. In exchange for these advantages, the company received 50 percent of each shop's gross profits. By the late 1860s this syndicate was earning between three and four hundred thousand dollars a year for its stockholders.[55]

Murray and Company fell apart from internal squabbling among the partners in 1868. It had shown the possibilities for greater profits inherent in centralization, however, and its example encouraged emulation. Its direct heir was a syndicate owned by six brothers, the Simmonses. The brothers bought the assets of their predecessors and remained in business in New York and Chicago until the 1880s. Other former members of the original association established a rival firm called Murray, France and Company in St. Louis. Elsewhere, a centralized organization emerged in Philadelphia by 1872, and the Simmonses had at least one competitor in Chicago by the mid-seventies.[56]

As new syndicates struggled with one another to control policy, some dealers resisted these centralizing tendencies. More independent-minded than their rivals, men like Frederick J. Luthey, a reputed dealer of Brooklyn's policy business, broke away from the old informational system and drew their own numbers to determine winners. This had the obvious advantage of increasing the odds against the bettor. A gig with a large amount of money wagered on it simply had no chance of appearing in these drawings.[57] It once again decentralized the policy business, making a dealer's success less dependent upon a single dominant organization in his particular city than upon the arrangements he might make with the local authorities.

Betting on horses was the last important form of gambling in the nineteenth century. Racing became increasingly popular after 1800, although most tracks were rather informal affairs often consisting of no more than a cleared field surrounded by a rude fence. More elaborate race courses, replete with clubhouse, restaurants, and nearby hotels, began to appear in the sixties.[58] Promoters organized all the major tracks which would dominate racing for the remainder of the century. Saratoga opened in 1864; Jerome Park (Westchester County, New York) in 1866; Monmouth Park (Long Branch, New Jersey) and Pimlico (Baltimore) in 1870; the New Orleans Fair Grounds in 1873; and Churchill Downs in 1875.[59]

Track owners sought to increase their revenues by introducing a more exciting form of racing. Prior to 1866 trotting had been the principal format for a race. Horses, running in tightly controlled circumstances, competed in a series of heats with the victor being determined on the basis of three out of five contests. Three or four matches in a day might be the maximum run with the trotting system. When Jerome Park opened, its promoters introduced sprints. These races, short in duration and featuring several horses, were more popular than trotting and permitted a large number of races in a single day. Sprints also increased the complexity and excitement of betting because the outcome became less predictable. For these reasons, the new racing format quickly rose to dominate the sport.[60]

Professional gamblers gradually became central figures in racing in two ways: first, by helping to develop some of the major tracks in the nation; second, by exercising increasing control over betting. John Morrissey and John Chamberlin illustrate the first trend. Both men were major gamblers in New York City by the early 1860s and were briefly partners with several other men in a syndicate of faro houses. In 1861, Morrissey opened a first-class gambling house at Saratoga and began to cultivate friendly relations with both the townspeople and wealthy visitors to this health resort. Between 1863 and 1865, Morrissey built a race track and helped organize the Saratoga Association for the Improving of the Breed of Horses. William R. Travers, John R. Hunter, and Leonard W. Jerome, all members of the state's social and financial elite, were among those who assisted Morrissey in his new venture.[61] In 1869, Chamberlin invested in an opulent gambling house at Long Branch, New Jersey, a summer resort for such notables as President Ulysses S. Grant. A year later Chamberlin used $150,000 of his own money and a large sum from such people as James Fisk, William M. Tweed, and Pierre Lorillard, to build Monmouth Park.[62] Morrissey and Chamberlin set the pattern for track ownership after 1870. By the eighties many race courses around the country were owned by gambling syndicates composed of socially prominent Americans in partnership with important gamblers.[63]

Beginning in the 1840s, betting underwent several changes which eventually permitted gamblers to control this crucial aspect of racing. Prior to that decade, private wagers dominated track gambling. Individuals simply made their own bets with friends and acquaintances. Growing dissatisfaction with these arrangements, perhaps because of the difficulty of collecting winnings from disgruntled losers, prompted the first major reform during the forties—the auction pool. Under this system an auctioneer "sold" each horse in a race to the highest bidder. The pool seller retained all the money until track officials declared a winner. At that point he gave the stakes, minus a commission for his labors, to the holder of the winning ticket. By the 1860s auction pools had become the recognized procedure for betting at most important tracks.[64] The professional gamblers' role in pools before 1860 is obscure. It is possible they helped introduce the system, but whether they dominated pool selling seems unlikely.[65]

The development of off-track betting gave gamblers their opportunity to infiltrate auction pools. Until the sixties pool selling occurred at the track on the day of the races. But by the middle of the decade some pool sellers began to offer their services at local hotels near the race courses.[66] Technology helped spread this practice. Gamblers located in the downtowns of major metropolitan areas could use the telegraph to obtain racing results from practically anywhere in the country. Firms began to replace individual pool sellers as the business prospered. Only the gamblers had the money, employees, and technical skills necessary for these more organized ventures. They set up "poolrooms" to accommodate customers who wanted to place a bet without going to the track itself. The first such establishment appeared as early as 1866.[67] By the seventies New York gamblers like Morrissey, Albert Cridge, Mike Murray, William Lovell, and James E. Kelley owned several of these businesses, and poolrooms had begun to appear in other cities as well.[68] Easily accessible, and extremely well patronized according to contemporary accounts, poolrooms helped make the professional gambler a central figure in betting on sports.

As racing increased in popularity, it attracted more and more people of limited financial means. The auction pool was ill-suited to the gambling instincts of these increasingly numerous fans. Only one person could hold a horse's ticket, so if a particular mount was favored to win a race, spirited bidding drove the cost of its ticket beyond the resources of the average customer. Pool selling, in sum, discriminated against the majority of racing addicts. Track owners tried to meet the needs of these people by introducing Paris mutuel machines in the early seventies. Mutuel tickets sold for five dollars, thus easing somewhat the frustrations of racing devotees. The holders of winning tickets, however, had to split the money bet on a particular race, thereby reducing their return. As a consequence, mutuels did not develop widespread popularity among bettors for many decades.[69] Some other more flexible betting system was needed.

Bookmaking proved to be the answer to the average bettor's problems. First introduced by the American Jockey Club at Jerome Park in 1871 or 1872, this betting system was initially too rigid to become popular. The club, following British precedent, reserved a room in its clubhouse which it leased to the highest bidder, who became the "bookmaker." Bettors wishing to use his services had to pay a special club fee, they could place their wagers only in a specified room, and the transaction had to be registered in a special ledger. Bookmaking in this form was more rigid than pool selling. The first experiment failed, and the Jockey Club returned to auction pools.[70]

In 1877, John Morrissey unintentionally precipitated an unusual sequence of events which led to the adoption of bookmaking in New York. Morrissey had acted as stakeholder for $350,000 in pools in the 1876 presidential election. When the election outcome became embroiled in political controversy, Morrissey called off all bets and returned the money. He did, however, subtract a 2 percent commission for his services. Other pool sellers followed suit. These maneuvers touched off a storm of controversy and provoked the state legislature into passing a law prohibiting pool selling of any kind on any sporting or electoral event.[71]

This new law threatened the existence of racing as a major business. Tracks had become important sources of profit for many people. Jockey clubs had to consider not only the expectations of their stockholders but also the needs of local businessmen who depended upon racing for their livelihoods. Hotels, saloons, and other small enterprises proliferated around every major race course. At Coney Island, for example, over one hundred businesses clustered near the track to serve the wants of thousands of visitors.[72] Both the clubs and their symbiotic neighbors required a large, steady flow of fans to earn a profit every year. But the "sporting classes" would not attend races unless they could gamble. Rising to this challenge, the American Jockey Club announced in the spring of 1877 that it would dismantle its pool selling stands at Jerome Park and replace them with bookmaking. The club explained that since bookmaking was not specifically prohibited by the new law, this was the only legal way to offer betting to the track's patrons.[73]

The old system of bookmaking had to be modified to meet the requirements of a mass market for betting. Although there is no evidence to determine precisely who suggested modifications, the structure of bookmaking in 1877 indicates that the American Jockey Club decided to adapt the basic features of English practice to a wider audience. The club auctioned off several bookmaker stands to the highest bidders. These men, who were probably former pool sellers, opened shop with a satchel full of money and cards upon which to record bets. This decentralized situation continued until 1881, when a syndicate of major gamblers (James Kelly, Charles Reed, T. B. Johnson, and Albert Cridge) negotiated with the Jockey Club for rights to all the bookmaking. This syndicate paid a fee to the track for its privileges and charged individual bookmakers or firms for the right to use the stands. The conduct of this business also became more elaborate. Bookmakers now stood on a raised dais and shouted the odds they were willing to offer, while three assistants moved about within a small ring taking in money, filling out tickets, and recording the bets.[74]

Bookmaking still had not spread very widely in 1881. A major breakthrough occurred the next year, when some New York sportsmen convinced Colonel M. Lewis Clark, founder of Churchill Downs, to allow their bookmaker friends to work at the Kentucky Derby. Clark made the bargain in order to obtain Runnymede, one of the era's champion thoroughbreds.[75] After this victory, bookmaking began to infiltrate into other cities. When Washington Park opened in Chicago in 1884, for example, twenty-four bookmakers appeared at the track. Within three years they dominated betting at Chicago's race courses.[76] Bookmaking achieved this popularity because it allowed the greatest number of bettors to participate in the excitement of gambling on a major sports event. As the acceptance of bookmaking spread, gamblers reaffirmed their crucial role in practically every form of betting-related urban recreation.

As professional gamblers gathered under their control all the important forms of public betting, they acquired the means to protect themselves from the demands for their suppression emanating from some parts of respectable society. Blacklegs and whores shared one asset in this regard: access to enormous sums of money. But gamblers had one advantage over their opponents which prostitutes could not hope to acquire: they enjoyed a great deal more legitimacy. Gamblers were important to the many thousands of people who depended upon their services to enhance the attractiveness of a wide range of entertainments. This acceptance established a basis for more complicated relationships to ordinary society than were possible for prostitutes.

Ties to respectable society assumed a variety of forms. Occasionally, individuals on opposite sides of the law were related. New York Mayor and Congressman Fernando Wood's brother, Benjamin, provided one of the better known examples of this situation. Editor of the *New York Daily News,* Benjamin Wood had a reputation as an avid gambler. His interest went beyond merely playing, however. In 1861 he helped organize the policy syndicate which attempted to dominate that business during the sixties.[77] Presumably, Fernando Wood's political influence contributed to that syndicate's early successes. On a less exalted level, a New York police superintendent's brother ran a gambling house which apparently suffered very little from police interference.[78] While not typical, familial ties probably did dilute some officials' enthusiasm for suppressing vice.

Corruption represented a notorious link between legitimate and illegitimate society. The origins of this type of behavior are obscure and almost impossible to trace. At times it is difficult to determine who exploited whom. Hence, any explanation of the development and progress of corruption can only be conjectural. Corruption may have originated with the fee system in law enforcement in the early nineteenth century. Constables earned part of their income from monies they received for such tasks as delivering court summonses and making some types of arrests. Perhaps some underworld figures adopted the practice of bribing a constable not to arrest them; or it may be that some officers made the suggestion themselves.[79] Whatever the origins, it is certain that by the 1840s some magistrates and court officers had developed the habit of exploiting criminals. Prostitutes, for example, would be arrested in a general roundup and robbed of whatever money and jewelry they possessed. Afterwards, they would be kept in jail until their madames or pimps could make "arrangements" to free them.[80] Salaries for court officers and the police replaced the fee system during the fifties, but habits formed under previous arrangements may have been hard to break.[81]

Another type of corruption may have derived from the services which the police performed for prostitutes. Whores sometimes called on officers to settle disputes among themselves, and madames occasionally had the local patrolman arrest unruly customers. Since prostitutes apparently paid the police for these favors, this practice may have evolved into a regular system. It appears to have become standard procedure to pay bribes of money or presents by the 1860s.[82] For their part, some public officials seem to have developed a proprietary attitude toward this graft. The St. Louis experiment in licensing prostitution failed in 1874 because politicians and policemen interested in restoring this source of income joined with outraged moralists to defeat the program.[83]

The structure of police departments sometimes provided graft-minded individuals with the opportunity to exploit the underworld. This was particularly true in New York, where not all the detectives worked from a single agency under the

direction of one person. Rather, each police captain was assigned two detectives who owed their appointment to him
and were responsible only to him. This arrangement, in effect, gave each captain personal servants who would do his
bidding. One of these detectives usually became his superior's
collector while the other worked on more legitimate concerns
such as keeping track of criminals in the precinct. Under New
York's decentralized police system the captains had most of
the actual power to determine general arrest policies; hence,
they also had the ability to blackmail prostitutes and gamblers who wanted to avoid harassment. This distribution of
power, and the presence of a tailor-made bagman, made many
New York captains wealthy.[84]

Chicago had a different departmental organization. The
chief of police dictated arrest policies, and the detectives operated as a distinct branch of the department. In this situation corruption seems to have been concentrated primarily in
the offices of the chief and the superintendent of the detectives. When Jacob Rehm became chief in 1874, for example,
he remarked that he assumed this burden to make money.
Rehm promptly ordered a massive roundup of prostitutes
and, to a lesser extent, gamblers. This pleased Chicago's moralists and established Rehm's power among those he was trying hardest to impress. The next year, arrest for vice activities
returned to normal levels and Rehm began to acquire his fortune. Ever the opportunist, he branched out into liquor graft,
becoming a key figure in the Whiskey Ring. The local investigation of that scandal forced him from office in 1875.[85] In
the meantime, Chicago's detectives reputedly developed close
relations with lower-class gamblers, especially bunko artists,
who specialized in a form of confidence game similar to modern bingo. By the mid-seventies the entire detective squad
was supposedly in the pay of these parasites. Accusations of
graft finally forced the retirement of Assistant Superintendent Joseph H. Dixon and Detective Isaac G. Lansing in
1879, but the problem of corruption did not disappear.[86]

Corruption did not always originate with the police. In
some instances vice figures decided to "normalize" relations
with the authorities by organizing their own associations to

regulate graft. Such a group appeared in Chicago about 1869 or 1870. For obvious reasons, the origins of this syndicate are obscure. Perhaps tiring of police exploitation, John Corcoran and Thomas Foley evidently decided to reduce the cost of corruption by making it more systematic. Corcoran, a major north side gambler who had been in town since 1863, and Foley, a billiards champion, baseball promoter, and saloonkeeper, chose Michael C. McDonald as their organizer.[87] At the time, McDonald was languishing in jail, unable to raise bail after his arrest for a major robbery. Prior to 1869 he had developed a reputation as a bunko artist, low-class gambler, and general roughneck. Why Corcoran and Foley chose McDonald for their venture remains a mystery, but they bailed him out of jail. A jury subsequently acquitted him of all charges.[88] In the next four years McDonald created a centralized graft syndicate composed of only the best faro houses in Chicago. Each gambling den paid a flat percentage of its gross income for protection; the amount varied with the profitability of each house. By 1873 this association had stabilized its relations with the police. As long as a corruptible chief held office, these particular establishments did not have to worry unduly about harassment by the authorities.[89]

Political connections offered yet another way to protect vice activities. Although prostitutes could not vote, their financial resources might have been very useful in elections. Some gamblers could provide help in addition to pecuniary contributions. They controlled large numbers of employees whose services could readily be adapted to the needs of local politics. Not every gambler or prostitute, however, developed close relations with local politicians. Many, if not most, such underworld denizens, had neither the money nor the manpower to become involved in politics. Only the more prosperous madames and gamblers whose business success depended upon fixed locations in the downtown areas had the resources to interest aldermen, mayors, and their political machines.

The symbiotic relationship between politics and vice developed at least by the 1840s. In keeping with the tumultuous nature of urban society at mid-century, no clear guidelines defining the nature of the partnership seem to have existed. With regard to gambling, this amorphousness may have been due to the character of the business during these years. Southern blacklegs had been moving into northern cities at a steady pace, but these men lacked roots in any particular city. Their faro houses no doubt attracted local politicians from time to time, and this patronage may have been the source of early contacts between the two groups. Whatever the origins, the success of these initial relationships probably depended upon the personalities involved. Political machines were not yet strong enough to impose tribute, and gamblers had no associational traditions which would impel them to cooperate with one another for the common good. In these circumstances gamblers might ally themselves with friendly politicians, or they might decide to hedge their bets by contributing money to both parties during an election.[90]

As the Irish began to move into gambling, the opportunities for important ties between vice and politics increased dramatically. John Morrissey's career illustrated the possibilities open to the talented. Born in Ireland in 1831, Morrissey came to America with his family at the age of three. During his youth in Albany, New York, his major asset was his enormous strength and endurance. He earned a reputation as a fearsome fighter while leading a local gang in several combats with rival organizations. Capitalizing on his experience, Morrissey became a prizefighter. He eventually won the title of U.S. champion, beating Yankee Sullivan in a controversial decision in 1853. While battling his way to that honor, Morrissey came to the attention of Isaiah Rynders, a sachem of Tammany Hall. Rynders employed Morrissey and his friends as shoulder-hitters during elections. Morrissey's fight purses provided him with the funds to buy a saloon, and his sporting fame ensured him of a large patronage. His political fortunes rose considerably when he joined Fernando Wood's successful mayoral campaign of 1854. By the end of the decade Morrissey had become an important politician, saloonkeeper, and sports figure.[91]

Not content with these accomplishments, Morrissey branched out into other areas. As a saloonkeeper he had learned something about gambling. In 1859 he sold his liquor interests and formed a partnership with Matt Danser, a noted New York blackleg, in a faro house. Building upon this beginning, Morrissey constantly sought more partners in other gambling establishments. By 1864 he had interests in sixteen first-class faro games; he had become the largest single stockholder in New York's policy syndicate; and he had emerged as a key figure in racing at Saratoga. These activities broadened his contacts with all levels of society and made him a rich man. By the end of the Civil War his circle of friends extended from the working-class Irish, who admired him for his ring exploits, to high society, whose members respected his wealth, political influence, and contributions to horse racing. Morrissey capitalized on this popularity by serving two terms (1866-1870) in Congress.[92]

Morrissey was at the height of his career in the seventies. He broke with the Tweed Ring, but returned to Tammany Hall when John Kelly and Samuel J. Tilden asked him to help sort out the shambles resulting from the Tweed scandals in 1872. Two years later he broke with Kelly and ran successfully for the state senate from a lower-class New York district. By the mid-seventies he had become a national figure in gambling. His racing odds were quoted as far west as Chicago, and his decision to return all bets on the 1876 presidential contest forced other gamblers to follow suit. Stung by Tammany accusations that he could not win an election in an upper-class district because of his reputation as a gambler, Morrissey demonstrated his extraordinary social and political power by severely trouncing Tammany's handpicked candidate for New York's silk-stocking state senatorial seat in 1877. The effort ruined his health, however, and he died in May 1878.[93]

While more spectacular than most, Morrissey's career as a major figure in gambling, sports, and politics was not unusual. Others enjoyed similar, if slightly less successful, lives. The organizers of Chicago's graft syndicate also sought ways to enhance their power by acquiring political influence. John Corcoran began this process by winning an aldermanic election in 1872, but the most important breakthrough came the next year. The Republican party found itself in shambles in 1873 because some members insisted upon enforcing the Sunday closing laws. German voters, who constituted one of the party's largest blocs, regarded those ordinances as an assault on their lifestyle and rebelled. The Democrats, hoping to forge a new voter alliance, joined with the Germans in a coalition called the People's party. Their mayoral candidate, Harvey D. Colvin, was well known among the sporting fraternity and promised a wide-open town if elected.[94]

Perhaps recognizing the possibilities which this situation offered, the gambling syndicate became extremely active in politics for the first time. Corcoran served as a member of Colvin's campaign committee; Foley ran for alderman of the 1st ward (the heart of the vice district); and McDonald served as commander of the gambling house runners and miscellaneous employees who acted as repeaters and shoulder-hitters during the election. Foley's supporters, other than Corcoran and McDonald, indicate how widespread the gamblers' political connections had become. Mark Sheridan, a police commissioner, and Daniel O'Hara, an Irish boss of considerable power, backed Foley. Both Colving and Foley won. This campaign, followed by the new mayor's tolerant administration, proved pivotal in solidifying the gambling influence in local politics. The gambling interests had formed friendships which included Anton C. Hesing, editor of the *Staats-Zeitung* and a major figure in the German community; Carter Harrison, Sr., county commissioner and future congressman and mayor; and Patrick Carroll, a county commissioner during the mid-seventies.[95]

These political relationships did not endow the central gambling association with absolute power in Chicago. There were distinct limits to their influence. The chaotic nature of local politics supplied one check. In the absence of a dominant machine, personalities more than organizations seem to have been the key to elections. Although the press quickly attributed sinister powers to McDonald, he frequently did not even carry his own ward for candidates who had his supposed blessing.[96] In a tumultuous political setting like Chicago's, friendship appears to have been crucial to pro-

tection. Thus, when Monroe Heath triumphed in the 1876
mayoral election, gambling entered an unsettled period of
frequent raids because the gamblers had little personal influence with the administration.[97] Money paid to the police,
when not supplemented by political clout, proved insufficient to ensure tranquillity. Harrison's mayoral victory in
1879, on the other hand, gave the sporting fraternity several
years of peace and prosperity.[98] Another disruption occurred
six years later. Harrison had to close the best-known houses
in the spring of 1885 because his corruption-tinged re-election
resulted in a long, bitter court fight during which he could
not afford to alienate public opinion by tolerating gambling.[99] Even with friends in power, gamblers had no absolute guarantee of immunity.

Chicago's syndicate leaders became involved in politics
voluntarily. Occasionally, however, gamblers and prostitutes
found themselves forced to participate. This was especially
true in those cities where politicians managed to develop very
powerful, centralized organizations. The Tweed Ring's power,
for example, enabled it to command, instead of solicit, support from the vice underworld by the late 1860s. Ordinarily
John Morrissey might have played a key role in this newer
kind of relationship, but he apparently was not involved.
Morrissey had broken with Tweed and was about to help
organize a revolt against the Ring. In spite of this rift between New York's most important gambler and its most
powerful politician, Tweed was able to impose his demands
upon local gamblers and prostitutes.[100] Mayor William S.
Stockley's Republican machine adopted the same approach
in Philadelphia. Stockley launched a vigorous campaign in
1873 against his city's gamblers which won widespread public approval and quickly subdued the blacklegs who had once
been independent of his organization.[101]

The alliance between politics and vice produced tangible
benefits for both. Politicians tapped an important source of
funds and organized manpower which helped them in local
elections. Within the underworld, prostitutes probably received fewer advantages for their contributions than gamblers
did. A madame who bribed the police or acquired political

influence through campaign contributions could expect her house to be immune from interference, and that was, of course, a substantial benefit. But gamblers received much more. Important politicians helped them in court, either as lawyers or bail bondsmen, if they were accidentally arrested.[102] Blacklegs sometimes found it possible to enlist their friends' aid in obtaining changes in the law which made it difficult to prosecute gambling.[103] Politicians consulted gamblers regarding police justice appointees, or candidates. The attitudes and practices of these officials, who were well situated to harm gambling activities, made them of special concern to the underworld. Putting the right man in those offices virtually nullified any ordinances governing gambling.[104] Finally, gamblers could seek and hold political positions themselves, thereby enhancing their own influence as well as that of their associates. In these ways gamblers became more important than prostitutes in the political and social life of their cities.

Ties between legitimate and illegitimate society did jeopardize the major legal tool available to the police for suppressing vice. Since prostitution and gambling were essentially victimless crimes, the police often could not obtain witnesses willing to testify in court. In order to secure convictions, patrolmen had to assume the role of complainant. But many obstacles prevented this strategy from being very effective. Corrupt policemen would not, of course, even make an arrest. If he did appear in court, an influential gambler easily obtained a dismissal. Judicial decisions in vice cases often maintained a precarious balance between protecting the defendant's rights and enforcing the law. Police justices frequently relied on the ineptitude of the arresting officer in manufacturing reasons for freeing gamblers. Local ordinances required that an offender be caught in the act, but judges would refuse to admit the evidence if an officer actually participated in a game on the grounds that such activities constituted entrapment.[105] The police had only one other way to obtain entry into a gambling den. They could either knock on the door and announce their presence, or break in; either way, the gambling paraphernalia disappeared before it could be confiscated. In an extreme example of the more polite, judicially correct approach to a gambling house, Chicago's police made a rare visit to McDonald's place of business and patiently knocked on his front door for twenty minutes before he asked them in for a drink. A diligent search of the premises produced no evidence of gambling in the city's most notorious den.[106] Frustrated by such conditions, the police never devised a satisfactory solution to the problem of obtaining admissible evidence on which to secure convictions.

Even if the protective ties between vice and legitimate society had not existed,the police would still have found the control of gambling and prostitution difficult. No single strategy could deal uniformly with an illicit urban subculture of such variety and size. If police commanders had ordered their men to arrest every whore and blackleg they encountered, the officers in some areas of the city would have been constantly walking prisoners back to the station house. Such a policy was simply not worth the effort because these offenses were misdemeanors carrying minimal penalties. With the aid of straw bail, most of the criminals would have been back at work within a matter of hours. In addition to that problem, constant harassment could have jeopardized the important role which gamblers, especially, played in police work. Since thieves as well as respectable people patronized vice establishments, the managers of these resorts could provide officers with valuable information on the whereabouts and activities of more serious lawbreakers. But this cooperation would have ceased if the police adopted the practice of continual arrest.[107]

Whatever the obstacles may have been in dealing with vice, significant segments of the population demanded that the police do something to attack these sources of crime. Recognizing that their existence depended to some extent on the goodwill of such people, the police sought to mediate between official morality and the realities of urban life. Casting about for a rationale which could justify a specific tactic, departmental commanders adopted a defensive posture. They argued that their principal function in vice control was merely to maintain order. As one New York captain explained, "so long as houses were not located in any neighborhood where they disturbed the peace, I think it would be better for them to remain there than to be removed to a place where they would disturb the public."[108]

The police relied upon raids as their primary tool for enforcing this policy. Brothels and gambling dens which conducted their affairs with decorum experienced little interference. But if a particular place became obnoxious to the surrounding neighborhood, the police descended upon the offender (unless, of course, bribes or political influence prevented a raid). The raid warned the inmates of such houses that they had overstepped the bounds of public civility and penalized those transgressions by disrupting business and embarrassing customers. Repeated disruptions could even on occasion drive the owners of these establishments out of business.[109] Gamblers and madames recognized the rationale behind raids of this type and acted accordingly. "In the interval between two 'raids,' the bad business goes on unmolested," one critic complained, "and the keepers, having perfect knowledge of this fact, accommodate themselves to the practice."[110] While true, this observer did not give enough credit to this technique as a regulatory mechanism. Chicago's houses of prostitution, for example, reportedly allowed their visitors to spend their money freely, "but they must restrain their debauchery so that the neighborhood shall not be disturbed."[111]

Raids also served a variety of other purposes. Occasionally, indignation over vice reached a fever pitch and various community spokesmen such as ministers or businessmen would demand the complete eradication of gambling or prostitution. A quick series of raids placated public opinion by demonstrating police efficiency. Ambitious officers sometimes used raids to promote their careers. In Chicago Captain John Nelson commanded the Armory Precinct located in the heart of the vice district. During the early sixties he won high praise as "one of the most discreet, yet faithful and daring men in the service," for his repeated attacks on gambling houses. This record enabled Nelson to become deputy superintendent of the department in spite of his precinct's reputation for corruption.[112] Finally, of course, raids were an important way to discipline madames and gamblers who failed to make the proper "arrangements" with local authorities.

Vice had always been present in American cities, but the pace of urbanization after 1830 offered this subculture innumerable possibilities for expansion and profit. Growth dictated changes, especially in the organization of prostitution and gambling. The freelance whore and blackleg did not disappear, but business methods became more widespread as sin developed into a major form of recreation. Elaborating on previous experience, madames probably introduced few genuinely new ideas into their enterprises, with the possible exception that recruitment became more systematic. But many gamblers discovered that they could improve their chances for success by combining resources. A faro game backed by a "bank" which had a great deal of money enhanced its excitement and profits by offering its patrons wider betting limits. As cooperation became common, gamblers evolved syndicates, roughly analagous to corporations, consisting of stockholders with investments in several faro houses and related activities, such as policy. The economic power of syndicates provided a base for individuals and groups of gamblers to establish a complex series of relationships between themselves and legitimate society. Coupled with the Irish influx into gambling, the syndicate was the most significant development in the underworld during the nineteenth century.

As vice became better organized and more prosperous, it required more elaborate ways of protecting itself from legal intervention. Its profits attracted the attention of venal, as well as ambitious, police officials and politicians. Corruption and political alliances can be construed as the two basic defenses which the purveyors of sin used to normalize their relations with the authorities. Investigators sometimes discovered conflicting evidence regarding the nature of these connections, indicating that various forms of protection coexisted with one another. One gambler, for instance, assured a reporter that he no longer had to pay for immunity. Instead, he claimed, "'we gain the friendship of the police through our political friends—Aldermen, Assemblymen, Congressmen, and others.'" At the same time, another blackleg asserted with equal conviction: "'How can a Captain, Inspector, or Commissioner of Police live on his salary? . . . They can't, and you can bet your life on it. . . .While gambling houses are prosperous the police officials will be able to buy real estate.'" [113] In effect, some gamblers were more successful than others in minimizing the cost of corruption.

If all prostitution and gambling had remained as unsystematic as it was before 1840, both might have been more vulnerable to police suppression. Certain characteristics of the relationship between vice and law enforcement as it existed prior to the introduction of crime prevention did continue; exploitation of streetwalkers, for example, appears to have been an established habit too profitable to break. But the growth of organized illegal enterprise enabled some of these criminals to protect themselves. The American version of crime prevention stressed decentralized political control of the police. In order for the model to work most effectively, there had to exist a general consensus as to which crimes should be suppressed. That consensus was lacking in regard to vice, and in this situation the amount of influence a particular group had determined whether its views of these offenses would prevail. Vice entrepreneurs formed one such bloc in the political spectrum, and their organizational advantages over incensed but disorganized moralists were often decisive in determining police policies toward their businesses. The structure of crime prevention thus created a dilemma for which there was no solution in the nineteenth century.

The material on gambling in this chapter is an adaptation of "A Sinful Business: The Origins of Gambling Syndicates in the United States, 1840-1887" by the author from *Police and Society*, a Sage Focus Edition, David H. Bayley, Editor, © 1977, by permission of the Publisher, Sage Publications, Inc. (Beverly Hills/London).

Conclusion

The complexity of law enforcement has usually been regarded as a consequence of the competition between legitimate interests jockeying for a dominant role in the formation of police policies and practices. Criminals, as people, have not figured prominently in these controversies. They have instead been symbols which those competing interests have manipulated as part of the rationale for their point of view. Thieves, gangs, gamblers, and prostitutes are real enough, of course, but since the earliest days of police reform their existence has been attributed to some impurity in the way the police fulfill society's mandate to eliminate them. Hence their symbolic uses, as proponents of new ideas for improving the performance of the police, point to corruption, public immorality, and other crimes as proof of law enforcement's imperfections. Improving the police by such means as civil service reform, professionalization, and higher educational standards would presumably contribute to the eventual triumph over crime.

Unfortunately, the history of the first major attempt to eliminate crime by police reform does not confirm that presumption. The advocates of preventive policing hoped for nothing less than the conquest of America's criminal classes, but in fighting the tedious, complicated battles to change the philosophy of nineteenth-century policing they overlooked the actual structure of the underworld as a major impediment to fulfilling their expectations.

Criminals as real people seriously compromised the idea of crime prevention because their social world was at least as complex as that of legitimate society. A "typical" criminal is hard to define or identify. More often than not, criminals were in most respects ordinary individuals who generally looked, thought, and behaved in ways which were indistinguishable from the rest of the population. This is even true of those who systematically committed crime. They might have families, own property, send their children to local schools, and work hard at their occupations. As a group, criminals were probably not any less or more intelligent than their fellow citizens. Some criminals did conform to the stereotypes of merciless parasites who committed violent acts routinely and without cavil. Whether they were more typical of all criminals is probably an unanswerable question, but in general the only important way to distinguish criminals from the rest of the population was by their specific acts.

The nature of those acts did, of course, set criminals apart to a certain extent. Their work required certain skills and commitments which other people did not have and were unwilling to assume. Burglars needed to know how to enter and leave buildings surreptitiously and how to fashion or obtain tools for their peculiar uses. They usually travelled a good deal, and in the least conspicuous manner possible. Patience and foresight were cardinal virtues in a situation which might involve weeks or months of meticulous planning before a particular burglary would succeed. The need for accomplices required a criminal to seek others who had similar skills and goals. His associates not only provided him with practical help, they also accorded him respect for his accomplishments, offered him companionship, and shared their knowledge of crime with him. An individual criminal was therefore part of a larger group which sustained and encouraged his behavior.

Criminals, moreover, did not exist as a separate social caste which had only predatory contacts with legitimate society. In the course of their lives they developed various relationships with non-criminals. If they married, their wives' (or husbands') relatives and friends became part of their circle of social contacts. Criminals who owned property or made investments had acquaintances in the business world. Some gamblers and thieves participated in politics, thereby acquiring useful friends whose friendship was not necessarily based upon an exchange of money. Politicians in many instances came to rely upon the voting and organizational activities of these criminals.

The variety of ties to legitimate society complicated the task of isolating and punishing criminals in America. Once the police made an arrest, the accused criminal could call upon any or all of these relationships to help him. Friends and business acquaintances who had no personal knowledge of his illegal behavior could provide bail, raise money for a defense, or otherwise act in his behalf. Politicians could arrange a quiet discharge or exert influence to have a friendly judge assigned to the case. Whatever the source of aid, the criminal often had the means to obstruct or mitigate efforts to deal with him by manipulating his contacts.

Coping with crime was therefore not a one-dimensional problem which involved simply finding the most effective method for apprehending and punishing criminals. Instead, coping encompassed multiple considerations, among which was the independent ability of criminals to resist or influence the outcome of any effort to deal with them. Whatever form the administration of justice took, it not only had to conform to the demands of those who supported its purposes; it also had to adapt itself to the realities of illegal behavior. In sum, both legitimate society and the underworld had an ability to shape law enforcement.

The police straddled the invisible boundary between these two worlds and tried to devise a coherent means of juggling the realities of both. They found the means to achieve that goal in America's emphasis upon a decentralized police controlled through local politics. Policemen would not be representatives of an impartial legal system, as they were in England. Patrolmen in the United States would have far more discretionary power than their British counterparts. The structure of American policing encouraged officers to ignore the standards of conduct dictated by legal strictures because they would not be required to apply the law to the urban underworld; they would only be asked to cope with crime by whatever means they found expedient.[1] Nineteenth-century policemen therefore evolved subtly intertwined policies of violence and tolerance as the best ways to meld the expectations of law-abiding citizens and the special capacities of the underworld. Whenever possible, the police relied upon criminals' cooperation to achieve the appearance of law enforcement; if cooperation did not or could not occur because of the nature of an offense, the police resorted to violence. This approach depended heavily upon each officer's ability to decide the proper applications of both policies. He decided when and how to use his authority against whom. Personalized decisions became the fundamental tool in policing the underworld.

A policeman's reception on the streets illustrates the circumstances in which officers resorted to force. Patrolmen began walking their beats at a time when violence seemed endemic to urban life. Ethnic, racial, and political hostilities fueled conflicts between individuals and neighborhoods, and the reliance upon firearms to settle these disputes increased the dangers of trying to suppress the disorders. Ostensibly representatives of civil order, policemen needed some practical means of impressing their authority upon people who were often hostile toward and quite willing to assault them. Brute force recommended itself so often not only as a quick way to restore peace but also as a means of establishing a patrolman's dominance and preserving his personal safety.

Street criminals came to fear the patrolman, as law-abiding Americans desired, less from the imminence of legal retribution than from the latent threat of violence. Unsure of how they would be treated when facing a policeman's stern or domineering demeanor, or perhaps convinced from experience that they would be abused, these offenders continued to resist arrest. The patrolman, on the other hand, had learned to be sensitive to any mannerisms which implied resistance, and to act accordingly. Each person in a confrontation had been conditioned to anticipate the worst in any encounter, and each therefore acted in ways which perpetuated the use of force as an important tool in making arrests.

Solving property crimes demonstrated the key role tolerance played in successful policing. Professional thieves, working alone or in small groups, represented a kind of aristocracy of talent in the underworld. Living by their wits and skill in a subculture marked by treachery, they expected, and often obtained, large monetary returns for their labors. Their specialized lifestyles shielded them from ordinary patrolmen, and their victims' frequent concern for the recovery of stolen property rather than the punishment of the thief further insulated them from the law. In contacting and bargaining with these thieves, detectives had to maintain a rapport with them in order to be effective. As negotiators between the principals involved in a theft, detectives provided an extralegal service which worked to the benefit of all concerned. Professional criminals committed many offenses which had to be ignored, however, in order for the detectives to sustain the ties between themselves and this portion of the underworld. These arrangements eventually evolved, with some modifications, into the practice of relying upon informers which characterizes some aspects of modern policing.

Although the complexity of prostitution and gambling's organization occasioned the growth of a variety of co-existing relationships, similar patterns of cooperation appeared in police contacts with vice. The many opportunities which vice offered for corruption obviously demanded tolerance. Both prostitutes and gamblers provided information to the police on the locations and activities of other criminals, thereby creating symbiotic ties between themselves and lawmen. On the other hand, some vice entrepreneurs dominated their relations with the police because they wielded more political power than their erstwhile suppressors. Knowing, furthermore, that the desire for neighborhood tranquillity and sinful pleasure was more widespread than the belief that vice should be eradicated, the police adopted a policy of maintaining public order to shield the more subtle (or noisome) aspects of their dealings with gamblers and prostitutes. While paying lip service to the idea of enforcing the law, the police assumed the role of mediators between the public's appetites and those who satisfied those urges.

Personalized law enforcement lent itself to the development of a peculiar kind of professionalism. The core of the patrolmen's concept of their work was not formal training; it was a mixture of practical experience and emotion—an emotion derived from the dangers of coping with crime. Since the structure of American preventive policing invited individual decisions, the police relied upon the lessons developed from daily contact with criminals rather than upon the law in performing their jobs. This version of professionalism separated the police from the legal system and the public. Having learned self-reliance in dealing with criminals, the police were, and are, loath to surrender any portion of the independence which they have been encouraged to foster.

The arrogance implicit in self-taught professionalism reduced police sensitivity to the excesses possible in policies based on violence and tolerance. Brutality and corruption blossomed among officers who worked under few effective restraints. Excessive force not only derived from the presence of misfits in every department; it also grew out of the problems patrolmen faced in defining appropriate force in making difficult arrests. Corruption was endemic in the policy of dealing with criminals who had useful information or services to offer. Too many temptations existed in situations governed only by the ethics of the parties directly involved. The eventually successful efforts to introduce civil service to policing did remove politically induced sources of corruption, but that campaign also left police matters more completely in the hands of the police. Not all policemen condoned gross corruption or brutality, but the emotional bonds between officers who constantly shared danger were stronger, historically, than the desire to purge themselves of men who abused their authority.

While time and circumstances have modified policing to some extent, the basic policies and attitudes which patrolmen adopted to perform their jobs remain fundamentally unchanged. This is not merely because politics, in more subtle ways, continues to guide police activities; nor is it because of the venality, ignorance, or callousness of some officers, although these problems have not been eliminated; rather it is because the nature of the policeman's job has not altered very much since the nineteenth century. The urban underworld has not disappeared. Criminals still plague society with their thefts and violence; the police still need ways to deal with them; and the tools of the past remain useful because no one has yet suggested viable alternatives which genuinely cope with the true complexity of law enforcement.

Appendixes

Gangs Named in the Public Ledger

Name	Dates Noted	Location	Type
Bleeders	6.17.51	Near Girard College	Combat
Blood Tubs	7.17.55		Street corner
Blossoms	2.1.48		Probably combat (associated with fire company)
Bouncers	2.1.48		Probably combat (associated with fire company)
Buffers	5.28.45		Street corner; combat
	6.4.45		
	7.17.55		
Bugs	7.17.55		Unknown
Bulldogs	2.21.48	Penn and Front	Combat
Chesapeakes	3.7.45		Street corner
Crockets	10.6.45	Moyamensing Rd. and 2nd	Combat
Darts	12.1.69	17th and Pine	Street corner
Deathfetchers	2.1.48		Probably combat (associated with fire company)
Dogs	6.21.60	15th ward	Combat
The Forty Thieves	9.21.68	Woods in northwest Philadelphia (28th ward)	Theft; violent
	12.29.69		
	1.24.70		
	7.15.71		
	2.23.77		

Appendix 1 (continued)

Name	Dates Noted	Location	Type
Garroters	2.29.60	7th and Tasker	Combat
Gumballs	10.29.44	6th and Brown	Combat;
	4.1.45		(associated with
	2.1.48		fire company)
Hyenas	12.19.44		Probably combat
	2.1.48		(associated with
			fire company)
Jack of Clubs	12.30.47		Theft
Jumpers	10.29.44	6th and Brown	Violent; combat;
	8.2.45	Green St. near	(associated with
	2.1.48	Old York Rd.	fire company)
Keystone No. 2	9.30.50		Combat
Killers	8.2.47		Violent; combat;
	2.1.48		(associated with
			fire company)
Lancers	1.20.54	Fitzwater below Broad	Theft
Neckers	8.10.48	Passyunk Rd. near prison	Violent
Pickwick Club	8.19.44	3rd and Walnut	Street Corner
Pluckers	2.1.48		Probably combat (associated with fire company)
Pots No. 2	9.30.50		Combat
Privateer Club No. 1	11.26.47	2nd and Dock	Street corner;
	1.22.50		violent
	3.18.50		
Rats	5.28.45		Street corner;
	10.16.45		combat;
	11.23.47		(associated with
	1.1.48		fire company)
Rangers	3.7.45	Penn and Front	Street corner;
	2.21.48		combat
Rebels	12.11.45	Shippen between 8th and 9th	Street corner
Red Roses	7.18.60	Coates St. RR Terminal at Fairmount Park	Violent
Reed Birds	6.22.50	Germantown RR near Girard Ave.	Violent

Appendix 1 (continued)

Name	Dates Noted	Location	Type
Schuykill Rangers	8.14.50 10.16.54 7.23.60 3.6.76 7.26.76		Theft; violent
Shifflers	5.28.45 6.4.45		Street corner; combat; probably associated with Shiffler fire company
Skinners	12.9.44 3.7.45 10.16.45		Street corner; combat
Smashers	6.22.50	Germantown RR near Girard Ave.	Violent
Snakers	2.1.48 8.11.55		Probably combat (associated with fire company)
Snappers	12.19.44 2.1.48		Probably combat (associated with fire company)
Spiggots	12.21.57 6.21.60	West part of 15th ward	Violent; combat
Sporters	12.9.44		Combat
Springers	1.3.55		Violent
Stockholders	5.12.54		Violent
Tormentors	2.1.48 2.8.50 6.17.51 6.17.51	Western Spring Garden	Violent; combat
Turks	8.15.50 11.20.50	Northern Liberties	Violent
Waynetowers	10.24.50	11th and Lombard	Street corner
Wildcats	5.28.45		Combat

Appendix 2   Distribution of Philadelphia Police

	1854			1856	
District	N*	%	District	N+	%
1	20	2.44	1	45	7.81
2	115	14.02	2	54	9.37
3	80	9.76	3	46	7.98
4	80	9.76	4	45	7.81
5	80	9.76	5	67	11.63
6	120	14.63	6	64	11.11
7	80	9.76	7	36	6.25
8	115	14.02	8	35	6.07
9	45	5.48	9	25	4.34
10	25	3.05	10	47	8.15
11	15	1.83	11	45	7.81
12	15	1.83	12	35	6.07
13	10	1.22	13	7	1.21
14	20	2.44	14	3	.52
			15	7	1.21
			16	15	2.60
Totals	820	100.00	Totals	576	99.94

*Patrolmen and officers.
+Patrolmen only.
Source: Public Ledger, July 19, 1854; May 21, 1856.

Appendix 3 Distribution of Chicago Police

Police precinct	1875 No.	1875 %	1876 No.	1876 %	1877 No.	1877 %	1878 No.	1878 %	1879 No.	1879 %	1880 No.	1880 %	1881 No.	1881 %	1882 No.	1882 %	1883 No.	1883 %	1884 No.	1884 %	1885 No.	1885 %
Central Station	55	9.7	54	10.9	53	10.9	42	10.2	37	8.6	38	8.5	52	10.9	65	12.2	70	11.5	101	11.5	107	12.3
Harrison St.	77	13.6	64	13.0	64	13.1	58	14.1	55	12.7	54	12.1	53	11.1	56	10.5	61	10.0	63	7.2	68	7.8
22nd St.	50	8.8	43	8.7	41	8.4	34	8.3	35	8.1	37	8.2	36	7.5	38	7.1	39	6.4	48	5.5	49	5.6
Cottage Grove Ave.	33	5.8	30	6.0	29	5.9	23	5.6	26	6.0	27	6.0	28	5.8	29	5.4	32	5.2	46	5.2	46	5.2
35th St.													17	2.9	20	2.6	19	3.1	34	3.9	22	3.9
West 12th St.	51	9.0	44	8.9	44	9.0	37	9.0	40	9.3	47	10.5	42	8.8	49	9.2	60	9.9	79	9.0	74	8.5
Hinman St.	23	4.0	23	4.6	23	4.7	21	5.1	23	5.3	23	5.1	23	4.8	25	4.7	28	4.6	49	5.6	46	5.2
Deering St.	25	4.4	19	3.8	18	3.7	14	3.4	17	3.9	18	4.0	15	3.1	18	3.4	23	3.4	35	4.0	34	3.9
West Lake St.	38	6.7	31	6.3	30	6.1	22	5.3	26	6.0	25	5.6	24	5.0	26	4.9	30	4.9	42	4.8	31	3.5
West Madison St.	86	15.2	75	15.2	74	15.2	64	15.6	66	15.3	69	15.4	59	12.3	20	3.7	23	3.8	31	3.5	44	5.0
West Chicago Ave.	27	4.7	24	4.8	22	4.5	22	5.3	22	5.1	24	5.3	25	5.2	26	4.9	29	4.7	61	7.0	62	7.1
West North Ave.																	19	3.1	27	3.1	28	3.2
Rawson St.	15	2.6	13	2.6	13	2.6	11	2.6	14	3.2	13	2.9	12	2.5	17	3.2	16	2.6	28	3.2	28	3.2
Chicago Ave.	51	9.0	43	8.7	42	8.6	36	8.8	42	9.7	41	9.1	38	7.9	42	7.9	48	7.9	64	7.3	64	7.3
Larrabee St.	19	3.3	17	3.4	19	3.9	15	3.6	15	3.4	17	3.8	21	4.4	25	4.7	27	4.4	48	5.5	48	5.5
Webster Ave.	15	2.6	12	2.4	13	2.6	10	2.4	12	2.7	13	2.9	17	3.5	15	2.8	19	3.1	42	4.8	42	4.8
Desplaines St.															64	12.0	64	10.5	73	8.3	63	7.2
West Madison St. Substation													14	3.5								
Totals	565	99.4	492	99.5	485	98.9	409	99.3	430	99.3	446	99.4	476	99.2	529	99.2	605	99.1	871	99.4	868	99.2

Source: Report of the General Superintendent of Police of the City of Chicago to the City Council (Chicago: The City Council of Chicago, 1875-1885).

Appendix 4 Data for the Calculation of R for the Correlation between Numbers of Patrolmen and Number of Arrests

Philadelphia

Complete arrest data are available only for July, 1856. The police department published arrest data by districts from 1873 to 1885, but these data did not include misdemeanor arrests.

Data for calculation of R, Philadelphia, July 1856 only

District	Patrolmen	Arrests
1	45	340
2	54	523
3	46	343
4	45	130
5	67	166
6	64	147
7	36	97
8	35	39
9	25	152
10	47	234
11	45	195
12	35	230
13	7	152
14	3	18
15	7	45
16	15	61
Totals	583	2872
$R = .534$		

Source: *Public Ledger.*

Chicago

While somewhat more complete, data for Chicago are hardly definitive. The following statistics were extrapolated from the *Report of the General Superintendent of Police*, using the information on the number of arrests made by the patrol wagon service. In the first table, NR represents the total number of arrests reported by the patrol service, NC is the number of arrests in each precinct calculated by first determining what percentage patrol service arrests were of the total number of arrests reported for the entire year; that percentage was then used as a multiple to obtain the statistic indicated for each precinct. The error in this method is below.

Appendix 4 (continued)
Arrests by Districts, Chicago, 1883-1885

District	1883		1884		1885	
	NR	NC	NR	NC	NR	NC
Central Station	1,208	3,897	1,913	5,170	2,071	4,706
Harrison St.	2,870	9,258	3,148	8,508	3,541	8,048
22nd St.	680	2,194	577	1,559	918	2,086
Cottage Grove Ave.	383	1,235	521	1,408	459	1,248
35th St.	431	1,290	415	1,22	473	1,075
West 12th St.	1,440	4,645	2,105	5,689	2,214	5,032
Hinman St.	300	968	752	2,032	952	2,164
Deering St.	NA	NA	179	484	415	943
West Lake St.	306	987	335	905	232	525
West Madison St.	180	581	232	627	178	405
West Chicago Avenue	446	1,439	702	1,897	1,397	3,175
West North Ave.	15	48	74	200	154	350
Rawson St.	108	348	126	340	314	714
East Chicago Ave.	882	2,845	937	2,532	1,845	4,193
Larrabee St.	509	1,642	692	1,870	581	1,320
Webster Ave.	NA	NA	NA	NA	NA	NA
Desplaines St.	1,772	5,716	1,884	5,092	2,208	5,018
Totals	11,530	37,193	14,592	39,435	17,952	41,004
Total arrests in annual report		37,187		39,434		40,938
Total arrests calculated		37,193		39,435		41,004
Calculation base		31%		37%		44%
N error		+6		+1		+66
% error		.02		.002		.16

Data for Calculation of R, Chicago, 1883-1885

District	1883		1884		1885	
	P*	A†	P*	A†	P*	A†
Central Station	66	3,897	99	5,170	105	4,706
Harrison St.	41	9,258	51	8,508	52	8,048
22nd St.	27	2,194	42	1,559	49	2,086
Cottage Grove Ave.	27	1,235	40	1,408	38	1,248
35th St.	NA+	NA+	NA+	1,122	NA+	1,075

Appendix 4 (continued)
Data for Calculation of R, Chicago, 1883-1885 (continued)

District	1883		1884		1885	
	P*	A†	P*	A†	P*	A†
West 12th St.	45	4,645	68	5,689	61	5,032
Hinman St.	21	968	43	2,032	40	2,164
Deering St.	15	NA+	29	905	25	527
West Lake St.	22	987	36	905	25	527
West Madison St.	15	581	25	627	38	405
West Chicago Ave.	21	1,439	52	1,897	52	3,175
West North Ave.	14	48	23	200	24	350
Rawson St.	11	348	24	340	24	714
Chicago Ave.	34	2,845	54	2,532	54	4,193
Larrabee St.	19	1,642	42	1,870	42	1,320
Webster Ave.	15	NA+	36	NA+	36	NA+
Desplaines St.	44	5,716	61	5,092	49	5,018
R	.711		.673		.641	

*Number of patrolmen assigned to duty, as reported in the *Report of the General Superintendent of Police of the City of Chicago to the City Council* (Chicago: The City Council of Chicago, 1883-1885).

†From Preceding table.

+Complete data not available. This row was eliminated from the calculation of R.

Notes

Introduction

1. Roger Lane, *Policing the City: Boston, 1822-1885* (Cambridge: Harvard University Press, 1967); James F. Richardson, *The New York Police: Colonial Times to 1901* (New York: Oxford University Press, 1970); Kevin E. Jordan, "Ideology and the Coming of Professionalism: American Urban Police in the 1920s and 1930s" (Ph.D. diss., Rutgers University, 1972); Jerald E. Levine, "Police, Parties, and Polity: The Bureaucratization, Unionization, and Professionalization of the New York City Police, 1870-1917" (Ph.D. diss., University of Wisconsin, 1971); Wilbur R. Miller, Jr., *Cops and Bobbies: Police Authority in New York and London, 1830-1870* (Chicago: University of Chicago Press, 1977); Maximillian Reichard, "The Origins of Urban Police: Freedom and Order in Antebellum St. Louis" (Ph.D. diss., Washington University, 1975); Allan E. Levett, "Centralization of City Police in the Nineteenth Century United States" (Ph.D. diss., University of Michigan, 1975); Joseph G. Woods, "The Progressives and the Police: Urban Reform and the Professionalization of the Los Angeles Police" (Ph.D. diss., University of California, Los Angeles, 1973).

2. The problems of enforcing liquor laws, and their effect on police behavior, have been treated so extensively that I have chosen to concentrate on other kinds of crime whose impact on the police has not been dealt with adequately. On the problems of liquor, see: Lane, *Policing the City,* passim; Richardson, *New York Police,* pp. 154-56, 181-85; Wilbur R. Miller, Jr., "Never on Sunday: Moralistic Reformers and the Police in London and New York City, 1830-1870," in *Police and Society,* ed. David H. Bayley, (Beverly Hills: Sage Publications, 1977), pp. 127-48.

3. An important study of urban geography which supplements this discussion is John Schneider, "Public Order and the Geography of the City: Crime, Violence and the Police in Detroit, 1845-1875," *Journal of Urban History* 4 (Feb. 1978): 183-208.

Chapter One   **Police Reform, 1830-1860**

1. For an elaboration of the conceptual basis of the preventive police movement in the antebellum era, see: Wilbur R. Miller, Jr., *Cops and Bobbies: Police Authority in New York and London, 1830-1870* (Chicago: University of Chicago Press, 1977); Maximillian Reichard, "The Origins of Urban Police: Freedom and Order in Antebellum St. Louis" (Ph.D. diss., Washington University, 1975); and Michael Feldberg, *The Philadelphia Riots of 1844: A Study of Ethnic Conflict* (Westport, Conn.: Greenwood Press, 1975). Allan E. Levett, in "Centralization of City Police in the Nineteenth Century United States" (Ph.D. diss., University of Michigan, 1975), makes an important distinction between criminal behavior and the desire to control particular persons as a motive for police reform. The two are not always distinguishable in contemporary evidence, nor are they, in my opinion, mutually exclusive.

2. Francis Lieber, *Encyclopedia Americana: A Popular Dictionary of Arts, Sciences, Literature, History, Politics and Biography* . . . (Philadelphia: Carey & Lea, 1832), 10:214; *The National Era* 3, no. 21 (May 24, 1849): 82; Miller, *Cops and Bobbies,* p. 4.

3. *Philadelphia Gazette,* June 6, 1795; Jacob Rush, *Charges and Extracts of Charges, on Moral and Religious Subjects* . . . (New York: Geo. Forman, 1804), pp. 18-20; *Hazard's Register* 12 (Nov. 2, 1833): 282; Francis Lieber, *Remarks on the Relation between Education and Crime* (Philadelphia: Philadelphia Society for Alleviating the Miseries of Public Prisons, 1835), p. 8; *Minutes of the Common Council of the City of New York, 1784-1831* (New York: City of New York, 1917), 7:72; ibid., 10:243-44 (hereafter cited as *M.C.C.*).

4. *Public Ledger,* May 9, 1836.

5. Ibid., July 13, 1844.

6. Mayor Matthew Clarkson, "An Address to the Citizens of Philadelphia Concerning the Better Government of Youth," reprinted in the *Philadelphia Gazette,* June 6, 1795.

7. *Pittsburg Gazette,* Nov. 28, 1823.

8. For further complaints see: *A Volume of Records Relating to the Early History of Boston Containing Minutes of the Selectmen's Meetings, 1799-1810* (Boston: City of Boston Printing Department,

1908), pp. 79-80, 329; ibid., *1811-1818*, pp. 101, 109; ibid., *1818-1822*, pp. 39-40; *Niles Weekly Register* n. s. 9, no. 17 (Dec. 15, 1821): 256; Charles Christian, *A Brief Treatise on the Police of the City of New York* (New York: Southwick & Pelsue, 1812), pp. 16-22, 29; *M.C.C.*, 14:298-99.

   9. Mayor William Milnor to the Councils, *Hazard's Register* 5 (Feb. 6, 1830): 87.

   10. Ibid. 6 (July 3, 1830): 6-7.

   11. James F. Richardson, "The Struggle to Establish a London-Style Police Force for New York City," *New-York Historical Society Quarterly* 49 (April 1965): 176; Roger Lane, *Policing the City: Boston, 1822-1885* (Cambridge: Harvard University Press, 1967), pp. 9-10, 21.

   12. Joseph M'Ilvaine's "Charge to the Grand Jury," reprinted in *Hazard's Register* 6 (July 3, 1830): 6-7. Emphasis in original.

   13. Girard arranged this bequest in 1830. The complete will is reproduced in Thomas Brothers, *The United States of North America as They Are; Not as They Are Generally Described: Being a Cure for Radicalism* (London: Longman, Orme, Brown, Green, & Longmans, 1840), app. 3, pp. 317-33. The quotation is from sec. 24, pt. 2, p. 331.

   14. *Hazard's Register* 12 (Nov. 2, 1833): 283, 285.

   15. See Chapter Two for a full discussion of the detective.

   16. *Hazard's Register* 12 (Nov. 2, 1833): 283, 285.

   17. *A Digest of the Ordinances of the Corporation of the City of Philadelphia, and of the Act of Assembly, Relating Thereto* (Philadelphia: S. C. Atkinson, 1834), p. 183; Charles Reith, *A New Study of Police History* (London: Oliver & Boyd, 1956), p. 147.

   18. *Hazard's Register* 6 (July 3, 1830): 6; ibid. 12 (Nov. 2, 1833): 282; *A Digest of Ordinances,* pp. 183-86.

   19. Louis H. Arky, "The Mechanics' Union of Trade Associations and the Formation of the Philadelphia Workingmen's Movement," *Pennsylvania Magazine of History and Biography* 76, no. 2 (April 1952): 169.

   20. Marcus Cunliffe, *Soldiers and Civilians: The Martial Spirit in America, 1776-1865* (Boston: Little, Brown, 1968), p. 102.

   21. See maps in Chapter Three.

   22. *Harper's* 6 (Dec. 1852): 125; *Brother Jonathan* 6, no. 12 (Nov. 18, 1843): 325; *Knickerbocker* 4, no. 3 (Sept. 1834): 246-47.

   23. *Weekly Chicago Democrat,* March 16, 1842.

   24. *Public Ledger,* Nov. 1, 1850.

   25. Howard O. Sprogle, *History of the Philadelphia Police* (Philadelphia: n.p., 1887), pp. 75-76; Richardson, *The New York Police: Colonial Times to 1901* (New York: Oxford University Press, 1970), p.

37; Edward H. Savage, *A Chronological History of the Boston Watch and Police, from 1631 to 1865* . . . (Boston: Published and Sold by the Author, 1865), pp. 77-78; John J. Flinn, *History of the Chicago* Police from the Earliest Settlement of the Community to the Present Time (Chicago: W. B. Conkey, 1887), pp. 54-55.

26. *New York Herald,* Feb. 14, 1840.

27. *Public Ledger,* Nov. 8, 1844; *New York Herald,* Jan. 14, 1840; Allan Nevins and Milton H. Thomas, eds., *The Diary of George Templeton Strong* (4 vols.; New York: Macmillan, 1952), 2:99, 403-4; Leonard L. Richards, *"Gentlemen of Property and Standing": Anti-Abolition* Mobs in Jacksonian America (New York: Oxford University Press, 1970).

28. *New York Herald,* Jan. 13, 1840.

29. S. G. Bulfinch, "Recent Acts of Popular Violence in Cincinnati," *Brother Jonathan* 1, no. 6 (Feb. 5, 1842): 161; Nevins and Thomas, *Diary of George Templeton Strong,* 3:425; Nicholas B. Wainwright, ed., *A Philadelphia Perspective: The Diary of Sidney George Fisher Covering the Years 1834 to 1871* (Philadelphia: Historical Society of Pennsylvania, 1967), p. 64.

30. *Public Ledger,* Jan. 1, 1844.

31. See Chapter Two.

32. *Documents of the Assembly of the State of New York, 63d session, vol. 3, no. 98 (1840).*

33. *New York Herald,* Jan. 28, 1840, emphasis added.

34. Ibid., Feb. 22, March 26, June 30, 1840.

35. *Public Ledger,* Feb. 4, 1840.

36. Ibid., June 29, 1840.

37. *New York Herald,* Feb. 22, 1840.

38. *Public Ledger,* May 18, 1844.

39. Ibid., May 21, 1844; *New York Herald,* Feb. 14, 1840; *Chicago Tribune,* March 8, 1853.

40. *Public Ledger,* Jan. 15, May 25, 1840.

41. *George A. Ketcham, "Municipal Police Reform: A Comparative Study of Law Enforcement in Cincinnati, Chicago, New Orleans, New York, and St. Louis, 1844-1877" (Ph.D. diss., University of Missouri, 1967), p. 72.*

42. The various plans can be found in Richardson, *New York Police,* pp. 38-40.

43. Ibid., p. 39.

44. *Public Ledger,* Jan. 5, 1844.

45. Richardson, *New York Police,* pp. 39-40.

46. *Public Ledger,* Jan. 2, 5, 11, 1844.

47. *Laws of the State of New York, Passed at the Sixty-Seventh Session of the Legislature* (Albany: C. Van Beuthuysen & Co., 1844), pp. 469, 473; Miller, *Cops and Bobbies,* pp. 16-17.

48. Feldberg, *Philadelphia Riots,* chaps. 2, 3.

49. *Public Ledger,* May 18, 20, 21, 1844; emphasis in original. Feldberg, *Philadelphia Riots,* pp. 162-63.

50. *Public Ledger,* Aug. 5, 1844.

51. Ibid., Nov. 12, 1844.

52. Sprogle, *History of the Philadelphia Police,* pp. 86-87.

53. *Laws of the General Assembly of the Commonwealth of Pennsylvania, Passed at the Session of 1845* (Harrisburg: J. M. G. Lescure, 1845), pp. 380-83.

54. *Laws of the State of New York, . . . 67th Sess.,* p. 471.

55. Mayor Peter McCall to the City Councils, printed in the *Public Ledger,* Oct. 18, 1845.

56. Richardson, *New York Police,* p. 54.

57. *New York Herald,* May 12, 1845.

58. Unspecified newspaper dated June 5, 1846, quoted in J. Thomas Scharf and Thompson Westcott, *History of St. Louis City and County* (2 vols.; Philadelphia: Louis H. Everts, 1883), 1:740.

59. Lane, *Policing the City,* p. 60.

60. Flinn, *History of the Chicago Police,* p. 57; *Weekly Chicago Democrat,* July 13, 27, 1847.

61. Compiled from the sample taken from the *Public Ledger,* as reported in Chapter Two. The distribution of reported gang incidents was: 1840-1844—17; 1845-1849—26; 1850-1854—24; 1855-1859—14; 1860-1864—8; 1865-1869—9.

62. J. Thomas Scharf and Thompson Westcott, *History of Philadelphia* (3 vols.; Philadelphia: L. H. Everts & Co., 1884), 1:691.

63. *Public Ledger,* March 12, 22, 1844.

64. *Philadelphia Almanac,* Aug. 2, 1847, quoted in Ellis P. Oberholtzer, *Philadelphia: A History of the City and Its People* (3 vols.; Philadelphia: S. J. Clarke, n.d.), 2:304.

65. *Public Ledger,* Jan. 26, March 3, April 17, 1848.

66. Scharf and Westcott, *History of Philadelphia,* 1:691-92.

67. *Public Ledger,* June 20, 1849.

68. Wainwright, ed., *A Philadelphia Perspective,* p. 226.

69. *Public Ledger,* Aug. 31, 1849.

70. Ibid., Oct. 1, 18, 1849.

71. Scharf and Westcott, *History of Philadelphia,* 1:692-93.

72. Public Ledger, Nov. 3, 8, 9, 15, Dec. 19, 1849.

73. Wainwright, ed., *A Philadelphia Perspective,* p. 179.

74. *Public Ledger,* Nov. 17, 1849. Concern over property values was, of course, only part of the reason for supporting consolidation. But among influential property owners and realtors it probably was a major consideration in their decisions to back reform.

75. Ibid., March 25, 1850.

76. Sprogle, *History of the Philadelphia Police,* pp. 93-94.

77. *Public Ledger,* Oct. 24, 1850.

78. Ibid., June 28, 1850.

79. Ibid., Aug. 21, 22, Sept. 11, 1850.

80. Ibid., Nov. 8, 1850.

81. Ibid., March 29, 1851.

82. Ibid., Nov. 21, 1850; ibid., Jan. 14, 1851; ibid., July 9, 1852.

83. Ibid., Nov. 26, 1852.

84. Scharf and Westcott, *History of Philadelphia,* 1:713-14.

85. *Public Ledger,* July 19, 28, 1854.

86. *Daily Journal* (Chicago), March 17, 1849.

87. *Gem of the Prairie,* Nov. 16, 1850; Flinn, *History of the Chicago Police,* p. 48; *Chicago Tribune,* March 8, 1853.

88. *Chicago Tribune,* March 31, April 11, 1853.

89. *The Revised Charter and Ordinances of the City of Chicago* (Chicago: Daily Democrat Office, 1851), pp. 34-43.

90. *Weekly Chicago Democrat,* Dec. 1, 1849.

91. *Chicago Tribune,* Dec. 23, 1853.

92. Bruce McK. Cole, "The Chicago Press and the Know-Nothings, 1850-1856" (M.A. thesis, University of Chicago, 1948).

93. *Chicago Tribune,* June 22, 24, 1854.

94. Ibid., March 14, 1855.

95. Flinn, *History of the Chicago Police,* pp. 76-78.

96. *Chicago Tribune,* May 2, 1855; Flinn, *History of the Chicago Police,* p. 71; George W. Thompson and John A. Thompson, comps., *The Charter and Ordinances of the City of Chicago, Together with the Acts of the General Assembly relating to the City, and Other Miscellaneous Acts, with an Appendix* (Chicago; D. B. Cooke & Co., 1856), pp. 310-20.

97. *Public Ledger,* June 15, 1855.

98. See Chapter Four for a discussion of these developments.

Chapter Two   **Professional Thieves and Policing**

1. Charles Christian, *A Brief Treatise on the Police of the City of New York* (New York: Southwick & Pelsue, 1812), pp. 21-22.

2. *Niles Weekly Register* ser. 4, 9, no. 2 (Sept. 7, 1833): 29-30.

3. [Philadelphia] *Aurora General Advertiser,* July 17, 1800;
Niles Weekly Register n.s., 2, no. 26 (Aug. 22, 1818): 429; ibid. ser. 3,
8, no. 26 (Aug. 25, 1827): 419.
      4. *Niles Weekly Register* 10, no. 16 (June 15, 1816): 263; ibid.
ser. 4, 2, no. 20 (July 10, 1830): 355; *National Gazette,* June 22, 1833
(story from New York).
      5. *Niles Weekly Register* n.s., 2, no. 8 (April 18, 1818): 135;
National Gazette, Feb. 15, 1825; ibid., Nov. 15, 1832; *The New-Yorker*
1, no. 22 (Aug. 20, 1836): 350.
      6. *National Gazette,* Feb. 15, 1825.
      7. *Public Ledger,* Nov. 15, 1836.
      8. *Aurora General Advertiser,* Jan. 6, 1803; ibid., July 3, 1810;
National Gazette, April 28, 1827; *M.C.C.,* 5:427; Christian, *A Brief
Treatise,* pp. 26-27. The receiver and the fence may have been the same
individual, but the evidence is not always clear on this point.
      9. Commonwealth v. Deacon, 8 Serg. & R. 48 (Pa. 1822); James
F. Richardson, "The Struggle to Establish a London-Style Police Force
for New York City," *New-York Historical Society Quarterly* 49, no. 2
(April 1965): 175.
      10. *M.C.C.,* 6:533-34.
      11. Rewards for the return of stolen goods appeared very irregu-
larly in the 1790s. For example, see the *Aurora General Advertiser,*
April 8, May 12, Aug. 15, 1791.
      12. Ibid., Oct. 18, 1800.
      13. Ibid., July 8, Oct. 4, 28, 1800; ibid., Sept. 5, 24, 1810;
Pittsburgh Gazette, June 5, 12, 1820.
      14. *Aurora General Advertiser,* July 17, 1800 (story from
New York).
      15. Ibid., Jan. 6, 1803; ibid., July 3, 1810.
      16. Seldon D. Bacon, "The Early Development of American
Municipal Police: A Study of the Evolution of Formal Controls in a
Changing Society" (Ph.D. diss., Yale University, 1939), pp. 175,
246-48.
      17. *Hazard's Register* 6 (July 3, 1830): 6-7.
      18. *Niles Weekly Register* ser. 2, 2, no. 26 (Aug. 22, 1818): 429;
Roger Lane, *Policing the City: Boston, 1822-1885* (Cambridge: Harvard
University Press, 1967), p. 10.
      19. "Police Report," *Hazard's Register* 12 (Nov. 2, 1833): 281.
      20. The phrase is James Richardson's, though he applies it to a
much later period. See Richardson, *The New York Police: Colonial
Times to 1901* (New York: Oxford University Press, 1970), p. 207.
      21. *Public Ledger,* Feb. 4, June 29, 1840; *New York Herald,*
Jan. 28, Feb. 7, 22, March 26, June 30, 1840.

204 Policing the Urban Underworld

22. *Public Ledger,* June 17, 1840.
23. *New York Herald,* Feb. 22, 1840.
24. Ibid., May 11, 1840.
25. Hatch v. Mann, 9 Windell 263; City Bank v. Bangs, 2 Edw. Ch. 96-97.
26. Hatch v. Mann, 15 Windell 45-48.
27. George F. Pool v. City of Boston, 59 Mass. (5 Cush.) 219-21; Smith v. Whilden, 10 Pa. St. R. 39-40.
28. *Laws of the State of New York, Passed at the Sixty-Seventh Session of the Legislature* (Albany: C. Van Beuthuysen & Co., 1844), p. 476; Lane, *Policing the City,* pp. 55-56; Howard O. Sprogle, *History of the Philadelphia Police* (Philadelphia: n.p., 1887), p. 104.
29. *Public Ledger,* April 17, 1845; ibid., Oct. 4, 1848; "Corrupt Police," *Journal of Prison Discipline 4, no. 2 (April 1849): 96.*
30. *Public Ledger,* Feb. 16, 1856; ibid., Feb. 4, 1863; ibid., April 5, 1865; *Chicago Tribune,* July 23, 1857.
31. *Public Ledger,* March 19, July 30, 1849; ibid., Nov. 8, 1866; *Democrat* (Chicago), Aug. 21, 1849.
32. *Public Ledger,* July 25, 1850; ibid., Nov. 21, 1860; ibid., Dec. 12, 1870; *Chicago Tribune,* May 18, 1858; ibid., Oct. 18, 1861; ibid., March 11, 1872; Edward Crapsey, *The Nether Side of New York; or, the Vice, Crime and Poverty of the Great Metropolis* (rpt. ed.; Montclair, N.J.: Patterson Smith, 1969), pp. 63-73.
33. *Chicago Tribune,* Nov. 13, 1858; *Public Ledger,* April 25, 1857; ibid., Oct. 24, 1861.
34. Lynn Glaser, *Counterfeiting in America: The History of an American Way to Wealth* (New York: Clarkson N. Potter, 1968), chap. 9.
35. *Brother Jonathan 4, no. 10 (March 11, 1843): 288; Public Ledger,* Jan. 18, 1851.
36. *Public Ledger,* March 22, 1867.
37. Benjamin P. Eldridge and William B. Watts, *Our Rival the Rascal: A Faithful Portrayal of the Conflict Between the Criminals of This Age and The Defenders of Society—the Police* (Boston: Pemberton Publishing Co., 1897), pp. 151-53; *Chicago Tribune,* Jan. 3, March 20, 1885.
38. *Public Ledger,* March 5, April 24, 1849; ibid., May 24, 1866; Ned Buntline [Edward Z. C. Judson], *The Mysteries and Miseries of New York: A Story of Real Life* (New York: Berford & Co., 1848), pp. 113-16; *New York Times,* July 2, 1866; George Matsell, *Vocabulum, or the Rogues Lexicon* (New York: George Matsell, 1859); John Landesco, "The Criminal Underworld of Chicago in the '80's and '90's,"

Journal of Criminal Law and Criminology 25 (May-June 1934): 343-45.
    39. *Chicago Tribune,* Aug. 19, 1857; *Public Ledger,* July 23, 1858; ibid., July 20, 1861; ibid., Dec. 24, 1862.
    40. Robert S. Pickett, *House of Refuge: Origins of Juvenile Reform in New York State, 1815-1857* (Syracuse, N.Y.: Syracuse University Press, 1969), p. 71; William W. Sanger, *The History of Prostitution* (New York: Eugenie's Publishing Co., 1939), p. 558.
    41. J. J. Tobias, *Crime and Industrial Society in the 19th Century* (New York: Schocken Books, 1967), pp. 92-96, describes robbery by English prostitutes as typical, but he does not refer specifically to the panel game; E. F. Vidocq, *Les Voleurs: Physiologie de leurs Moeurs et de leur Langage* (2 vols.; Paris: Chez L'Auteur, 1837), 2:28, similarly referred to *Pontonniers* as prostitutes who always stole from their customers, but not in the prescribed manner of the panel game.
    42. For example, *Public Ledger,* April 16, 1840; ibid., Oct. 20, 30, 1857; Buntline, *Mysteries and Miseries of New York,* p. 113-16; *Daily Tribune* (New York), Sept. 5, 1845.
    43. *Public Ledger,* Feb. 5, 1851; *Journal of Prison Discipline* 3, no. 1 (Jan. 1858): 38-40.
    44. "Robbery as a Science," *Harper's New Monthly Magazine* 26, no. 155 (April 1863): 744-45; *Public Ledger,* Jan. 31, 1848; ibid., Oct. 29, 1867. "Playthings" were burglar tools. See Matsell, *Vocabulum.*
    45. *Weekly Chicago Democrat,* Nov. 7, 1848; *Chicago Tribune,* March 24, 1855; ibid., July 24, 1861; ibid., Dec. 20, 1885; *Public Ledger,* Dec. 31, 1849; ibid., Jan. 24, 1871; ibid., June 1, 1878.
    46. *Public Ledger,* Jan. 31, 1848.
    47. Ibid., May 25, 1857. See also: *Chicago Tribune,* Feb. 15, 1853; ibid., June 10, 1857; *Public Ledger,* Jan. 26, 1861; ibid., June 24, 1865.
    48. Crapsey, *The Nether Side,* p. 16; *Public Ledger,* March 27, 1877.
    49. *Public Ledger,* Jan. 31, 1848; Matsell, *Vocabulum;* Eldridge and Watts, *Our Rival the Rascal,* pp. 38, 394-95, 397.
    50. "Robbery as a Science," p. 745; *Public Ledger,* March 30, 1877.
    51. "Robbery as a Science," p. 745.
    52. For one such controversy see: *Chicago Tribune,* Jan. 21 to March 14, 1870.
    53. Langdon W. Moore, *Langdon W. Moore: His Own Story of His Eventful Life* (Boston: Langdon W. Moore, 1893), pp. 167-68; Eldridge and Watts, *Our Rival the Rascal,* p. 45.

54. *Public Ledger,* March 27, 1877.
55. Eldridge and Watts, *Our Rival the Rascal,* pp. 410-13.
56. *Chicago Tribune,* March 20, 1872; *Chicago Times,* July 21, 1875; *Public Ledger,* March 24, 1859; ibid., Jan. 19, 1863; ibid., Nov. 7, 1874 (supp.); ibid., Aug. 14, 1878.
57. [New York Detective] William H. Bell, unpublished diary, May 2, 3, 1851, New-York Historical Society; *New York Times,* Aug. 26, 1866; *Public Ledger,* Nov. 12, 1839; ibid., Feb. 11, 1851; ibid., Feb. 12, 1863; ibid., July 28, 1870.
58. Crapsey, *The Nether Side,* p. 84.
59. *Public Ledger,* July 7, 1857.
60. Ibid., Jan. 31, 1865.
61. *New York Times,* July 6, 1866.
62. George W. Walling, *Recollections of a New York Chief of Police* (New York: Caxton Book Concern, 1887), pp. 279-91, 472-75; *Chicago Tribune,* Oct. 10, 1880.
63. *Public Ledger,* July 7, 1857.
64. *Brother Jonathan* 6, no. 4 (Oct. 28, 1843): 242; *Weekly Chicago Democrat,* Aug. 21, 1849; *Public Ledger,* June 14, 1856; ibid., June 30, 1860; ibid., Feb. 25, 1862; ibid., Aug. 23, 1866; ibid., July 2, 1870: John J. Flinn, *History of the Chicago Police from the Earliest Settlement of the Community to the Present Time* (Chicago: W. B. Conkey, 1887), p. 358; Landesco, "The Criminal Underworld," pp. 343-44.
65. The number and frequency of public reward notices declined after 1830, probably because the victims knew how the stool pigeon system worked by that time and so did not need to advertise. But the practice persisted in modified form. See for example: *Public Ledger,* March 9, 1840; ibid., Nov. 17, 1849; ibid., Nov. 13, 1863; *Brother Jonathan* 6, no. 15 (Dec. 9, 1843): 410; *Chicago Tribune,* April 9, 1857.
66. *New York Daily Tribune,* June 20, 1845.
67. Unspecified newspaper dated June 5, 1846, quoted in J. Thomas Scharf and Thompson Westcott, *History of St. Louis City and County* (2 vols.; Philadelphia: Louis H. Evarts, 1883), 1:740; "Baltimore Correspondence," *The National Era* 1, no. 32 (Aug. 12, 1847): 3; *Public Ledger,* Sept. 29, 1848.
68. A comparison of early police rosters published in the newspapers and the city directories which listed occupations revealed that some private policemen after 1855 had no prior law enforcement experience. Cf. *McElroy's Philadelphia City Directory* (Philadelphia: Joseph Monier, 1859), pp. 151, 255, 322, and various rosters in the *Public Ledger,* for example, Jan. 2, 1844, March 3, 1848, Dec. 30,

1852, and March 9, 1855. See also *D. B. Cooke & Co.'s City Directory* (Chicago: D. B. Cooke & Co., 1858), pp. 58, 219, 230, and *Chicago Tribune*, May 25, 1855, and March 20, 1857.

69. Pinkerton's early career can be traced in the following: *Daily Democratic Press* (Chicago), Sept. 9, 1853; ibid., Oct. 5, 1854; ibid., March 17, July 28, 1855; *Chicago Tribune*, Feb. 29, 1856; ibid., Jan. 21, 1857. Additional details are in photostatic copies of the Allan Pinkerton Papers, Chicago Historical Society.

70. Crapsey, *The Nether Side*, chap. 7.

71. See below.

72. *Public Ledger*, June 9, 1855.

73. *Chicago Weekly Times*, June 14, 1855.

74. *Daily Democratic Press*, June 12, 1855; George W. Thompson and John A. Thompson, comps., *The Charter and Ordinances of the City of Chicago, Together with the Acts of the General Assembly relating to the City, and other Miscellaneous Acts, with an Appendix* (Chicago: D. B. Cooke & Co., 1856), p. 320.

75. Flinn, *History of the Chicago Police*, p. 79; *Chicago Tribune*, April 18, May 10, 1856; Feb. 17, 18, 24, March 14, April 6, 1857.

76. *Chicago Daily Democrat*, March 11, 1857.

77. *Chicago Tribune*, July 18, 21, 1857; *Weekly Chicago Democrat*, July 25, 1857.

78. *Chicago Tribune*, May 16, June 24, 1857.

79. Ibid., June 26, 1857.

80. For example see ibid., Jan. 4, 8, 15, April 23, May 19, 1858.

81. Ibid., Oct. 7, 1858.

82. *Chicago Western Democrat*, Jan. 22, 1859; *Chicago Daily Times*, Oct. 25, 1859; *Chicago Tribune*, April 30, 1864.

83. *Chicago Daily Times*, Oct. 25, 1859.

84. *New York Daily Tribune*, Aug. 13, 1845; *Public Ledger*, Feb. 15, 1850; Bell, unpub. diary, July 3, 1851; Mayor Robert J. Conrad to Edward Gratz, March 27, 1855, Edward Gratz Collection, Pennsylvania Historical Society.

85. Lane, *Policing the City*, p. 60; Richardson, *New York Police*, p. 122; Sprogle, *History of the Philadelphia Police*, pp. 116-17; Flinn, *History of the Chicago Police*, p. 96.

86. *Chicago Tribune*, April 18, May 10, 1856; Flinn, *History of the Chicago Police*, pp. 79, 96-97; Richardson, *New York Police*, p. 62.

87. *Chicago Tribune*, Oct. 8, 1857; ibid., Aug. 31, 1858; ibid., Oct. 8, 28, 1859; ibid., Aug. 7, Dec. 10, 1860; *Chicago Daily Times*, Oct. 25, 1859; *New York Times*, July 2, 1866; Matsell, *Vocabulum*, pp. 66, 71.

88. *Chicago Tribune,* April 30, 1864; *New York Times,* Aug. 9, 1866; Lane, *Policing the City,* pp. 156-57, 200.

Chapter Three   **Street Crime: Philadelphia as a Case Study**

1. *Public Ledger,* Jan. 20, 1863.

2. This study uses one newspaper, the *Public Ledger,* to examine the geographic incidence of crime. Surviving court records and precinct arrest books did not provide information concerning the addresses where offenses occurred. The *Ledger,* unlike Chicago's local press, consistently reported such addresses throughout the period from 1840 to 1870. The *Ledger* had one other advantage over official records. The latter contained data only for those cases where an arrest and/or conviction was made. Since newspapers noted crimes which, in many cases, were never acted upon by any official agency, the *Ledger's* coverage of crimes is more likely to have been representative than were official records.

3. W. E. B. DuBois, *The Philadelphia Negro: A Social Study* (New York: Schocken Books, 1967), pp. 302-3; Sam B. Warner, Jr., *The Private City: Philadelphia in Three Periods of Its Growth* (Philadelphia: University of Pennsylvania Press, 1968), chap. 3; Stuart Blumin, "Mobility and Change in Antebellum Philadelphia," in *Nineteenth-Century Cities: Essays in the New Urban History,* ed. Stephen Thernstrom and Richard Sennet (New Haven: Yale University Press, 1969), pp. 187-90.

4. Nicholas B. Wainwright, ed., *A Philadelphia Perspective: The Diary of Sidney George Fisher Covering the Years 1834 to 1871* Philadelphia: Historical Society of Pennsylvania, 1967), p. 202.

5. Kenneth T. Jackson, "Urbanization in the Nineteenth Century: A Statistical Inquiry," in *The New Urban History: Quantitative Explorations by American Historians,* ed. Leo F. Schnore (Princeton, N.J.: Princeton University Press, 1975), pp. 110-43; *North American and United States Gazette,* Sept. 12, 1859.

6. The movement of the downtown has been traced through accounts in the *Public Ledger.* See, for example, Nov. 11, Dec. 15, 1847; March 29, 1848; Dec. 19, 1850; April 4, 1851; Jan. 13, Feb. 23, 27, 1855; June 17, 1856; Aug. 31, 1857; Jan 14, Feb. 29, March 20, April 12, 14, 1860; July 26, 1864; Aug. 30, 1865; July 23, 1869; April 26 (supp.), 30 (supp.), May 3 (supp.), 1873.

7. The discussion of crimes against both property and persons is based on a sample taken from the *Public Ledger* at five-year intervals. In each year, I examined every other day's (January 1, 3, 5 . . . ,

February 2, 4, 6 . . . , etc.) catalogue of crimes and recorded every incident in which a geographic location was given. This method resulted
in a record of the following number of offenses:

Year	Property	Personal
1840	122	68
1845	120	71
1850	117	116
1855	151	51
1860	143	47
1865	164	55
1870	272	104

On the accompanying maps each dot therefore represents *one*
crime. The sample is in all probability statistically insignificant, but it
was impossible to record any offenses which were not located geographically by the *Ledger*.

8. Pickpockets and shoplifters also plagued storeowners, but by
the 1840s they tended to be professional thieves and are therefore
omitted from this discussion. See Chapter One.

9. John F. Watson, *Annals of Philadelphia, Being a Collection
of Memoirs, Anecdotes, & Incidents of the City and Its Inhabitants
from the Days of the Pilgrim Founders* (Philadelphia: E. L. Carey & A.
Hart, 1830), p. 201.

10. Ibid., pp. 218-19; *Public Ledger*, Nov. 12, 1839; ibid., Jan. 5,
1844; Sept. 15, 1871; ibid., letter to editor signed "Honest Dealer,"
Feb. 14, 1875 (supp.). A similar situation existed in Chicago and New
York, See, for example: *Chicago Tribune,* Aug. 20, 1856; ibid., Aug. 6,
1859; *New York Times,* July 6, Aug. 26, 1866; William H. Bell, unpublished diary, May 2, 3, 1851, New-York Historical Society.

11. On the general assault pattern see the accompanying maps.
For race riots see Leon F. Litwack, *North of Slavery; The Negro in the
Free States, 1790-1860* (Chicago: University of Chicago Press, 1961), p.
100. The raids and reprisals can be followed in the *Public Ledger*. See,
for example: July 1, 27, 31, 1840; Dec. 4, 28, 1840; Feb. 3, 25, 27,
1845; May 7, 29, Aug. 2, 12, 26, 1850; Jan. 23, Feb. 27, Sept. 17,
1855.

12. Computed from the *Sixth Census of Enumeration of the
Inhabitants of the United States, 1840* (Washington, D.C.: Government
Printing Office, 1840), p. 150.

13. See Appendix 1.

14. Letter to the editor signed "A Corner Lounger," *Public
Ledger,* July 25, 1856. Examples of complaints against corner loungers

210   Policing the Urban Underworld

can be found in: ibid., July 19, 1859; March 29, 1867; March 8, 1873 (suppl.).

15. Ibid., Aug. 7, 1856.

16. Ibid., Dec. 12, 1870. The dugouts were segregated according to age, with 13- to 18-year-olds in some, 18- to 21-year-olds in others.

17. Ibid., Oct. 13, 1875.

18. Ibid., March 7, 1845; ibid., Dec. 1, 1869.

19. Ibid., Jan. 20, Oct. 16, 1854; ibid., Dec. 30, 1857; Jan. 15, 1877. Such groups were by no means unique to Philadelphia. For similar gangs elsewhere see: *Chicago Weekly Times,* June 14, 1855; *Chicago Tribune,* Feb. 11, 1860; ibid., Aug. 26, 1861; ibid., May 26, 1863; Clifford Thompson, "Burglars," *Galaxy* 4 (Aug. 1867): 428; Edward Crapsey, *The Nether Side of New York; or the Vice, Crime and Poverty of the Great Metropolis* (rpt.; Montclair, N.J.: Patterson Smith, 1969), p. 121.

20. *Public Ledger,* Dec. 28, 1840; ibid., Sept. 12, Dec. 19, 1844; ibid., Feb. 25, 27, 1845; ibid., Aug. 10, Nov. 1, 1848; ibid., June 22, 1850; ibid., Jan. 16, 1854; ibid., July 18, 1860; ibid., Sept. 4, 1876.

21. George R. Taylor, ed., "Philadelphia in Slices: Slice III: The Rowdy Clubs, by George C. Foster," *Pennsylvania Magazine of History and Biography* 93 (Jan. 1969): 37. This account originally appeared in the *New York Tribune,* Oct. 30, 1848.

22. The *Public Ledger* first mentioned the use of brass knuckles on December 18, 1854. Within three months this weapon had appeared in Chicago. See the *Chicago Times,* March 13, 1855.

23. *Public Ledger,* April 8, 1840; ibid., Jan. 22, 1850.

24. See Map 1.

25. *Public Ledger,* April 30, 1850.

26. Ibid., May 28, 1845; ibid., Feb. 21, 1848.

27. Foster, "Philadelphia in Slices," p. 36.

28. Alice F. Tyler, *Freedom's Ferment: Phases of American Social History from the Colonial Period to the Outbreak of the Civil War* (New York: Harper & Row, Harper Torchbooks, 1962), pp. 308-95; Ray A. Billington, *The Protestant Crusade, 1800-1860: A Study of the Origins of American Nativism* (Chicago: Quandrangle Books, 1964).

29. Bruce Laurie, "Fire Companies and Gangs in Southwark: The 1840s," in *The Peoples of Philadelphia: A History of Ethnic Groups and Lower-Class Life, 1790-1940,* ed. Allen F. Davis and Mark H. Haller (Philadelphia: Temple University Press, 1973), p. 74.

30. Andrew J. Neilly, "The Violent Volunteers: A History of the Volunteer Fire Department of Philadelphia, 1736-1871" (Ph.D. diss., University of Pennsylvania, 1959), p. 28.

31. *Public Ledger,* Jan. 14, 1853; Foster, "Philadelphia in Slices," pp. 35-36.

32. J. Thomas Scharf and Thompson Westcott, *History of Philadelphia* (3 vols.; Philadelphia: L. H. Evarts & Co., 1884), 3:1887-88, 1899-1901, 1910; Neilly, "The Violent Volunteers," pp. 130, 143.

33. *Public Ledger,* Jan. 30, 1844; ibid., Jan. 25, 1848; ibid., April 19, 1850; ibid., July 1, 1850; ibid., Sept. 24, 1858; ibid., Nov. 7, 1865; ibid., Sept. 17, 1866; Scharf and Westcott, *History of Philadelphia,* 2:691-92; Neilly, "The Violent Volunteers," p. 88.

34. *Public Ledger,* May 28, Oct. 6, 16, Nov. 29, 1845.

35. Ibid., Nov. 23, 1847, identifies Paul as the Rats' leader.

36. Ibid., Aug. 13, 1846; Laurie, "Fire Companies and Gangs in Southwark," p. 78.

37. Anonymous, *Life and Adventures of Charles Anderson Chester, the Notorious Leader of the Philadelphia "Killers"* (Philadelphia: Yates & Smith, 1850), pp. 27-28.

38. Neilly, "The Violent Volunteers," pp. 70-72.

39. *Public Ledger,* Aug. 13, 1846.

40. *The National Era* 3, no. 42 (Oct. 18, 1849): 167.

41. Laurie, "Fire Companies and Gangs in Southwark," p. 81.

42. *Public Ledger,* April 16, 19, 1850.

43. Letter to editor signed T. S., *Public Ledger,* April 19, 1850.

44. This explanation of the conduct and activities of combat gangs differs significantly from recent analyses of this form of deviance. Mid-nineteenth-century gangs, in a fluid urban situation which did not yet have institutions such as police forces and schools to impose "correct" behavior patterns, responded to the values of their neighborhoods or ethnic groups. Thus, at this time, there were no "subcultures" in the sense that Albert Cohen (for example) employs in his *Delinquent Boys: The Culture of the Gang* (Glencoe, Ill.: Free Press, 1955). Cf. Gerald D. Suttles, *The Social Construction of Communities* (Chicago: University of Chicago Press, 1972), pp. 21-43.

45. Cf. David Ward, *Cities and Immigrants: A Geography of Change in Nineteenth-Century America* (New York: Oxford University Press, 1971), pp. 118-20, and Gerald D. Suttles, *The Social Order of the Slum: Ethnicity and Territory in the Inner City* (Chicago: University of Chicago Press, 1968).

Chapter Four   Organizing for Crime Prevention

1. Roger Lane, *Policing the City: Boston, 1822-1885* (Cambridge: Harvard University Press, 1967), p. 119.

2. *St. Paul Daily Minnesotan*, n.d., quoted in the *Chicago Tribune*, Feb. 3, 1858. Emphasis in original. *Chicago Tribune*, May 28, 1855; *Journal of Prison Discipline* 6, no. 1 (Jan. 1851): 88.

3. *Chicago Tribune*, April 9, 1861.

4. *Public Ledger*, July 31, 1860.

5. This analysis is based upon an examination of the following department rulebooks: *By-Laws and Ordinances of the Mayor, Aldermen, and Commonalty of the City of New York* (New York: J. S. Voorhies, 1845); Robert S. Reed, *Police Manual: Being Rules and Regulations for the Organization and Government of the Consolidated Police of the City of Philadelphia* (Philadelphia: King & Baird, 1855); *Police Ordinance and Rules and Regulations for the Government of the Police Department, and Instructions as to the Powers and Duties of Police Officers of the City of Chicago* (Chicago: Daily Democrat Office, 1855).

6. *By-Laws and Ordinances*, p. 207.

7. *Police Ordinance and Rules and Regulations*, p. 74.

8. *Public Ledger*, Aug. 13, 1856; "Report of the Joint Committee on Police Matters in the City and County of New York, and County of Kings," *New York State Senate Documents*, 1856, 2, no. 97 (Albany: Charles Van Benthuysen, 1856), p. 130 (hereafter cited as *New York Senate Documents* 1856); *Police Ordinances and Rules and Regulations*, p. 62.

9. *Chicago Tribune*, July 12, 1861.

10. *Police Ordinance and Rules and Regulations*, p. 23.

11. George A. Ketcham, "Municipal Police Reform: A Comparative Study of Law Enforcement in Cincinnati, Chicago, New Orleans, New York, and Saint Louis, 1844-1877" (Ph. D. diss., University of Missouri, 1967), pp. 232-35; *Public Ledger*, Feb. 8, March 16, 1854; ibid., Jan. 28, 1859; Edward H. Savage, *A Chronological History of the Boston Watch and Police, from 1631 to 1865* . . . (Boston: Published and Sold by the Author, 1865), p. 102.

12. William H. Bell, unpublished diary, passim, New-York Historical Society; Lane, *Policing the City*, p. 66; *Public Ledger*, Dec. 12, 1861.

13. James F. Richardson, *New York Police: Colonial Times to 1901* (New York: Oxford University Press, 1970), p. 122; Howard O. Sprogle, *History of the Philadelphia Police* (Philadelphia: n. p., 1887), p. 117; *Chicago Tribune*, Nov. 16, 1858; Savage, *Boston Watch and Police*, p. 101.

14. *Public Ledger*, Jan. 14, 1840.

15. *New York Daily Tribune*, June 26, 1845.

16. *Public Ledger*, Jan. 25, 1848.

17. Ibid., Feb. 28, 1855.

18. *Chicago Times*, March 19, 1855.

19. *Public Ledger*, May 22, 1845; *Laws of the State of New York . . . 67th Sess.*, p. 471.

20. *Public Ledger*, May 22, 1845.

21. *New York Daily Tribune*, July 30, 1845.

22. *Public Ledger*, Nov. 11, 1853.

23. Ibid., July 8, 1855.

24. Ibid., March 5, 1855.

25. Richardson, *New York Police*, p. 64; *Public Ledger*, May 22, 27, 1845.

26. *Public Ledger*, Jan. 1, 1850.

27. In 1848 the Philadelphia councils passed an ordinance requiring a uniform coat, but it was ignored; see *Public Ledger*, March 10, 1848.

28. Augustine E. Costello, *Our Police Protectors: History of the New York Police from the Earliest Period to the Present Time* (New York: A. E. Costello, 1885), pp. 128-29.

29. *Public Ledger*, Jan. 4, 14, 23, Feb. 2, April 3, 1854.

30. Ibid., Aug. 15, Sept. 29, 1854. Sprogle, *History of the Philadelphia Police*, p. 103.

31. *Public Ledger*, March 5, 1855.

32. Ibid., May 20, 1856.

33. Sprogle, *History of the Philadelphia Police*, p. 107; *Public Ledger*, Sept. 23, Nov. 11, 1858.

34. *Public Ledger*, Aug. 3, 11, Sept. 15, Dec. 20, 1860; ibid., Jan. 4, 1861.

35. Savage, *History of the Boston Watch and Police*, p. 99; Lane, *Policing the City*, p. 105.

36. John J. Flinn, *History of the Chicago Police from the Earliest Settlement of the Community to the Present Time* (Chicago: W. B. Conkey, 1887), pp. 88-94; *Chicago Tribune*, April 5, Sept. 29, 1859; ibid., March 28, May 9, July 6, 1861.

37. Costello, *Our Police Protectors*, p. 114.

38. *Public Ledger*, Oct. 17, 1854.

39. Ibid., Nov. 16, 1854.

40. *Chicago Tribune*, June 7, 1858; *Public Ledger*, Oct. 16, 1863; ibid., April 25, 1864; Richardson, *New York Police*, pp. 66-67.

41. *Public Ledger*, May 26, 1877 (supp.); Richardson, *New York Police*, p. 173.

42. *New York Times*, Feb. 9, 1856.

43. Ketcham, "Municipal Police Reform," pp. 218-21; *Public Ledger*, April 11, 1866; ibid., Dec. 13, 1878.

44. Bell, unpub. diary, April 14, 1851; *Public Ledger*, July 2, 1851; *Chicago Tribune*, June 12, 1857.

45. *Chicago Tribune*, Oct. 28, 1857; *Public Ledger*, July 21, 1854.

46. *Public Ledger*, Dec. 23, 25, 1857; Richardson, *New York Police*, p. 60.

47. George W. Thompson and John A. Thompson, comps., *The Charter and Ordinances of the City of Chicago, Together with the Acts of the General Assembly relating to the City, and Other Miscellaneous Acts, with an Appendix* (Chicago: D. B. Cooke & Co., 1856), pp. 316-18; *Laws and Ordinances Governing the City of Chicago* (Chicago: E. B. Myers and Chandler, 1866), p. 635; *Municipal Code of Chicago: Comprising the Laws of Illinois Relating to the City of Chicago, and the Ordinances of the City Council; Codified and Revised* (Chicago: Beach, Bernard & Co., 1881), pp. 208-11; Richardson, *New York Police*, pp. 60, 80, 204.

48. Reed, *Police Manual*, p. 28; *Public Ledger*, Aug. 18, 1856; ibid., Jan. 30, 1863.

49. See below.

50. Richardson, *New York Police*, p. 193; *Chicago Tribune*, April 10, 22, 1856; ibid., June 12, 1857; *Public Ledger*, July 21, 1854; ibid., Aug. 14, 1856; ibid., Aug. 18, Oct. 28, 1869.

51. E. g., letter to the editor signed "Tax-payer," *Public Ledger*, May 30, 1855; *Chicago Tribune*, Jan. 5, 1862.

52. *Public Ledger*, July 19, 1854; Crime Pattern Map for 1850, Chapter Three. Percentages calculated from newspaper data; see Appendix 2. Lane, *Policing the City*, pp. 99-100, comes to similar conclusions for Boston.

53. *Public Ledger*, Oct. 6, 1854.

54. Ibid., Nov. 3, 14, 1854.

55. Ibid., Nov. 9, 1854.

56. Ibid., Aug. 3, Oct. 26, Nov. 2, 1855. Percentages calculated from newspaper data; see Appendix 2.

57. *Chicago Tribune*, June 23, 1865.

58. Ibid., Aug., 23, 1865.

59. This analysis is based on calculations from Appendix 3.

60. *Public Ledger*, Sept. 14, 1854; Sprogle, *History of the Philadelphia Police*, pp. 115-16; *Report of the General Superintendent of Police of the City of Chicago to the City Council for the Year 1884* (Chicago: The City Council of Chicago, 1884), pp. 4-16; Richardson, *New York Police*, p. 172.

61. *Report of the General Superintendent . . . 1883* (Chicago: The City Council of Chicago, 1883), p. 22. *Report of the City Marshall*

... *1875* (Chicago: The City Council of Chicago, 1875), p. 16.

62. Arrests per patrolman, calculated from the *Annual Reports* of the Chicago police department, were as follows: 1875, 38.9; 1876, 65.6; 1877, 67.9; 1878, 77.9; 1879, 76.6; 1880, 78.7; 1881, 83.7; 1882, 87.5; 1883, 82.5; 1884, 52.4; 1885, 55.5. Cf. Theodore N. Ferdinand, "Politics, the Police and Arresting Practices in Salem, Massachusetts, since the Civil War," *Social Problems* 19 (Spring 1972); 572-87. Ferdinand argues that a decline in the allocation of financial resources to the Salem police produced a corresponding decline in police willingness to make arrests. Presumably, an increase in those resources should have resulted in an increase in arrests. In Chicago, the opposite seems to have occurred: a decline in manpower (1876-1881) resulted in an increase in arrests per patrolmen; a very large increase in manpower (1884) precipitated a sharp drop in arrests. For the correlations between the number of patrolmen and the number of arrests, see Appendix 4.

63. See below, Chapter Five.

64. Lane, *Policing the City*, p. 100; Richardson, *New York Police*, p. 53; Sprogle, *History of the Philadelphia Police*, p. 123.

65. *Chicago Tribune*, Jan. 1, 1866.

66. Sprogle, *History of the Philadelphia Police*, p. 107, 112; Richardson, *New York Police*, p. 68; Lane, *Policing the City*, p. 103.

67. *Public Ledger*, April 1, 1858.

68. Costello, *Our Police Protectors*, p. 439; Richardson, *New York Police*, pp. 136-37.

69. Flinn, *History of the Chicago Police*, pp. 398-99.

70. Ibid., p. 400; *Report of the General Superintendent . . . 1883*, p. 69.

71. Flinn, *History of the Chicago Police*, pp. 406-7.

72. *Chicago Tribune*, Nov. 12, 1880.

73. Ibid.; *Report of the General Superintendent . . . 1881*, p. 41.

74. *Chicago Tribune*, Dec. 22, 1880.

75. Ibid.; Flinn, *History of the Chicago Police*, p. 400. *Report of the General Superintendent . . . 1881* (Chicago: The City Council of Chicago, 1881), p. 41; *Report of the General Superintendent . . . 1884* (Chicago: The City Council of Chicago, 1884).

76. Letter from Police Superintendent William J. McGarigle to the Public, printed in the *Chicago Tribune*, Dec. 19, 1880; the Municipal Signal Co., *Police and Fire Alarm Systems and Apparatus* (Boston: Municipal Signal Co., 1888), pp. 16-17.

77. Calculated from the *Report of the General Superintendent of Police* from 1881 to 1885.

78. Lane, *Policing the City*, pp. 203-4, 210; *New York Times*,

Sept. 29, 1884; Richardson, *New York Police,* p. 170; Sprogle, *History of the Philadelphia Police,* p. 170; *Annual Message of the Mayor, 1885,* p. 305.

79. *Public Ledger,* July 11, 1859.

80. Costello, *Our Police Protectors,* pp. 114-15; De Francis Folsom, *Our Police: History of the Baltimore Force* (Baltimore: Ehlers, 1888), p. 34.

81. Richardson, *New York Police,* p. 55; Jerald E. Levine, "Police, Parties, and Polity: The Bureaucratization, Unionization, and Professionalization of the New York City Police, 1870-1917" (Ph. D. diss., University of Wisconsin, 1971), p. 23.

82. Levine, "Police, Parties, and Polity," pp. 21-22; Flinn, *History of the Chicago Police,* p. 95; Don E. Fehrenbacher, *Chicago Giant: A Biography of "Long John" Wentworth* (Madison, Wis.: American History Research Center, 1957), pp. 173-80.

83. *Public Ledger,* May 19, 25, 1858.

84. Cf. King's remarks on tenure in his inaugural address, reproduced in Sprogle, *History of the Philadelphia Police,* p. 166, with those of the Chief of Police in the *Annual Message of the Mayor, 1884,* p. 282.

85. *Laws and Ordinances Governing the City of Chicago, 1866,* p. 635; Richardson, *New York Police,* p. 202.

86. *New York Senate Documents* 1856, p. 45; *Chicago Tribune,* Oct. 29, 1885; Flinn, *History of the Chicago Police,* p. 382; Levine, "Police, Parties, and Polity," pp. 23, 37.

87. Calculated from the *Report of the General Superintendent of Police* from 1875 to 1885:

Year	Total strength		Patrolmen	
	No.	% change	No.	% change
1875	565		493	
1876	492	−12.9	416	− 15.6
1877	485	− 1.4	414	− .04
1878	409	−15.6	349	− 15.7
1879	430	5.1	357	2.2
1880	446	3.7	362	1.4
1881	476	6.7	379	4.6
1882	529	11.1	375	− 1.0
1883	605	14.3	451	20.2
1884	871	43.9	753	66.9
1885	868	− .03	737	− 2.1

88. *New York Times,* June 29, 1866; Levine, "Police, Parties, and Polity," p. 87.

89. This tentative conclusion is based upon a 20 percent random sample of the arrest data reported in the mayor's *Annual Messages,* 1873 to 1885. An analysis of patrolmen's attendance records for that period revealed no discernible policy of frequent transfers. These reports were badly biased, however. Of all reported arrests, 52.9 percent were for larceny. More common arrests, for offenses such as drunkenness and vagrancy, were severely underrepresented. A complete statistical picture of the Philadelphia police's arrest practices is therefore missing.

90. *Municipal Code of Chicago,* 1881, p. 209. The evidence on rotation was derived from a study of the First Precinct Arrest Book, January 2, 1875, to June 30, 1885, in the manuscript collection of the Chicago Historical Society. This daily blotter, which is the only extant precinct book of its kind for Chicago, actually contains data on two precincts. An analysis of the attendance records (100 percent sample) for one of these precincts reveals the following:

Effectiveness	*1875*	*1876*	*1877*	*1878*	*1879*	*1880*
Authorized strength	35	28	28	20	22	20
Number of different patrolmen who made arrests	34	NA	36	33	43	39

For more detailed analysis see David R. Johnson, "Law Enforcement in Chicago, 1875-1885," unpublished paper, 1968, pp. 49-62.

91. *New York Times,* Feb. 25, April 7, 1852; ibid., July 6, 1857; "Report of the Select Committee Appointed to Inquire into the Practice of Arrest, Detention and Discharge of Persons by Metropolitan Police Force," *New York State Senate Documents* 1861, 2 no. 71 (Albany: Van Benthuysen & Sons, 1861), pp. 6, 11, 12, 16. *Chicago Tribune,* Aug. 6, 1885, contains a number of letters from aldermen to police justices asking for favors to their constituents who were in trouble.

92. *New York Senate Documents* 1856, pp. 8-9; Richardson, *New York Police,* p. 204.

93. *Weekly Chicago Democrat,* Feb. 6, 1858.

94. *Public Ledger,* Oct. 9, 1856; ibid., May 19, 1863.

95. Ibid., Sept. 18, 1865.

96. Ibid., April 22, 1870.

97. J. Thomas Scharf and Thompson Westcott, *History of Philadelphia* (3 vols.; Philadelphia: L. H. Everts & Co., 1884), 3:1735.

98. G. T. Moore, letter to the editor, *Chicago Tribune,* Oct. 6, 1858.

99. Costello, *Our Police Protectors,* p. 125; *Weekly Chicago Democrat,* July 13, 1847; *Chicago Tribune,* March 17, 1857; Flinn, *History of the Chicago Police,* pp. 96, 98; *Annual Message of the Mayor, 1884,* p. 289. For obituaries of other career officers see: *Public Ledger,* July 20, 1868; ibid., Jan. 2, 1875; ibid., Jan. 15, 1877; Savage, *History of the Boston Watch and Police,* p. 5. See Table 2.

Chapter Five   **The Patrolman on the Street**

1. *Police Ordinance and Rules and Regulations for the Government of the Police Department, and Instructions as to the Powers and Duties of Police Officers of the City of Chicago* (Chicago: Daily Democrat Office, 1855), p. 26.

2. M.C.C., 15:238-41.

3. See, for example, the debate on this point between the *Public Ledger,* and the *Philadelphia Gazette* during April 1836.

4. *The Ariel* 5, no. 15 (Nov. 12, 1831): 230.

5. William H. Bell, unpublished diary, Aug. 19, 1851, New-York Historical Society.

6. *Brother Jonathan* 6, no. 4 (Sept. 23, 1843): 100; *Harbinger* 6, no. 3 (Nov. 20, 1847): 19; *Journal of Prison Discipline* 16, no. 4 (Oct. 1861): 208; *Public Ledger,* Sept. 26, 1862.

7. *Public Ledger,* Oct. 7, 1864.

8. *North American Review* 9 (Sept. 1819): 307.

9. *Public Ledger,* April 12, 1855.

10. Stephen Thernstrom, *Poverty and Progress: Social Mobility in a Nineteenth-Century City* (Cambridge: Harvard University Press, 1964), p. 31.

11. Charles Christian, *A Brief Treatise on the Police of the City of New York* (New York: Southwick & Pelsue, 1812), p. 8; *Public Ledger,* Nov. 2, 1847; *Chicago Tribune,* Jan. 6, 1864.

12. *Public Ledger,* Sept. 1, 1849; ibid., July 7, 1855. Emphasis in original.

13. *Journal of Prison Discipline* 6, no. 1 (Jan. 1851): 103.

14. On early liquor problems, see Carl Bridenbaugh, *Cities in the Wilderness: The First Century of Urban Life in America, 1625-1742* (New York: Alfred A. Knopf, 1964), pp. 271-74. For a discussion of juvenile delinquency, see Robert S. Pickett, *House of Refuge: Origins of Juvenile Reform in New York State, 1815-1857* (Syracuse, N.Y.: Syracuse University Press, 1869), and Chapter Two above.

15. Cf. James Q. Wilson, *Varieties of Police Behavior: The Management of Law and Order in Eight Communities* (Cambridge: Harvard University Press, 1968), p. 140.

16. *New York Senate Documents* 1856, p. 14.

17. Bell, unpub. diary, Nov. 11, 1850.

18. *Public Ledger,* March 17, 1845.

19. Ibid., June 21, 1855; *Chicago Tribune,* Sept. 10, 1857.

20. *Public Ledger,* Feb. 5, 1853.

21. *New York Senate Documents* 1856, p. 129; *Chicago Tribune,* April 5, 1859; ibid., May 28, 1873.

22. *Chicago Tribune,* Jan. 25, 1873.

23. *Public Ledger,* April 13, 1850.

24. Robert S. Reed, *Police Manual: Being Rules and Regulations for the Organization and Government of the Consolidated Police of the City of Philadelphia* (Philadelphia: King & Baird, 1855), pp. 49-50.

25. See, for example, *Public Ledger,* April 8, 1851; ibid., July 21, 1852; ibid., Jan. 1, 1859.

26. For some examples of the shifting nature of complaints against corner loungers, see the map of gang activity in Chapter 2. Street-corner gangs, the most short-lived of those groups, are well scattered over the city, and their locations are rarely based on more than one complaint regarding their behavior, indicating the migratory nature of this problem facing the police.

27. *Public Ledger,* May 28, 1866.

28. *Chicago Tribune,* July 17, 1880.

29. Bell, unpub. diary, May 19, 1851.

30. *Public Ledger,* Aug. 30, 1870.

31. George A. Ketcham. "Municipal Police Reform: A Comparative Study of Law Enforcement in Cincinnati, Chicago, New Orleans, New York, and Saint Louis, 1844-1877" (Ph.D. diss., University of Missouri, 1967), p. 238.

32. *Laws and Ordinances Governing the City of Chicago* (Chicago: Bulletin Printing Co., 1873), p. 100; Bell, unpub. diary, May 14, 1851.

33. *Public Ledger,* Sept. 2, 1840; ibid., Sept. 5, 1848; ibid., April 8, 28, 1851; ibid., July 21, 1852.

34. *Chicago Tribune,* July 20, 1857; *Public Ledger,* Feb. 20, 1861; ibid., Sept. 27, Nov. 19, 26, 27, 1875; ibid., Jan. 9, 1877.

35. *Chicago Tribune,* Sept. 1, 1859.

36. *Public Ledger,* May 24, 1836. See also ibid., May 16, 30, 1836; *New York Herald,* Jan. 23, 1840.

37. E. F. Vidocq, *Les Voleurs: Physiologie de leurs Moeurs et de leur Language* (2 vols.; Paris: Chez L'Auteur, 1837), 1:45-46.

38. Bell, unpub. diary, April 12, May 5, 1851; *Chicago Tribune,* Jan. 21, 1880. See also *Public Ledger,* Dec. 19, 1849; *Chicago Tribune,* Sept. 25, 1857.

39. Bell, unpub. diary, May 14, 1851, and passim.

40. *Chicago Tribune,* July 9, 1880.

41. From an account reprinted in the *Chicago Democrat,* Aug. 10, 1847.

42. *Chicago Tribune,* April 9, 1858.

43. *Public Ledger,* May 25, 1849; Bell, unpub. diary, June 11, 1851.

44. Shanley v. Wells, 71 Ill. 78.

45. In 1883 a Chicago judge had to issue an order forbidding arrests of suspicious persons on charges of vagrancy. *Chicago Tribune,* March 30, 1883.

46. *Public Ledger,* March 13, 1862.

47. Ibid., Aug. 9, 1856. ibid., April 21, 1860.

48. Ibid., May 17, 1862.

49. Ibid., Oct. 31, 1865.

50. Ibid., June 12, 1851; ibid., July 23, 1852; ibid., June 1, 1874; Edwin H. Fitler to [?], July 25, 1877, Edwin H. Fitler Collection, Historical Society of Pennsylvania.

51. Nicholas B. Wainwright, ed., *A Philadelphia Perspective: The Diary of Sidney George Fisher Covering the Years 1834 to 1871* (Philadelphia: Historical Society of Pennsylvania, 1967), pp. 341, 344; Bell, unpub. diary, July 24, 1851.

52. Technological change also contributed to the decline of rioting. See David R. Johnson, "Crime Patterns in Philadelphia, 1840-70," in *The Peoples of Philadelphia: A History of Ethnic Groups and Lower-Class Life, 1790-1940,* ed. Allen F. Davis and Mark H. Haller (Philadelphia: Temple University Press, 1973), pp. 103-4.

53. Assaults on officers can be followed in the daily press of practically any city. For example: *Public Ledger,* June 16, 1840; ibid., Jan. 4, 18, 1845; ibid., April 8, 1850; ibid., Dec. 1, 1857; ibid., Feb. 7, 1860; ibid., June 27, 1866; ibid., July 6, 1871; *Chicago Tribune,* June 6, 7, Dec. 6, 1853; ibid., Aug. 13, 1861; ibid., March 11, 1872; *New York Times,* Jan. 23, April 13, 1852; ibid., July 13, 1857; *Atlanta Constitution,* May 4, 1875; ibid., June 28, 1885.

54. On police arrogance, see *Public Ledger,* May 2, July 11, 1859; *Chicago Times,* Aug. 8, 1865; *Chicago Tribune,* July 31, 1866; William R. Balch, "The Police Problem," *International Review* 13 (Dec. 1882): 507-8. The failure to search prisoners was a distinctive feature in many news accounts of arrests; see the *Public Ledger,* Oct. 14, 1863; Aug. 23, 1875; and note 53 above for further examples.

55. An important exception is Lee Kennett and James La-Verne Anderson, *The Gun in America: The Origins of a National Dilemma* (Westport, Conn.: Greenwood Press, 1975). Pp. 145-51 are especially pertinent to my discussion. Wilbur R. Miller, Jr., *Cops and Bobbies: Police Authority in New York and London, 1830-1870* (Chicago: University of Chicago Press, 1977), pp. 21-22, 51-54, 145-47, 169, also discusses firearms, but not from the perspective of social attitudes and uses of weapons.

56. *Kentucky Gazette,* Aug. 29, 1798, quoted in James M. Smith, "The Grass Roots Origins of the Kentucky Resolutions," *William and Mary Quarterly* ser. 3, 27, no. 2 (April 1970): 235.

57. Quoted in the *Public Ledger,* Nov. 29, 1844, emphasis in original.

58. *New York Courier* and *Enquirer,* quoted in the *New York Herald,* Oct. 1, 1844. The *Herald* also reprinted editorials from other Whig newspapers on the same day, all containing similar advice.

59. *New York Herald,* Oct. 1, 1844.

60. Wainwright, ed., *A Philadelphia Perspective,* pp. 167-68. Also see the *Public Ledger,* Nov. 15, 1844, for an eyewitness account of the distribution and use of firearms during the riots.

61. For example, *Public Ledger,* Jan. 11, Oct. 8, 1840.

62. Ibid., July 25, 1844.

63. *New York Daily Tribune,* June 11, 1845.

64. Allen Nevins and Milton H. Thomas, eds., *The Diary of George Templeton Strong* (4 vols.; New York: Macmillan, 1952), 2:320.

65. *Chicago Tribune,* Feb. 7, 1860, letter to editor signed "North Division." See also ibid., May 23, 1855; ibid., Jan. 14, 1856; ibid., Aug. 8, 1861.

66. *Public Ledger,* Nov. 14, 26, 28, Dec. 18, 1849.

67. Ibid., May 27, 1850. See also the *Albany* (N.Y.) *Evening Journal,* n.d., quoted in the *Public Ledger,* Aug. 19, 1850, for the use of firearms against police in that city.

68. Ibid., May 2, 1859.

69. *Chicago Tribune,* Aug. 21, 1873. For views in favor of arming, see also the letter to the editor signed "Many Citizens of the S.W. District," *Public Ledger,* May 1, 1850; R. Ludlow to Alexander Henry, Aug. 24, 1865, Alexander Henry Papers, HSP. The *Chicago Tribune* consistently favored the use of firearms; see for example June 16, July 20, 1857; ibid., March 19, 1873. Anti-arming view are expressed in a letter to the editor signed "The Public Good," *Public Ledger,* Aug. 24, 1850, and in an editorial in ibid., Oct. 15, 1849.

70. Quoted in the *Public Ledger,* March 31, 1873.

71. Ibid., Sept. 9, 1854; ibid., Aug. 17, 31, 1855.

72. James F. Richardson, *The New York Police: Colonial Times to 1901* (New York: Oxford University Press, 1970), p. 113; Roger Lane, *Policing the City: Boston, 1822-1885* (Cambridge: Harvard University Press, 1967), p. 104.

73. A rare instance where an officer flourished a pistol was recorded in the *Public Ledger*, Jan. 4, 1845. But see the *New York Daily Tribune*, Aug. 9, 1845, and the *New York Herald*, April 10, 1848, for examples of more typical arrests.

74. For examples see the *Public Ledger*, Sept. 12, 1849; ibid., July 6, 1850; ibid., April 25, 1851; ibid., July 7, 1852; ibid., May 4, 1853; ibid., Jan. 21, 1856; ibid., Aug. 24, 1859; *Chicago Tribune*, Sept. 19, 1854; ibid., Aug. 7, 1858.

75. *Public Ledger*, April 25, 1851; ibid., Nov. 3, 1859.

76. *Chicago Tribune*, Sept. 19, 1854.

77. Benjamin T. Sewell, *Sorrow's Circuit, or Five Years' Experience in the Bedford Street Mission, Philadelphia*, rev. Rev. J. B. McCullough (Philadelphia: Jespar Harding & Son, 1859), p. 333; *Public Ledger*, July 15, 1872. Other examples of abuse appeared regularly in the press. See the *Public Ledger*, Aug. 11, 1855; ibid., April 1, 1861; ibid., Dec. 17, 1875; *Chicago Tribune*, July 31, 1866; ibid., April 29, 1873; ibid., Sept. 11, 1884; *Leslie's Illustrated* 22 (Sept. 15, 1866): 402.

78. *Chicago Times*, Feb. 1, 1864; John J. Flinn, *History of the Chicago Police from the Earliest Settlement of the Community to the Present Time* (Chicago: W. B. Conkey, 1887), p. 359.

79. Langdon W. Moore, *Langdon W. Moore: His Own Story of His Eventful Life* (Boston: Langdon W. Moore, 1893), p. 126.

80. *Public Ledger*, Dec. 29, 1870.

81. Ibid., Dec. 23, 1872.

82. Howard O. Sprogle, *History of the Philadelphia Police* (Philadelphia: n.p., 1887), p. 108.

83. George W. Walling, *Recollections of a New York Chief of Police* (New York: Caxton Book Concern, 1887), p. 48.

84. *Public Ledger*, Sept. 17, 1850; ibid., Dec. 31, 1852; ibid., Jan. 17, 1859; ibid., April 22, 1874; *Chicago Tribune*, March 12, April 3, 1856; ibid., June 8, 1858.

85. *Public Ledger*, Nov. 28, 1855.

86. Edward H. Savage, *A Chronological History of the Boston Watch and Police from 1631 to 1865* . . . (Boston: Published and Sold by the Author, 1865), p. 346, emphasis in original.

87. *Chicago Tribune*, March 19, 1873.

Notes   223

88. Police departments unfortunately did not keep consistent records of disturbances suppressed without arrests. Boston's former police chief J. L. C. Amee claimed that in two years (1861-1863) his department quieted 15,500 incidents in this manner, and escorted home 4,367 drunks. Chicago began keeping track of this tactic in 1881. J. L. C. Amee, *Farewell Address to the Boston Police Department* (Boston: n.p., 1863), p. 5; *Report of the General Superintendent of Police of the City of Chicago to the City Council for the Year 1881* (Chicago: The City Council of Chicago, 1881).

89. [?] Daughin to Mayor Alexander Henry, Dec. 30, 1863, Henry Papers, HSP.

90. *Public Ledger,* Aug. 3, 1854.

91. Walling, *Recollections,* pp. 507, 509.

92. I do not mean to imply here that the police were the *only* means of establishing a greater degree of order in post-Civil War America than had existed before. Other important social trends, such as continuing urbanization and industrialization, also contributed to that development. For a provocative analysis of the role these trends played in reducing disorder, see Roger Lane, "Urbanization and Criminal Violence in the Nineteenth Century," *Journal of Social History* 2, no. 2 (Dec. 1968): 156-63, and Howard Zehr, "The Modernization of Crime in Germany and France, 1830-1913," *Journal of Social History,* 8 (Summer 1975): 117-41.

93. For a discussion of professionalism see Everett C. Hughes, "Professions," *Daedalus* 92 (Fall 1963): 655-68.

94. Walling, *Recollections,* p. 100. The statue was noted in the *Public Ledger,* Feb. 5, 1872.

95. *Public Ledger,* March 8, 1860.

96. *Chicago Times,* Aug. 8, 1865.

97. *New York Times,* July 18, 1866.

98. *Chicago Tribune,* July 31, 1866.

99. *Public Ledger,* March 4, 5, 1869.

100. *New York Times,* July 24, 1875.

Chapter Six   Policing Sin

1. *Chicago Tribune,* Nov. 24, 1865.

2. John S. Haller, Jr., and Robin M. Haller, *The Physician and Sexuality in Victorian America* (Urbana: University of Illinois Press, 1974), pp. 237-38.

3. For typical condemnations of gambling see Jonathan H. Green, *Gambling Exposed: A Full Exposition of All the Various Arts,*

Mysteries and Miseries of Gambling (Philadelphia: T. B. Patterson & Bros., 1857), and John P. Quinn, *Fools of Fortune; or, Gambling and Gamblers, Comprehending a History of the Vice in Ancient and Modern Times* (Chicago: The Anti-Gambling Association, 1892).

4. *Public Ledger,* June 10, 1840.

5. The following discussion of prostitution draws upon the evidence presented in: William W. Sanger, *The History of Prostitution* (New York: Eugenie's Publishing Co., 1939), pp. 549-74; Edward Crapsey, *The Nether Side of New York; or the Vice, Crime and Poverty of the Great Metropolis* (rpt.; Montclair, N. J.: Patterson Smith, 1969), pp. 138-39, 142-43; *A Guide to the Stranger, or Pocket Companion for the Fancy, Containing a List of the Gay Houses and Ladies of Pleasure in the City of Brotherly Love and Sisterly Affection* (Philadelphia: n. p., 1849); *Sporting and Club House Directory* (Chicago: n.p., c. 1890). I have rearranged classifications somewhat to account for distinctions noted in contemporary press commentary. See, for example, *New York Post,* Sept. 5, 1857, reprinted in *Chicago Tribune,* Sept. 10, 1857.

6. Robert S. Pickett, *House of Refuge: Origins of Juvenile Reform in New York State, 1815-1857* (Syracuse, N.Y.: Syracuse University Press, 1969), pp. 70-71.

7. William H. Bell, unpublished diary, June 10, 1851, New-York Historical Society.

8. *Public Ledger,* March 15, 1850; ibid., March 14, 1851; ibid., Feb. 14, 1863; *Chicago Tribune,* April 11, 1853.

9. Sanger, *History of Prostitution,* pp. 523-524; *Public Ledger,* Feb. 27, 1855; *Chicago Tribune,* July 2, 1861.

10. *Public Ledger,* Dec. 29, 1855; *Chicago Tribune,* Feb. 22, 1858; *Chicago Times,* Oct. 19, 1865.

11. *Public Ledger,* March 6, 1857; ibid., Nov. 14, 1874 (supp.); *Chicago Tribune,* Feb. 12, 1864.

12. Letter to the editor signed "A Woman," *Chicago Tribune,* March 15, 1862.

13. *Public Ledger,* March 6, 1857; *Chicago Tribune,* Feb. 12, 1864; Sanger, *History of Prostitution,* p. 496.

14. Sanger, *History of Prostitition,* pp. 460, 491-92, 524; Guardians of the Poor, Prostitutes Register [c. 1868], Philadelphia Department of Records, Archives Division, passim; *New York Times,* Aug. 4, 1866. For an extended discussion of this point see Jacqueline B. Barnhart, "Working Women: Prostitution in San Francisco from the Gold Rush to 1900" (Ph.D. diss., University of California, San Francisco, 1976).

15. Crapsey, *The Nether Side,* p. 138.

16. *Public Ledger,* May 21, 1866; ibid., Aug. 10, 1872; ibid., Feb. 15, July 2, 1878. See Chapter Two for the location of the business district. Boardinghouse concentrations were plotted from a business directory for 1859-1860.

17. Federick F. Cook, *Bygone Days in Chicago: Recollections of the "Garden City" of the Sixties* (Chicago: A. C. McClurg & Co., 1910), pp. 130-31, 134-35; Walter C. Reckless, "Natural History of Vice Areas in Chicago" (Ph.D. diss., University of Chicago, 1925), p. 21; *Chicago Tribune,* Nov. 5, 1885.

18. I am assuming here that streetwalkers generally charged less than the cheapest rate in parlor houses. In 1890 the lowest rate in Chicago's brothels was three dollars. See *Sporting and Club House Directory,* passim. On the rate for the lowest sort of prostitute, see Crapsey, *The Nether Side,* p. 138.

19. An analysis of Chicago's prostitutes in 1870 estimated that 5,500 women did not reside in parlor houses. Of that number, over half operated in squads of two or three in order to defray rent costs. But there was no mention of pimps directing these squads. *Chicago Times,* Feb. 20, 1870.

20. An exception to this may have been in cases where prostitutes allied with thieves to operate panel houses. Crapsey, *The Nether Side,* p. 141, recounts the story of King Badger, who behaved much like a pimp in his dealings with his prostitutes.

21. Matthew H. Smith, *Sunshine and Shadow in New York* (Hartford: J. B. Burr & Co., 1868), p. 378. In New York 73.10 percent of the women had been prostitutes for four years or less; 87.65 percent in Philadelphia. Calculated from Sanger, *History of Prostitution,* p. 484; Philadelphia Guardians of the Poor, Prostitutes Register.

22. *Public Ledger,* May 22, 1850; ibid., Nov. 30, 1852; *Chicago Tribune,* March 23, 1859.

23. Sanger, *History of Prostitution,* pp. 518-19; *Chicago Tribune,* May 24, 1865.

24. *Chicago Tribune,* July 2, 1861; *Public Ledger,* Nov. 6, 1874.

25. *Chicago Tribune,* Feb. 22, 1860.

26. Ibid., April 25, 1873.

27. *Public Ledger,* Jan. 8, 1874.

28. Ibid., April 10, 1875.

29. George C. Edwards, *A Treatise on the Powers and Duties of Justices of the Peace,* rev. D. McMaster (4th ed.; Ithaca: Mark, Andrus, and Woodruff, 1840), p. 219.

30. Copy of a letter from "Lizzie" to Thomas Hall, reprinted in the *Chicago Tribune,* July 25, 1863; Sanger, *History of Prostitution,* p. 519.

31. This analysis is based upon the sources cited in note 5 above.

32. *Public Ledger,* Dec. 19, 1840; ibid., Sept. 4, Nov. 15, 1854; ibid., March 28, 1855.

33. *A Guide to the Stranger . . . North of Market Street: Being the Adventures of a New York Woman in Philadelphia* (Philadelphia: Avil Printing Co., 1896).

34. *Chicago Tribune,* May 14, Dec. 27, 1855; ibid., Feb. 13, April 4, July 21, Nov. 28, 1857; ibid., Sept. 29, 1862; ibid., July 14, 1875; *Chicago Times,* Feb. 20, 1870; *Morris' Dictionary of Chicago and Vicinity* (Chicago: n.p., 1891), p. 48; Reckless, "Natural History of Vice Areas in Chicago," pp. 31-32.

35. These estimates are based upon the following calculations: One woman entertained a minimum of two customers per day at five dollars each. Working a six-day week, she would earn a gross income of sixty dollars from which the madame would subtract twelve dollars for customer service fees and sixteen for boarding, leaving the net income of thirty-two dollars. There is no evidence that madames doubled their service fees by 1890. I am assuming that for purposes of illustration. See Sanger, *History of Prostitution,* p. 554; *Sporting and Club House Directory* for pricing information.

36. Assuming six customers per day since this class had to depend on a large volume of business.

37. Cf. wages reported in Norman Ware, *The Industrial Worker, 1840-1860: The Reaction of American Industrial Society to the Advance of the Industrial Revolution* (Chicago: Quandrangle Books, 1964), p. 119; Stanley Buder, *Pullman: An Experiment in Industrial Order and Community Planning, 1880-1930* (New York: Oxford University Press, 1967), pp. 164-65.

38. Sanger, *History of Prostitution,* p. 554; Herbert Asbury, *Gem of the Prairie; an Informal History of the Chicago Underworld* (New York: Alfred A. Knopf, 1940), pp. 135-40.

39. Sanger, *History of Prostitution,* p. 600. Figures for Chicago were calculated on the basis of twelve customers per prostitute per week at five dollars each for fifty weeks. This produced an estimate of $1,212,000 per year for Chicago's top houses, which had a total of 404 women. See the *Sporting and Club House Directory.*

40. Sanger, *History of Prostitution,* p. 601. The *Chicago Times,* February 20, 1870, estimated there were 4,000 prostitutes in Chicago.

Using Sanger's calculation of ten dollars a week as the average earnings of all prostitutes produced a total estimated income of $3,640,000.

41. Sanger, *History of Prostitution,* pp. 627-76; Crapsey, *The Nether Side,* p. 145; "Report of the Select Committe Appointed by the Assembly of 1875 to Investigate the Causes of the Increase of Crime in the City of New York," *Documents of the Assembly of the State of New York,* vol. 6, no. 106 (1876): 31 (hereafter cited as *New York Assembly Documents* 1876); James Wunsch, "Licensing Prostitution in New York City," paper in the author's possession, p. 7; Haller and Haller, *The Physician and Sexuality in Victorian America,* pp. 243-43.

42. See below.

43. For a more detailed analysis of the growth and organization of gambling, see David R. Johnson, "A Sinful Business: The Origins of Gambling Syndicates in the United States, 1840-1887," in *Police and Society,* ed. David Bayley (Beverly Hills: Sage Publications, 1977), pp. 17-48.

44. George H. Devol, *Forty Years a Gambler on the Mississippi* (2nd ed.; New York: G. H. Devol, 1892), passim; Henry E. Hugunin, *Life and Adventures of Henry Edward Hugunin, or Thirty Years a Gambler* (New York: R. J. Oliphant, 1879), pp. 14-16, 40-41.

45. *Hoyle's Games* (Philadelphia: n.p., 1857), pp. 99-104; William B. Dick, *The American Hoyle; or Gentleman's Hand-Book of Games* (New York: Dick & Fitzgerald, 1880), pp. 272-80; Herbert Asbury, *Sucker's Progress; an Informal History of Gambling in America from the Colonies to Canfield* (New York: Dodd, Mead, & Co., 1938), pp. 6, 10-11, 12-14.

46. *New York Herald,* July 30, 1835; *Chicago Tribune,* March 31, 1857; ibid., Jan. 28, 1858; ibid., Jan. 9, 1865; ibid., July 7, 1870; Crapsey, *The Nether Side,* pp. 93-95; Smith, *Sunshine and Shadow,* pp. 394-98, 406-7.

47. *New York Times,* July 10, 1871; ibid., Feb. 15, 1885; *Chicago Daily Democrat,* March 26, 1860; *Chicago Tribune,* Nov. 1, 1873; ibid., Nov. 22, 24, 1874; ibid., May 26, Aug. 13, 1875; George Foster, *New York in Slices: By an Experienced Carver* (New York: William H. Graham, 1849), pp. 28-29, 30; Jonathan H. Green, *Gambling Exposed,* p. 158n; Jonathan H. Green, *Twelve Days in the Tombs; or, a Sketch of the Last Eight Years of the Reformed Gambler's Life* (New York: T. W. Strong, 1851), pp. 104-5; Ferdinand Longchamp, *Asmodeus in New York* (New York: Longchamp & Co., 1868), p. 142; Crapsey, *The Nether Side,* pp. 92-93, 97; Quinn, *Fools*

of Fortune, pp. 405, 423-24; Asbury, *Sucker's Progress,* pp. 14, 161.
   48. *Chicago Tribune,* Aug. 13, 1875; ibid., July 22, 1885;
Reckless, "Natural History of Vice Areas in Chicago," p. 24; *New
York Times,* March 19, 1871; ibid., May 4, 1883; ibid., Jan. 21, 22,
1885; *Public Ledger,* March 16, 1855; ibid., Dec. 10, 1859.
   49. I am indebted to Professor Mark Haller of Temple University for pointing out Irish attitudes toward gambling.
   50. Johnson, "A Sinful Business," pp. 24-27, 36-37. Also, see
below.
   51. John Aston, *The History of Gambling in England* (1898
ed.; Montclair, N.J.: Patterson Smith Publishing Co., 1969), chaps.
17-18; John S. Ezell, *Fortune's Merry Wheel: The Lottery in America*
(Cambridge: Harvard University Press, 1960), pp. 95-98; Asbury,
Sucker's Progress, pp. 89, 92-95; *Public Ledger,* June 12, 1845. A gig
was three numbers bet to appear anywhere on a lottery drawing list.
   52. *New York Senate Documents* 1856, pp. 29-31; Asbury,
Sucker's Progress, pp. 91-92.
   53. Asbury, *Sucker's Progress,* p. 97; *New York Times,* Nov.
28, 1869; *Public Ledger,* Dec. 19, 1872; Edward W. Martin [James D.
McCabe], *The Secrets of the Great City; a Work Description of the
Virtues and the Vices, the Mysteries, Miseries, and the Crimes of New
York City* (Philadelphia: Jones, Brothers & Co., 1868), p. 518; Ezell,
Fortune's Merry Wheel, p. 231.
   54. This analysis is based upon the evidence of two detailed
inquiries into policy. See: letter to the editor signed Phil., *New York
Times,* April 26, 1856; *Chicago Tribune,* Nov. 21, 1875.
   55. Johnson, "A Sinful Business," pp. 31-32.
   56. Ibid., pp. 33-34.
   57. *New York Times,* Dec. 31, 1869; ibid., Dec. 27, 1873.
   58. Mark Haller, "The Rise of Urban Crime Syndicates, 1865-
1905," unpublished paper, p. 12.
   59. John Hervey, *Racing in America, 1665-1865* (2 vols.; New
York: Privately Printed by the Jockey Club, 1944), 2:377-79; Charles
P. Parmer, *For Gold and Glory: The Story of Thoroughbred Racing in
America* (New York: Carrick and Evans, 1939), chap. 7; *New York
Times, Sept. 22, 1866.*
   60. *Chicago Tribune,* Aug. 8, 1870.
   61. Asbury, *Sucker's Progress,* pp. 382-84; Hugh Bradley, *Such
Was Saratoga* (New York: Doubleday, Doran & Co., 1940), pp. 142-45.
   62. *Chicago Tribune,* July 28, 1870; ibid., Aug. 1, 1875; Asbury,
Sucker's Progress, pp. 121-22, 391-92, 396.

63. Haller, "The Rise of Gambling Syndicates," unpublished paper, pp. 5, 11.

64. Johnson, "A Sinful Business," pp. 35-36.

65. Letter to the editor signed "G," *New York Times,* April 13, 1868. Not much is known about the origins and backgrounds of pool sellers prior to 1860. For a typically cryptic comment on the careers of these men, see *Chicago Tribune,* Aug. 1, 1875.

66. *New York Times,* Aug. 4, 1864; *Chicago Tribune,* July 7, 18, 1865.

67. *New York Times,* Sept. 25, 1866; John R. Betts, "The Technological Revolution and the Rise of Sports," *Mississippi Valley Historical Review* 40, no. 2 (Sept. 1953): 238-40.

68. These men were all first identified with faro or other forms of gambling before the local press tied them to pool selling. See: *New York Times,* May 17, July 10, 1871; ibid., April 14, 29, 1875; ibid., July 26, Aug. 1, 1878; ibid., July 23, 1880. On poolrooms and their connection with gamblers in Chicago see: *Chicago Tribune,* March 6, 1870; ibid., Sept. 11, 18, 1875.

69. Johnson, "A Sinful Business," pp. 37-38.

70. Letter to the editor signed "Fielder," *New York Times,* June 6, 1875; Bradley, *Such Was Saratoga,* pp. 281-82.

71. *New York Times,* Dec. 10, 11, 12, 1876; ibid., Jan. 11, 12, 19, 27, Feb. 7, March 8, 1877; *Laws of the State of New York* (Albany: Weed, Parsons & Co., 1877), 1:192.

72. *New York Times,* June 6, 1885.

73. Ibid., May 21, 23, 1877.

74. Ibid., Sept. 29, 1881.

75. Frank G. Menke, *The Story of Churchill Downs and the Kentucky Derby* (Louisville: n.p., 1940), pp. 20-21.

76. Washington Park Jockey Club, *History of the American Derby* (Chicago: n.p., 1940), n.p.; *Chicago Tribune,* July 24, 31, 1887.

77. M. R. Werner, *Tammany Hall* (Garden City: Doubleday, Doran & Company, Inc., 1928), pp. 84-85; Longchamp, *Asmodeus in New York,* pp. 143-144; Commonwealth v. City of Frankfort, Simmons and Dickinson, E. S. Stewart, & c., 76 Ky. (13 Bush) 185, 345.

78. *New York Times,* July 13, 1875.

79. *Public Ledger,* March 5, 1853, and Aug. 2, 1855, illustrates the possibility of arranging to pay officers to avoid arrest or to obtain release from jail.

80. George Wilkes, *The Mysteries of the Tombs, a Journal of Thirty Days Imprisonment in the New York City Prison* (New York: George Wilkes, 1844), pp. 39ff; *New York Senate Documents 1856,* pp. 28-29, 31, 37-38; *Chicago Tribune,* May 28, 1857.

81. For indications that this kind of corruption persisted in spite of salary reforms, see *Public Ledger,* March 14, July 27, 1860; ibid., Aug. 16, 1862; *Chicago Tribune,* Dec. 20, 1864.

82. *New York Senate Documents 1856,* pp. 37, 209-12; *New York Times,* May 4, 1880; *Chicago Tribune,* May 20, 1858; ibid., Jan. 15, 19, 27, 1868; ibid., July 10, 1873; ibid., Jan. 2, 1880.

83. Haller and Haller, *The Physician and Sexuality in Victorian America,* p. 243.

84. *New York Assembly Documents 1876,* pp. 7, 15-16; *New York Times,* July 9, 1882; ibid., Aug. 2, 1883; ibid., May 11, 1884; George W. Walling, *Recollections of a New York Chief of Police* (New York: Caxton Book Concern, 1887), p. 380; Alexander B. Callow, Jr., *The Tweed Ring* (New York: Oxford University Press, 1966), p. 147.

85. *Chicago Times,* Aug. 15, 1874. Arrest data on Rehm's roundup of vice figures came from an analysis from the *Report of the Board of Police, in the Police Department, to the Common Council of the City of Chicago, 1873-1875.* Rehm's role in the Whiskey Ring is noted in George A. Ketcham, "Municipal Police Reform: A Comparative Study of Law Enforcement in Cincinnati, Chicago, New Orleans, New York, and Saint Louis, 1844-1877" (Ph.D. diss., University of Missouri, 1967), p. 202.

86. *Chicago Times,* Aug. 15, 1874; ibid., July 19, 21, 1879; *Chicago Tribune,* July 18, 19, 20, 25, 1879.

87. Alfred T. Andreas, *History of Chicago: From the Earliest Period to the Present* (3 vols.; Chicago: A. T. Andreas, 1884-1886), 2:505; *Chicago Daily News,* Nov. 4, 1926.

88. McDonald was a famous Chicago character in later years. The best synopsis of his early career appeared in the *Chicago Herald,* Oct. 27, 1882.

89. *Chicago Tribune,* Feb. 2, Nov. 2, 1873; ibid., Feb. 14, 1875; ibid., Oct. 27, 29, 1882; *Chicago Times,* Feb. 8, 1874; *Chicago Herald,* Oct. 27, 1882.

90. Foster, *New York in Slices,* pp. 29-30; *New York Senate Documents 1856,* pp. 280-81, 286; *Chicago Tribune,* Dec. 19, 1860.

91. William E. Harding, comp., *John Morrissey, His Life, Battles, and Wrangles, from His Birth in Ireland until He Died a State Senator* (New York: The Police Gazette, 1881) pp. 7-9, 13-15; Werner, *Tammany Hall,* p. 68; *New York Times,* May 2, 1878; Bradley; *Such Was Saratoga,* p. 139-40.

92. Bradley, *Such Was Saratoga,* pp. 140, 142-45; Asbury, *Sucker's Progress,* pp. 382-84; 388; *New York Times,* Oct. 3, 4, 1868; ibid., May 2, 1878.

93. Matthew P. Breen, *Thirty Years of New York Politics Up-to-Date* (New York: Published by the Author, 1899), pp. 529, 533; Werner, *Tammany Hall,* p. 288; *New York Times,* Dec. 10, 11, 12, 1876; ibid., May 2, 1877; ibid., May 2, 1878; *Chicago Tribune,* Feb. 28, March 21, 1875.

94. Andreas, *History of Chicago,* 3:101; Asbury, *Sucker's Progress,* pp. 300-301; Bessie L. Pierce, *History of Chicago* (3 vols.; New York: Alfred A. Knopf, 1937-1957), 3:343.

95. *Chicago Tribune,* Oct. 15, 31, 1873; ibid., Feb. 20, Nov. 7, 1875; ibid., Feb. 19, 1880; *Lakeside Annual Directory of the City of Chicago, 1876-1877* (Chicago: The Lakeside Press, 1877), p. 30.

96. Cf. *Chicago Tribune,* April 7, Oct. 20, Nov. 3, 1875; ibid., Nov. 3, 1880; ibid., April 6, 1881; ibid., March 1, 1885.

97. *Chicago Times,* Nov. 25, 1878.

98. *Chicago Tribune,* Dec. 4, 1879; ibid., Jan 7, 1880.

99. Ibid., June 3, 1885.

100. *New York Times,* May 2, 1877; Callow, *The Tweed Ring,* p. 145.

101. *Public Ledger,* Dec. 27, 1872; ibid., Jan. 2, 6, 18, 24, 25, Feb. 3, 7, 8, 18, 1873. The assault on the gamblers continued through the year, but at much reduced levels after February.

102. *New York Times,* Feb. 12, 1856; *Chicago Tribune,* Feb. 20, 1875.

103. *Chicago Tribune,* Feb. 8, 11, 1865.

104. *New York Senate Documents* 1856, pp. 280-81, 286; *Chicago Tribune,* March 27, April 18, 1875.

105. *Chicago Tribune,* March 23, 1865; *Chicago Staats-Zeitung,* quoted in ibid., Feb. 1, 1875; *New York Times,* May 5, 1879; ibid., Feb. 17, 1885.

106. *Chicago Tribune,* Jan. 6, 1880.

107. *New York Times,* March 20, 1858; Martin, *Secrets of the Great City,* p. 387; Langdon W. Moore, *Langdon W. Moore: His Own Story of His Eventful Life* (Boston: Langdon W. Moore, 1893), pp. 494-95; Quinn, *Fools of Fortune,* p. 190.

108. *New York Senate Documents* 1856, p. 142.

109. Devol, *Forty Years a Gambler,* pp. 14-15.

110. *Public Ledger,* Aug. 26, 1872.

111. *Chicago Times,* Feb. 20, 1870.

112. *Chicago Tribune,* July 12, 1863; Cook, *Bygone Days in Chicago,* pp. 150-51; John J. Flinn, *History of the Chicago Police*

from the Earliest Settlement of the Community to the Present Time
(Chicago: W. B. Conkey, 1887), pp. 99, 104-6.
    113. *New York Times,* April 22, 1883.

Conclusion

    1. Wilbur R. Miller, Jr., *Cops and Bobbies: Police Authority in
New York and London, 1830-1870* (Chicago: University of Chicago
Press, 1977), pp. 140-41.

Bibliographical Note

An interest in American law enforcement is a relatively recent development among historians. Systematic research and publication in this area began only in the 1960s, spurred perhaps by the social and political turmoil of that decade. The study of crime in this country is an equally recent phenomenon which is even less well developed than the analysis of policing because only a handful of historians have been working on ordinary criminal behavior (as distinguished from the study of violence). Our understanding of both the police and the criminal is therefore in its formative stages, although enough has been done to indicate some fruitful directions for research. My purpose here is to indicate the most important studies which contributed to my understanding of these subjects, and to suggest areas which need further research.

Sociologists have produced many important works on policing and crime which proved crucial to my early struggles with the basic framework for this study. The best works on the police for my purposes proved to be: Wayne R. LaFave, *Arrest: The Decision to Take a Suspect into Custody* (Boston: Little, Brown, 1965), the best study of the intricacies involved in the use of police discretion in contemporary society; Jerome H. Skolnick, *Justice without Trial: Law Enforcement in Democratic Society* (New York: Wiley, 1966), an important examination of actual police behavior in modern America; William A. Westley, *Violence and the Police: A Sociological Study of Law, Custom, and Morality* (Cambridge, Mass.: M.I.T. Press, 1970), the classic study of police violence; and James Q. Wilson, *Varieties of Police Behavior: The Management of Law and Order in Eight Communities* (Cambridge, Mass.: Harvard University Press, 1968), which argues that differences between "legalistic" and "watchmen" styles of law enforcement derive

233

from the character and expectations of the communities which the
police serve. Two other excellent studies were Michael Banton, *The
Policeman in the Community* (New York: Basic Books, 1964), and
Jonathan Rubenstein, *City Police* (New York: Farrar, Straus, and
Giroux, 1974). Collectively, these stimulated my thinking about the
behavioral characteristics of policemen in the nineteenth century.
The sociological literature on crime is staggeringly large, especially to an outsider. I found Albert K. Cohen, *Deviance and Social
Control* (Englewood Cliffs, N.J.: Prentice-Hall, 1966), and Donald R.
Cressey with Edwin H. Sutherland, *Principals of Criminology* (Philadelphia: J. B. Lippincott, 1966), the most useful guides for orienting
myself in this literature. Although the theories which attempt to
explain criminal behavior must be applied to historical research with
great care because of frequently inadequate evidence, the questions
which sociologists ask about crime can provide an extremely interesting
framework for analysis of the evidence which is available. In that
regard, I found the most stimulating works were: Howard S. Becker,
Outsiders: Studies in the Sociology of Deviance (New York: Free Press
of Glencoe, 1963); Peter Letkemann, *Crime as Work* (Englewood Cliffs,
N.J.: Prentice-Hall, 1973); Ned Polsky, *Hustlers, Beats, and Others*
(Garden City, N.Y.: Doubleday & Company, 1969); Edwin H. Sutherland, *The Professional Thief* (Chicago: University of Chicago Press,
1937); Gerald D. Suttles, *The Social Order of the Slum: Ethnicity and
Territory in the Inner City* (Chicago: University of Chicago Press,
1968); Gerald D. Suttles, *The Social Construction of Communities*
(Chicago: University of Chicago Press, 1972); and Frederick M. Thra-
sher, *The Gang: A Study of 1,313 Gangs in Chicago* (Chicago: University of Chicago Press, 1927). Taken together, these studies alerted me
to the complex social milieu in which crime occurs and helped define
some important characteristics of criminal behavior.

Historians have produced a number of excellent studies of policing and crime which contributed in various ways to my own thinking
about these topics. Those works which deal with the police presently
fall into three general groups. Departmental biographies appeared first.
Both Roger Lane, *Policing the City: Boston, 1822-1885* (Cambridge:
Harvard University Press, 1967), and James F. Richardson, *The New
York Police: Colonial Times to 1901* (New York: Oxford University
Press, 1970), deal with the administrative development and political
problems of two large city departments. Scholars dissatisfied with the
somewhat mechanistic interpretation which Lane and Richardson use
to explain the origins of preventive policing have written studies
analyzing the roles of community conflict and ideology in the reform

of law enforcement. The best examples of this approach are: Michael Feldberg, *The Philadelphia Riots of 1844: A Study of Ethnic Conflict* (Westport, Conn.: Greenwood Press, 1975); Allan E. Levett, "Centralization of City Police in the Nineteenth-Century United States" (Ph.D. diss., University of Michigan, 1975); and Maximillan Reichard, "The Origins of Urban Police: Freedom and Order in Antebellum St. Louis" (Ph.D. diss., Washington University, 1975). The last group of historians interested in the police have adopted some theme, such as professionalization, reform, or the implementation of authority as their perspective. Wilbur R. Miller, Jr., *Cops and Bobbies: Police Authority in New York and London, 1830-1870* (Chicago: The University of Chicago Press, 1977), is the best of these studies. Others include: Kevin E. Jordan, "Ideology and the Coming of Professionalism: American Urban Police in the 1920s and 1930s" (Ph.D. diss., Rutgers University, 1972); Jerald E. Levine, "Police, Parties, and Polity: The Bureaucratization, Unionization, and Professionalization of the New York City Police, 1870-1917" (Ph.D. diss., University of Wisconsin, 1971); and Joseph G. Woods, "The Progressives and the Police: Urban Reform and the Professionalization of the Los Angeles Police" (Ph.D. diss., University of California, Los Angeles, 1973). With few exceptions, these works share one common failing. They concentrate on case studies rather than upon a comparative analysis which would enable us to assess the general trends in the development of the police. The administrative history of police departments in the large cities seems to have followed a similar pattern everywhere, but as yet we do not know a great deal about the general reasons for the successes and failures of efforts to mold the police to our notions of an ideal law enforcement agency. Our knowledge of actual police behavior, how it changes over time, and the reasons for such changes, also needs more study.

The problems with the historiography of the police are relatively minor in comparison to the present state of our knowledge about crime and the underworld. Most scholars who have studied crime regard it as a dependent phenomenon which is shaped by changing conditions in the host society. These works include: Douglas Greenberg, *Crime and Law Enforcement in the Colony of New York, 1691-1776* (Ithaca: Cornell University Press, 1976); Roger Lane, "Crime and Criminal Statistics in Nineteenth Century Massachusetts," *Journal of Social History* 2 (Dec. 1968) 157-63; Eric H. Monkkonen, *The Dangerous Class: Crime and Poverty in Columbus, Ohio, 1860-1885* (Cambridge, Mass.: Harvard University Press, 1975); and Howard Zehr, "The Modernization of Crime in Germany and France, 1830-1913," *Journal of Social History* 8 (Summer 1975) 117-41. While useful in understanding the effect of broad social processes on crime, none of these studies deals effectively with the behavior of criminals or the structure of the underworld. In order to gain an appreciation of those aspects of crime, one must turn to Mark H. Haller's work. Among his most important articles are: "Organized Crime in Urban Society: Chicago in the Twentieth Century," *Journal of Social History* 5 (Winter, 1971-1972) 210-34; "Bootleggers and American Gambling, 1920-1950," in the Commission on the Review of National Policy toward Gambling, *Gambling in America,* App. 1 (Washington, D.C.: Government Printing Office, 1976), 102-43; and, with John V. Alviti, "Loansharking in American Cities: Historical Analysis of a Marginal Enterprise," *The American Journal of Legal History* 21 (1977) 125-56. Humbert Nelli, *The Business of crime: Italians and Syndicate Crime in the United States* (New York: Oxford University Press, 1976), is also an important work.

These were the most influential studies in shaping my own research on crime. In general, however, the historical study of crime remains in its infancy. There is a great need for a general survey of the American underworld, as well as for special attention to such matters as ethnic succession in crime, the interaction between law enforcement and criminal behavior, the nature of the ties between politics and the underworld, and the changing responses of criminals to the opportunities of urbanization and industrialization.

Index

237